Postmodernism
Rightly Understood

American Intellectual Culture

Series Editors: Jean Bethke Elshtain, University of Chicago,
Ted V. McAllister, Hillsdale College, and Wilfred M. McClay,
Tulane University

The books in the American Intellectual Culture series examine the place, identity, and public role of intellectuals and cultural elites in the United States, past, present, and future. Written by prominent historians, philosophers, and political theorists, these books will examine the influence of intellectuals on American political, social, and cultural life, paying particular attention to the characteristic forms, and evolving possibilities, of democratic intellect. The books will place special, but not exclusive, emphasis on the relationship between intellectuals and American public life. Because the books are intended to shape and contribute to scholarly and public debates about their respective topics, they will be concise, accessible, and provocative.

When All the Gods Trembled: Darwinism, Scopes, and American Intellectuals
    by Paul K. Conkin, Vanderbilt University
Heterophobia: Sexual Harassment and the Future of Feminism
    by Daphne Patai, University of Massachusetts, Amherst
Postmodernism Rightly Understood: The Return to Realism in American Thought
    by Peter Augustine Lawler, Berry College

Forthcoming Titles:
Modern Inconvenience: The Social Origins of Antifamily Thought
    by Elisabeth Lasch-Quinn, Syracuse University
Academic Politics: The Colonial Colleges and the Shaping of American Intellectual Culture
    by J. David Hoeveler, University of Wisconsin, Milwaukee
History and Public Memory in America
    by Wilfred M. McClay, Tulane University
Integrating the World: Cold War Intellectuals and the Politics of Identity
    by Christopher Shannon, George Eastman House
A Pragmatist's Progress? Richard Rorty and American Intellectual History
    by John Pettegrew, Lehigh University
Ralph Waldo Emerson and the Problem of Democracy
    by Peter S. Field, Tennessee Technological University
The Murder of Joy: Paul Goodman and the American Battle over Maturity
    by Robert Oliver, University of Wisconsin, Madison
The Public and Protagonist: Tocqueville and American Intellectuals, 1835–2000
    by Matthew Mancini, Southwest Missouri State University

Postmodernism Rightly Understood

The Return to Realism in American Thought

PETER AUGUSTINE LAWLER

ROWMAN & LITTLEFIELD PUBLISHERS, INC.
Lanham • Boulder • New York • Oxford

ROWMAN & LITTLEFIELD PUBLISHERS, INC.

Published in the United States of America
by Rowman & Littlefield Publishers, Inc.
4720 Boston Way, Lanham, Maryland 20706

12 Hid's Copse Road
Cumnor Hill, Oxford OX2 9JJ, England

British Library Cataloguing in Publication Information Available

Library of Congress Cataloging-in-Publication Data

Lawler, Peter Augustine.
    Postmodernism rightly understood : the return to realism in
American thought / Peter Augustine Lawler.
        p.   cm. — (American intellectual culture)
    Includes bibliographical references and index.
    ISBN 0-8476-9425-9 (alk. paper). — ISBN 0-8476-9426-7 (pbk. : alk. paper)
    1. Postmodernism—United States.   2. Philosophy, American—20th
century. 3. United States—Intellectual life—20th century.
B944.P67L38   1999
149'. 97—dc21   99-13633
                                                                CIP
Printed in the United States of America

♾ ™The paper used in this publication meets the minimum requirements of American National
Standard for Information Sciences—Permanence of Paper for Printed Library Materials,
ANSI/NISO Z39.48–1992.

CONTENTS

v

ACKNOWLEDGMENTS

I t is only realistic and common courtesy to acknowledge your debts. But it is equally realistic to realize that you can never get the job done. So all I claim to do is to mention a few.

For turning my life to the study of political philosophy, I am grateful to Delba Winthrop. For providing an endless supply of fascinating discussion on the themes of this book and for sharing some of his comprehensive knowledge about philosophers, statesmen, scholars, and books, I owe Dan Mahoney. For listening to and talking with me on those same themes year after year, I must thank the students of Berry College. For reading this book carefully and critically and convincing me it is worth reading, I am indebted to Paul Seaton.

A rather large number of Berry College students helped to improve this book, most notably Darrell Sutton, Lynsey Morris, Carrie Sumner, Robbie Crowe, Ryan Rakness, and Matt Barrett. Alisa Ray whipped the text into its final form. And Steve Wrinn at Rowman & Littlefield once again helped me more than I deserved.

Generous funding from the Earhart Foundation gave me much of the time I needed to write this book.

For plenty of evidence for the goodness of life, I thank Rita, Catherine, and my parents.

Earlier versions of parts of this book were published by Rowman & Littlefield, Praeger, *Perspectives on Political Science, The Political Science Reviewer,* and the Carolina Academic Press. Thanks to each for the permission to reuse and refine my work here.

INTRODUCTION

This book is about signs of a movement from modern to postmodern thought in contemporary American writing. By modern thought I mean the attempt to master or to overcome nature through action directed by thought. Modern thought, roughly speaking, can be called pragmatism. The point of thought, as Karl Marx said, is not to understand the world but to change it. That project of transformation through mastery, based on the premise that human beings can only understand what they control and so the truth is the "effectual truth," began centuries before Marx with Niccolò Machiavelli.[1]

Marx's conclusion that the mystery and misery that is human existence could be completely overcome practically or historically merely radicalizes Machiavelli's beginning. Historical struggle can come to an end with the complete abolition of the human dissatisfaction that brought it into being. Then human beings also become wise, because they are in position to comprehend all they have made, and, strictly speaking, there is nothing else for them to know.

Postmodern thought rightly understood is human reflection on the failure of the modern project to eradicate human mystery and misery and to bring history to an end. One form of postmodern thinking is found in the writing of the anticommunist dissidents Václav Havel and Aleksandr Solzhenitsyn. The fall of communism, Havel said, should be understood as a lesson about the resistance of being and human being to human manipulation. And Solzhenitsyn, of course, told Americans at Harvard that if human beings were born only to be happy, they would not be born to die. Postmodern thought begins with the news, perhaps both good and bad, about the intractable limits to any pragmatic project to make human existence predictable, tranquil, secure, and carefree.

Postmodernism rightly understood is not postmodernism as it is usually understood. All postmodernists rightly reject the systematic or reductionistic

1

rationalism of modern thought. But, properly understood, postmodernism is not antifoundationalism or a celebration of endless self-creation out of nothing. Antifoundationalism, the assertion of the groundlessness of human existence, is really hypermodernism, or the exaggeration to the point of caricature of the modern impulse to self-creation. Havel and Solzhenitsyn, true postmodernists, write of human beings living in light of the truth, meaning primarily the truth about human purpose and limits.[2]

Postmodernism rightly understood rejects the illusion of self-creation in favor of the reality of conscientious responsibility. So postmodernism is not a rejection of Socratic or Thomistic rationalism. Human reason exists primarily not to transform reality but to understand and to come to terms with it. There is some correspondence between human thought and the way things really are. Postmodernism is the return to realism.

But realism is not to be confused with the possibility of comprehensive human wisdom, which would only be possible if man became God or history came to an end. Postmodernism rightly understood includes a realistic acknowledgment of the limits of human understanding. Being and the human self, or soul, necessarily elude to some extent both human comprehension and human control. We know something, and enough to live well as human beings, but not everything about nature and human nature. So the mystery of being and human being is not really threatened by human reason, as some alleged postmodernists say.

The philosophers Friedrich Nietzsche and Martin Heidegger, at least as they are often understood, are not postmodernists rightly understood. They write against the coming of a wasteland inhabited by "last men." They dread the possibility that human beings might immerse themselves completely in unselfconscious contentment. So Nietzsche and Heidegger reject the whole metaphysical or Socratic tradition in the name of the greatness of human life or liberty. They lack confidence in the capability of nature or reality to resist manipulation, because they seem to understand human liberty to be a historical manifestation with no natural foundation or direction.

At the center of postmodernism rightly understood is such confidence, and so optimism about the beneficence of the modern project's inevitable failure. Human beings are not becoming and cannot become "last men," or wretchedly content. And human reality is never primarily a wasteland, or without goodness and greatness. Postmodernism is the recognition of the indestructibility of the good that is human life or liberty.

. TOCQUEVILLE'S POSTMODERNISM

Arguably the first postmodern thinker was Alexis de Tocqueville, the author of *Democracy in America*.[3] He wrote of Americans restless in the midst of abundance, of human beings who were not becoming apathetically content but progressively more perverse or deranged and unhappy. Tocqueville observed that Americans act as if they have unsatisfied spiritual needs, and he asserted that they are evidence that the needs of the soul cannot be eradicated and so must be satisfied one way or another. He described the Americans in Pascalian fashion, as miserable in God's absence. And their fundamental experience is one of deprivation, especially being deprived of the language to express their soul-based experiences. Tocqueville wrote to deny the truth of modern progressivism, or the pragmatic ability of history to transform radically human nature on behalf of wisdom and happiness.

But Tocqueville also wrote of the tendency of democracy to culminate in individualism, an apathetic existence without the social or heart-enlarging passions of love, hate, and so forth. Individualism is the return to Jean-Jacques Rousseau's asocial brutish state of nature. As a doctrine, individualism is based on the judgment that social and political life are misery-producing errors more than anything else. Tocqueville also said he feared the coming of a provident, gentle, administrative despotism that would relieve people of the burden of thinking about and caring for the future, of their humanity, for their own good.

Tocqueville predicted the possible coming of history's end. He even admitted that his resistance to that conclusion is partisan or questionable. His devotion to human liberty as an unquestionable human good eludes rational analysis. He suggested that liberty might be overcome in the name of reason. Tocqueville left us uncertain whether human liberty or distinctiveness has a natural or a historical foundation, and so he gave us reason to be both optimistic and pessimistic about the future of human liberty.

We, postmodernists rightly understood, today believe that we should be more confident and consistent than Tocqueville. We note that when Tocqueville describes actual Americans, he uses the psychological language of Blaise Pascal about the human condition or human nature. When he describes the theory of democracy, its egalitarian leveling of all that is distinctively human in the direction of homogeneity or pantheism, he uses the language of Rousseau. The practice of American democracy, the real world of human beings, contradicts modern democratic theory, which culminates in unempirical misanthropy. Tocqueville's singular brilliance is to understand how Rousseau radically secularized Pascal's fundamental insight. Rousseau turned Pascal's human psychology, which he presents as the mysterious creation of God, into history, which is wholly a human creation.

Both Pascal and Rousseau say, in effect, that the greatness of man lies in his misery. He is miserably restless or anxiously dislocated. He experiences himself as somehow alienated from his true being. Pascal says that alienation is a permanent feature of human existence without God's grace. It cannot be overcome by human effort. Rousseau's view is that human beings have made themselves miserable over time, and so they might overcome their misery by bringing history to an end. Radical despair comes with the recognition that what Christians believe about man's special creation is an illusion, and so the truth is that human freedom is just a worthless accident. But for Rousseau that despair is overcome with the radical hope that comes with the thought that the human being was not and need not always be an accident.

So Rousseau provides the historical theory—the radical distinction between brute or mechanical nature and human history or freedom—and the moral impetus for G. W. F. Hegel, Karl Marx, and the various twentieth-century socialist tyrants and pragmatic therapists. But for Tocqueville, Rousseau did not really prove Pascal wrong. He did not prove that the Creator-God does not exist, or that the human or spiritual longings that point in His direction have no natural foundation. The history of America and modern democracy generally, according to Tocqueville, might well provide evidence, perhaps decisive evidence, for either Pascal's psychology or Rousseau's history.

We postmodernists acknowledge that the really decisive evidence would be in Rousseau's favor, and we would not be self-conscious enough to acknowledge it. Still, the history of America and the West in our century has tended to support Pascal. The tyrannical projects to transform humanity have failed. Therapeutic evolution toward the administrative state in America and Western Europe is also in the process of collapsing. Americans are more restless and troubled, more miserably deprived, than ever.

History has not come to an end, and human nature in its greatness and perversity continues to resist historical manipulation. Human liberty still exists in its mysterious elusiveness, and human beings are still required to live responsibly in light of the truth if they are to live well. Contemporary Tocquevillians have more reason than Tocqueville himself to choose for Pascal and against Rousseau, for the real experiences of Americans against abstract, egalitarian theory.

But much American thought remains modern, despite the facts. The therapeutic, pragmatic effort still continues the attempt to bring history to an end, and there are those who celebrate consciously or semiconsciously history's end. Among the latter are the "politically correct" who believe that the American educational task has been reduced to rooting out residual racism, sexism, and classism. But a more consistent and experienced version of Tocqueville's postmodernism is also found among some American thinkers today. The purpose of this book is to explore the relationship in America today between modern and postmodern thought.

SOME THEORETICAL CLARIFICATIONS

Before I become more specific about the book's contents, a few more theoretical comments might well spare readers some confusion and irritation. So far, I have identified Pascal with postmodern and Rousseau with modern thought. It might be objected that Pascal's Augustinian psychological realism is something quite different from Aristotelian or Thomistic scientific realism. Christian realism is basically the person's knowledge of his own limits and so of his need for God. Scientific or philosophic realism concerns the human mind's access to the truth about nature and human nature. It is more about human capability than human limitation.

Modern or pragmatic thought begins with premises about both human capability and human limitation. Human beings are not fitted by nature to understand nature, and they are dissatisfied with what they experience as their natural limitations. So they have no reason not to believe that those apparent limitations cannot be overcome through their free and thoughtful mastery of nature.

The Pascalian criticism of these modern premises is that they are based on a denial of what human beings really know. They know that they have been somehow given the greatness and misery of self-conscious mortality and that they cannot really overcome the misery of their mortality through their own efforts. The pragmatic project is a diversion from the truth, and the diversion becomes progressively less successful over time. Pascal predicted in advance what actually happened: Pragmatism culminates in existentialism.

Existentialism is a form of realism: We are stuck with our human freedom. But it is not a complete form. Scientific realism begins to return with the thought that the denial of realism was part of the modern diversion. Only Christian moral or psychological realism, the truth about the human individual, is compatible with philosophical realism, or the truth about science and the scientist.

The modern denial of realism depends on the ontological dualism of nature and history. I call Rousseau *the* modern thinker because, in his *Discourse on Inequality,* he attempts with great success to articulate all that is implied in this dualism. Human beings are free or historical beings, not determined by nature. Nature is what obeys unconsciously mechanical, impersonal laws. So human nature is an oxymoron. And all that is distinctly human, including language, is a self-creation or historical acquisition. Language is not a natural capability and gives us no reliable access to any reality beyond human making.

Human beings began, according to Rousseau, qualitatively no different from the other animals. They were stupid, instinctually determined, and solitary or self-sufficient beasts. So their behavior was predictable and tranquil or, in a sense, reasonable, and they were content. Their movement away from their reasonable and contented natural existences must have been a misery-producing accident. Human beings become increasingly miserable and restless over time as they move away from nature. Their misery is largely their increasing awareness of time and so death. Over time, human beings also become more self-conscious, conscious of what they have made, and the lesson of history, which becomes more clear, is that history or human liberty is an error.

History had a beginning, and it should have an end. According to Hegel's best student, thinking through all that is implied in Rousseau's dualism, the true human ethics is to work to bring history to an end, and that is what pragmatists or Marxists do. So as Tocqueville suggested, democratic intellectual progress culminates in individualism; the end of history is a return to the beginning, to Rousseau's pure state of nature. The lesson of history is that the human being, the being with time in him, had a beginning and ought to have an end. History is man becoming conscious of himself as an error and working to eradicate that error. Twentieth-century political revolution and scientific therapy, as Tocqueville so clearly predicted, have been consciously or semiconsciously against human liberty or individuality as such.

The identification of modern thought with Rousseau and Hegel and with history as opposed to nature might well be confusing to Americans. I might begin by saying that American pragmatists, such as John Dewey and Richard Rorty, explicitly take their bearings from Hegel, but it is more instructive still to begin with the leading American Founders. Insofar as founding American thought was modern, it was mostly Lockean, and Lockean thought, it is commonly held, is easily distinguished from Rousseau's.

The Lockeanism of the founding is present in Thomas Jefferson's Declaration of Independence. There the human being seems to be presented as a natural being, as bound by natural laws, which are also God's laws, and as possessing natural or inalienable or not merely historical or transient rights. So the Declaration of Independence seems compatible with some form of realism, especially moral realism. Jefferson surely does not accept the ontological dualism between nature and history.

But in truth the American Founders should be viewed as, at best, accepting an incoherent anthropology. Their thought was a confusing mixture of realistic and modern elements. And obvious incoherence is even found in John Locke's own writing. Locke presents human beings as natural beings, existing by nature as individuals in a prepolitical state of nature. So it would seem that human efforts, including the creation of government, are shaped and limited by nature.

But Locke presents human history as a movement away from nature, as human freedom or pragmatic invention overcoming what only appeared to be natural constraints. The invention of money, for example, overcame the perception that there are natural limits to the human acquisition of property. By nature, or prior to such work, human existence is miserable and worthless. Everything of value, including knowledge, human beings have made for themselves. Locke's very comprehensive labor theory of value (presented most cogently in the chapter on property in his *Second Treatise*) is really a doctrine of free or historical self-creation in opposition to nature. And Locke presents no limits that can be determined in advance to such self-creation. The only guidance nature gives to human beings is negative: They should do everything they can to overcome it.

For Rousseau, Locke's antinatural pragmatism is based on confusion. Locke, following Thomas Hobbes, presents nature negatively only because the human beings he describes in the state of nature already have social or historical qualities. Natural man, an asocial, stupid being, would be neither fearful nor bellicose. This confusion causes Locke to believe that the antidote to human misery is the escape from nature. But the effort he encourages actually worsens that misery. Human beings become more anxiously and restlessly preoccupied with time and death. The true antidote to that misery is the return to nature, and so human beings, in truth, ought to work to negate history, not nature. Rousseau brings to the surface the misanthropy latent in Locke's antirealism, his negative view of nature. Once Rousseau clarifies Locke, it becomes clear, at least for theorists, that American thought and life ought to conclude with apathetic individualism, or what Rousseau calls natural goodness.

The relationship between Hobbes and Locke and contemporary pragmatists (including, among others, linguistic therapists, behaviorists, pharmacological psychotherapists, New Age pantheists, radical environmentalists, and California Buddhists) in America is the relationship between Hobbes's and Locke's confused and Rousseau's consistent views of the relationship between nature and history. According to Hobbes, human beings consent to government to alleviate their fear of death. But that invented or historical solution to an allegedly natural problem does not work particularly well. Its effectiveness is uncertain, and in fact human beings tend to feel more afraid when they are actually more secure. Death remains a necessity, and human beings become more conscious of it when they have time to think about it and more to lose when it comes. So Hobbes's bourgeois—or intelligently, timidly fearful—person actually becomes more haunted by death when living under the good government he cleverly created through his consent. Tocqueville and Solzhenitsyn are right when they say that what distinguishes bourgeois Americans, above all, is their inability to live calmly with death.

Today's American pragmatist, sharing Hobbes's goal of freeing human beings from fear of death and the cruelty it engenders, says that the human goal must be to free human beings from being moved by death at all. They acknowledge that Rousseau is right. The individual human being must be purged of the effects of history. The pragmatic solution cannot be merely political or limited. It must transform all of human existence. Death must be talked or drugged to death.

But the actual history of America has not been a straight line from Locke to Rousseau. The American Founders' confusion was greater than Locke's. Their mishmash anthropology included non-Lockean or premodern and biblical elements. And so America has always had an openness to Pascalian, realistic criticisms of pragmatism that come not only from human nature but from American history. Pragmatism, in any case, is always countered by human nature, and despite the testimony of many experts, I say that the solution of Rousseauean pragmatists is not really being implemented in America.

These theoretical remarks will strike most readers as far from self-evident. And for some they will be particularly questionable because of their obvious debt to Leo Strauss. To avoid all sorts of tedious notes, I will simply say that I accept the nerve of Strauss's interpretation of Hobbes, Locke, and Rousseau in *Natural Right and History*.[4] And the modern, ontological dualism between nature and history first came to my attention through reading that book. But I must add that this so-called Straussian view is also Tocqueville's and that it makes sense of the modern and postmodern elements I have found in contemporary American thought.

Also consider that the place of that dualism in defining consistently modern thought was taught brilliantly by Strauss's friendly antagonist, Alexandre Kojève, in the 1930s. And so perhaps Strauss owes to Kojève his fundamental insight concerning modern thought, and Kojève is the semisecret intellectual founder of what is called European postmodernism. The least we must acknowledge is that the Straussian view turns out not to be very idiosyncratic or even sectarian at all.

This book's debt to Strauss is fundamental but limited. He and I agree that modern, mechanical science leaves no room for a teleological account of human nature, or finally for any account of distinctively human nature at all. But what natural scientists know today is more complex than Rousseau or Strauss would have us believe. Some sort of realistic account of human nature, some sort of Thomism, may actually be the most plausible way of accounting for what we really know. I do not agree with Strauss that all contemporary Thomists accept thoughtlessly the dualism between mechanical science and moral teleology, and my view of what is right according to nature is much more compatible with Christianity than Strauss's. Strauss and most Straussians and I disagree on the character of postmodernism rightly understood as well as on the connection between moral realism and scientific realism.

These theoretical remarks are meant only to give an orientation, and many of them are no more than deliberatively provocative assertions. To know more, read on.

AN OVERVIEW

This book concerns five best-selling contemporary American authors who combine theoretical depth with moral and political concern. Two are clearly modern, Francis Fukuyama and Richard Rorty. One, Allan Bloom, is ambiguously modern. Two others, Walker Percy and Christopher Lasch, are defenders of postmodernism rightly understood.

Fukuyama's *The End of History and the Last Man* considered the possibility that the fall of communism had brought history to an end.[5] Nobody believed him because he did not make clear what the end of history would have to be. His book had the merit of introducing Kojève's wonderfully consistent Hegelianism to an American audience. For Kojève, writing at the Cold War's

beginning, America was already at the end of history. In chapter 1, I try to fulfill Fukuyama's intention of presenting Kojève's account of the ontological dualism clearly, showing what the modern pragmatic alternative to realism is. For
Kojève, the human being is a historical or temporary stranger in a cosmos that
is better off without him.

Chapter 2 explains that Rorty, America's leading, most accessible, and
most clever professor of philosophy, actually writes to bring history to an end.
For Rorty, pragmatism is the whole of philosophy, and its task is to eradicate
human cruelty and construct a classless society. Without realizing it, Rorty
agrees with Kojève that the coming of that society requires that death be put to
death. Rorty's method of suppressing death is not violent revolution but sentimental, linguistic therapy.

Rorty agrees with Kojève that language is both the cause and the effect of
self-creation, and that it gives human beings no access to any reality beyond the
self. The self has no stable identity. All human experience depends upon language, and so experience can be described into and out of existence. Human
beings have reason to hope that they can create a world pretty much as Kojève
describes at history's end.

Bloom wrote his unexpected best-seller, *The Closing of the American
Mind,* to preserve the twinship of love and death against pragmatic therapy.[6]
Bloom makes clear what Rorty obscures; the death of death would also be the
end of all distinctively human eros. He shouts the truth about death in the name
of love. But Bloom seems too open to the truth of Rousseau's ontological dualism in two ways. The American students he describes seem actually to live at
the end of history, and it is hard to tell whether his description is based on empirical observation or on what he learned from Kojève. Bloom's students are
presented as nice or politely apathetic animals moved by neither love nor death,
and so they seem to be proof that human beings do not have distinctive natures
after all. They seem to have been cured of their human misery by history.
Bloom also seems, finally, to agree with Rorty and Rousseau that most human
beings would be better off if they lost their capacity to be moved by death.
Bloom and Rorty, by agreeing on the level of description, both tend to accept
Kojève's view that history has ended in America.

Chapter 3 begins the presentation of the realistic alternative to the possibility of history's end. Percy is best known as a novelist, but he also wrote a
large amount of theoretical prose, and he is arguably the best indigenous American thinker of this century. Percy disagrees with Rorty's and Bloom's description of Americans as clever, nice animals. He agrees with Tocqueville that

they are restless, deranged, and deprived—deprived especially by therapeutic experts of the language to express their fundamental experiences. The example of contemporary Americans shows that Rorty is wrong to say that if words disappear, the experiences they describe will also do so. The Americans remain beings with human natures and so with ineradicable spiritual needs. They still long to know and love each other and God. The prosperous, isolated American individual is much more angry and lonely than apathetic and content.

Percy's realism begins with his rejection of the Rousseauean view that language is a historical acquisition with no natural foundation. He shows that language is a natural human capacity, and so both human love and human knowledge of nature are not illusions. Human beings are languaged and so social and rational beings by nature. But the human self, or soul, itself is also elusive. The distinctiveness of human nature causes human beings to experience themselves as leftovers in a cosmos they can otherwise comprehensively understand.

Percy says that modern science, insofar as it depends on the untenable dualism between history and nature, is incomplete as natural science. Modern scientists characteristically cannot explain how human beings can know and take pleasure in understanding nature. There must be a natural connection between the human being and the world that opens him to the truth about being and human being. That connection is language. Man exists between pure mind, or freedom, and mere body, or wholly determined matter. The experiences of the particular individual cannot really be explained by either the historical idealist or the scientific materialist. For Percy, the human being is a stranger in the cosmos by his nature.

The inexplicable heterogeneity of nature, which exists because of the distinctiveness of human nature, offends reason and leads to anxiety, and so the understandable tendency of modern science and scientists or philosophers is self-negation or self-forgetfulness in thought. The scientist inspiring modern, pragmatic political efforts actually aims quite futilely to extinguish human reality by divinizing himself and brutalizing others. But the unself-forgetful, realistic scientist knows that his theoretical knowledge cannot free him from his human troubles, and he does not forget what connects him to other, flawed mortals. He also knows that Christianity may well provide the most plausible explanation for otherwise mysterious natural facts.

Chapter 4 is an interpretation of Percy's last novel, *The Thanatos Syndrome*.[7] This novel, although not Percy's best, is the one that is most politically and theoretically astute. Percy describes an effort to overcome death by actually changing human nature. The scientists who conceive this pragmatic project make an important theoretical correction to Rousseau in accord with Rousseau's intention. Rousseau holds that men originally are unhaunted by death and so good by nature. The scientists understand that nature would have to be altered by chemicals for human beings to become good in Rousseau's sense.

Percy agrees with Rorty that the pragmatic project of modern science is to turn moody, anxious, death-haunted selves into clever animals and nothing more. He makes clear the self-deception and murderous misanthropy at the core of the project. Percy's political message is an American defense of the rule of law and personal sovereignty. But he adds that our understanding of human liberty has to be relocated on a realistic foundation.

Chapter 5 concerns another contemporary realist, the social historian and cultural critic Lasch. The similarities between his thought and Percy's are stunning. They both describe the transformation of psychoanalysis (or the Socratic search) into psychotherapy (or the use of words and chemicals to dull symptoms), the therapeutic, misanthropic intention of the contemporary scientific or knowledge elite, the self-deceptive or death-denying character of that elite, the foundation of the revival of moral responsibility or realism in the courageous experiences of ordinary people, the connection between truthful personal sovereignty and the admirable practice of virtue, and the dogmatic atheism of modern thought in much the same way. What makes the extent of this agreement most remarkable is that Lasch never quite writes as a Christian, and he moved in the direction of the truth of Thomism almost in spite of himself.

Lasch and Percy affirm Christian interpretations of the human situation only when the interpretations correspond to what they have experienced for themselves. They agree that the end of modern thought—or therapeutic efforts to overcome death—points to the return of the Socratic or genuinely "psycheiatric" tradition of an introspective, dialogic search for the truth about one's own existence. It is also a return to an acceptance of the ineradicability of the experience, described by Christian psychology, of the mystery and alienation of being human.

This book, in large measure, concerns the question of whether self-conscious mortality, or language and awareness of death, is given to human beings by nature or acquired historically. But perhaps most of all it is about love. Kojève, following Rousseau, says that at history's end love, or specifically human eros, disappears. What remains is only the mechanical rutting of animals. Love is historical, not natural, and the experience of history is that we would be better off without it. Rorty indirectly but insistently agrees with this conclusion.

The world he works to construct would be one without cruelty and so at least largely without love.

Bloom writes eloquently about the twinship of love and death, explaining that if one disappears, so does the other. He affirms the human goodness of love, but he does not regard it as an adequate compensation for death for most people. Percy and Lasch also write of that twinship. But they view the love of other, mortal selves and of God as, usually, more than adequate compensation for death. They have a much clearer view of what makes even ordinary people lovable. The good that is human life, one that is always mixed with misery and evil, is worthy of much more than our pity.

I have tried to write clearly and for a wide and varied audience, following the fine examples set by the American best-selling writers about whom I write. Percy, Lasch, and Bloom each had the wonderful and enviable talent of writing profound, thought-provoking prose while very rarely resorting to footnotes. I have not quite been able to do the same. But neither have I allowed myself to become bogged down in the controversies that animate scholarly literature.

NOTES

1. See Václav Havel, *Open Letters: Selected Writing 1965–90* (New York: Knopf, 1991), 256: "Machiavelli . . . first formulated . . . a theory of politics as the rational technology of power."

2. On Havel and Solzhenitsyn, see my "The Dissident Criticism of America," in *The American Experiment,* ed. P. Lawler and R. Schaefer (Lanham, Md.: Rowman & Littlefield, 1994). Let me say here that most of the authors and ideas discussed in this introduction are treated more fully in other places in the book. So I have not introduced what would end up being redundant notes here.

3. The remarks on Tocqueville here are based on my reading of volume 2 of *Democracy.* See my *The Restless Mind: Alexis de Tocqueville on the Origin and Perpetuation of Human Liberty* (Lanham, Md.: Rowman & Littlefield, 1993).

4. Leo Strauss, *Natural Right and History* (Chicago: University of Chicago Press, 1953).

5. Francis Fukuyama, *The End of History and the Last Man* (New York: Free Press, 1992).

6. Allan Bloom, *The Closing of the American Mind* (New York: Simon and Schuster, 1987).

7. Walker Percy, *The Thanatos Syndrome* (New York: Farrar, Straus, and Giroux, 1987).

1

FRANCIS FUKAYAMA VERSUS
THE END OF HISTORY

The revolution of 1989, which brought down most existing socialist regimes and discredited the idea of socialism, was arguably the last of the modern revolutions. There are two extreme or radical interpretations of its significance.

The first is that the end of the modern world may signal the coming of the postmodern world. This new world will be a rebirth of human liberty or plurality, one free from the pretentious and misanthropic illusions of modern rationalism. This postmodern view is found in many places today. One of its most striking formulations is found in the speeches of Václav Havel, the Czech former dissident and current president. According to Havel and his fellow former dissident Aleksandr Solzhenitsyn, the collapse of socialist totalitarianism was part of the modern world revealing itself to itself as an error.[1]

The second extreme interpretation of 1989 is radically modern. Socialism failed because it contained reactionary "idealism," which opposed the free development of human liberty and prosperity. Its failure shows that human beings were already definitively satisfied with the "classless society" of the United States, which is imitated by the other "advanced" nations of the world. Socialism and the revolution against it were the last manifestations of human spiritedness, that which produces human action or history, in the world. History, or human liberty, has now come to an end. Human beings will now come to live everywhere as docile members of a "welfare state," gradually surrendering the details of the humanity or human liberty they have already surrendered in principle. Eventually, even the state itself will wither away. This end of history, with its eradication of the disorder of modern liberty, is the culmination of modern or systematic rationalism. This view is found in the thought of Alexandre Kojève, the greatest Hegelian of our century. It was also anticipated by the musing of Alexis de Tocqueville about "soft despotism."

The American Francis Fukuyama achieved some notoriety by writing a book presenting a middle way between Kojève's misanthropic rationalism and the postmodern rejection of that rationalism on behalf of human dignity.[2] He claims to present an account of the end of history that is full of free and dignified human beings. Fukuyama fails, although perhaps nobly. The middle position he defends is indefensible, and he convinced virtually nobody.

I want to give the possibility that history has ended, Kojève's argument, the hearing it deserves.[3] Thinking about history and its end flows quite reasonably from the characteristically modern premise that human beings are defined by their freedom from nature and God. If God is dead, then human beings can no longer orient themselves according to an image of divine perfection. They cannot help but turn their eyes and their hopes to history. Said properly, the death of God is not some piece of Nietzschean fanaticism, but the implicit premise of a free, individualistic, secular society. That society's progressivism can only be justified, finally, by some conception of history's end.

AN INTRODUCTION TO HISTORY

History is human beings freely making themselves and their world. It is, as G. W. F. Hegel said, "spirit" opposed to "matter." It is what is uniquely human, what is not according to nature. It is the effort to make a world or political community completely satisfying to free and rational beings. So the end of history would be the completion of the human project. It would be the unfettered reign of human freedom on earth.

Human beings are inexplicably free from control by a nature indifferent or hostile to their existence. They are also, in truth, free from the God who denies the worthiness and possibility of definitive success of merely human efforts. The political community or state that exists at history's end owes nothing to nature or God. It is a wholly human creation. Its existence is proof that human beings can make for themselves in this world what God promises in the imaginary world to come.

More fundamentally, the end of history is the completion of the rationalist project to turn philosophy into wisdom. Modern philosophy, beginning with Niccolò Machiavelli, made the possibility of this completion seem realistic by identifying knowledge with power. It aimed to eradicate human uncertainty, to create a world in which there would be no need for faith or illusion. The aim was nothing less than to dispel the mystery of being, to make being—all that exists—comprehensible to the human mind. The only way such wisdom is possible is if being is identified with history, with what human beings have freely made. Wisdom is possible only if history is all there is. For history to be over, the human mind must be completely satisfied with its contemplation of history's complete rationality or circularity.

Modern rationalism is the effort to eradicate the mystery of being through historical or political reform. It is pragmatism at war with both religion and atheistic fatalism, or existentialism. As Karl Marx says, its premise is that all theoretical mysteries can be resolved by transforming the world into a place where human beings can live rationally and happily. The fact that human desire really points to this result is clear. Reason knows of no other world in which human beings could really live. The achievement of this result would be the only definitive, empirical evidence of human freedom. Consciousness of that freedom is wisdom. Because human beings have freed themselves from God and nature, wisdom is essentially complete self-consciousness. That consciousness is also essentially atheistic; man has replaced God as the free or omnipotent and wise being.

FUKUYAMA'S TRICKY ATHEISM

Fukuyama's most misleading incoherence is his combination of a seemingly moderate defense of human dignity and liberal democracy with radical atheism. He seems to hold that human liberty, or uniqueness, can be perpetuated in the absence of the distinction between human being and God. He asserts that religion has been banished from the West by liberalism,[4] but he does not agree with Kojève that religion's disappearance signals the end of human liberty.

According to Kojève, there was no difference worth considering between today's triumphant liberal democracies and the socialist societies that used to make up the Soviet bloc. The Soviets were, in principle, poor Americans trying to catch up.[5] Both the American and Soviet constitutions are forms of the universal and homogeneous state, the goal of millennia of historical development of political forms. They both, in principle, recognize the dignity, or liberty, of all human beings equally well. Each human being is seen as a free individual and not as merely a member of a tribe, race, class, gender, nation, or species.[6] Both societies, Kojève adds, have the effect of reducing human beings to "automatons," to cogs in a machine or system.[7] In Kojève's eyes, both these observations could be true only if the atheistic recognition of the true or historical ground of human dignity is a momentary prelude to its disappearance.

But Fukuyama believes he can distinguish radically between liberal democracy's encouragement of freedom and dignity and communism's effort to impose systematic uniformity in their place. He affirms Havel's heroic defense of human dignity against communism's futile effort to negate it. He disguises his disagreement with Havel by not saying that, for Havel, "living in the truth" means in large part living with the awareness that one is not fundamentally a historical being.[8] It means rejecting the pretentious view that human beings could ever bring heaven to earth, or history to an end. In Fukuyama's hands, Havel's account of dignity becomes merely an assertion of spirited freedom from fear. But, for Havel, it is much more. It is the freedom to acknowledge one's moral responsibility to "the order of Being," that which was neither made by human beings nor wholly knowable by them. It is the freedom to acknowledge that one is not God.[9]

Havel learned something quite different than Fukuyama from the human victory in his nation. His people's successful resistance against efforts at systemization ought to inspire the people in the Western nations to resist the systematic tendencies that animate their own societies. Human beings act humanly, or in accord with their dignity and openness to the truth, precisely when they resist all efforts to bring history to an end.

Havel sees the effects of pretentious, systematic rationalism in the Western, impersonal, media-manipulated mass democracies, and he presents the perspective of the dissident and, more recently, that of the responsible intellectual as the postmodern antidotes to modern excesses throughout the world.[10] He sees liberal democracy as superior to socialism only because it is not completely animated by the thought that history can or should end. For Fukuyama, liberal democracy is superior to socialism because it may be history's true end. But Fukuyama cannot help but say sometimes that the end of history cannot be simply systematic. To perpetuate itself over time, history must make room for expressions of human irrationality or disorder, including national chauvinism, religion, and a work ethic. History can come to an end and stay there only if it does not really come to an end.[11] Such subtle thinking is really equivocation. It is possible only by obscuring what it means to say that humans are historical beings. So Fukuyama makes it possible for us to believe what Alexandre Kojève, Václav Havel, and Friedrich Nietzsche do not: Man can live in freedom and dignity without God. Fukuyama, from one view, is finally a naive secular humanist. He does not see that secular humanism, radically expressed, is an oxymoron.

HISTORY AND NATURE

Fukuyama says, again incoherently, that Kojève was wrong not to use a teleological view of nature to support his conclusion that human desire is definitively satisfied at the end of history. A transhistorical—natural—standard is required to assess the results of historical change. For that purpose, Fukuyama employs the Socratic tripartite account of the soul, or human nature.[12]

We can judge the end of history as humanly satisfying if the rational, spirited, and desiring parts of the soul are all satisfied. Science has conquered nature in the sense of overcoming scarcity; it has produced the material prosperity required to satisfy bodily desire. The spirited part of the soul, realistically or historically defined as the desire for recognition, is satisfied by the universal and homogeneous recognition of citizen by citizen in a world of liberal democracies. The rational part of the soul is satisfied by the fact that history is a system comprehensible at history's end. At the end of history, philosophy is replaced by wisdom. What the wise man possesses, according to Fukuyama, is a complete account of the satisfaction or perfection of human nature over time. With this comprehension of this natural yet historically won freedom, Fukuyama can affirm history's success.

Fukuyama deliberately confuses us by presenting his teleological view of nature and history in the text, while leaving Kojève's empirical objection to it for the notes.[13] For Kojève, human nature is an oxymoron. The evidence indicates that what distinguishes humans is their historical being, not their nature. Their nature is really the same as that of other bodies in motion. It obeys the same predictable, mechanical laws. Nature, so understood, has no telos. If human beings have a purpose, it must be historical. And it can only be known at the end of history. The human purpose is historical success, the historical satisfaction of distinctively human desire.

The idea of history and its end presupposes the truth of the Baconian-Newtonian-Cartesian account of natural motion. Nature is "stuff" or matter. Spirit, distinctively human motion, opposes itself to matter. It cannot be explained by the impersonal laws of science. To be spirited, for the Hegelian, is to act humanly or historically. It is the overcoming of one's determination by nature or instinct for some uniquely human purpose. That purpose, Kojève says, is to have one's freedom recognized by other free beings. Spiritedness is the source of political distinctions, those between master and slave and ruler and ruled. At history's end, spirited longing is satisfied, and so spirited striving disappears. Political distinctions, Kojève says, also disappear. They are replaced by the automatic control of automatons, by the same impersonal order that characterizes nature.

Kojève would call Fukuyama an Aristotelian. Aristotle, he explains, was an "areligious" thinker, willing, unlike Plato, "to be satisfied with the here and now." He described political distinctions—such as the one between master and slave—correctly. But he misunderstood them as natural, or biological. Aristotle viewed human beings as by nature political animals, because he viewed social life as natural. But what Aristotle called human nature is really a mixture of nature and history. Because he could not see human freedom for what it is, he could not really account for moral choice or human responsibility.

Aristotle's ethics, Kojève says, is really a "treatise of the veterinary art," designed to produce ethical health. But for Kojève, ethical health is an oxymoron for the same reason natural man is one. So Aristotle was confused; he could not distinguish between human and natural reality. His incoherent idea of human nature made it impossible for him to conceive not only of the end of history but of history itself.[14] The Aristotelian who conceives of the end of history is even more confused than Aristotle. Fukuyama has mixed up two radically different conceptions of nature.

It is easy to see why those who speak clearly about the end of history do not speak about human nature. Fukuyama's attempt to combine natural and historical teleology is impossible. He relies on the authority of one of Leo Strauss's letters to Kojève to support his innovation.[15] The letter's main point is that only a teleological conception of human nature can keep human existence from seeming radically contingent. That observation is true enough, but it is not clearly a criticism of Kojève. The radical contingency of human existence is a necessary consequence of the radical distinction between history and nature.

Strauss does add that without a teleological conception of nature Kojève cannot know whether the historical process he describes is unique. It may repeat itself here on earth or somewhere else. But Kojève does not deny that history might occur again. There is no reason why or why not. That fact has nothing to do with the rationality or circularity of Kojève's description of human freedom, and so of his satisfaction at history's end. Although history emerges accidentally against nature, it can still be shown to have become a rational, human whole.

Human beings, according to Kojève, are given a nature, as is every other animal. They make themselves human through their action. The motion of a particular member of the species *Homo sapiens,* at least until history's end, is actually a mixture of natural givenness and historical acquisition. With the disappearance of historical action at history's end, human beings once again become determined, like every other animal, by nature.

THE END OF HISTORY AS RETURN
TO ROUSSEAU'S STATE OF NATURE

Fukuyama does see clearly that the identification of human with historical existence was first made not by Alexandre Kojève or G. W. F. Hegel, but by Jean-Jacques Rousseau. He does not assess the significance of this fact or show the relationship between Rousseau and Hegel and Kojève. The connection, although quite obvious, usually goes unnoticed.

It has often been observed, perhaps first and certainly best by Leo Strauss, that the Hegelian account of history presupposes Thomas Hobbes's state of nature.[16] It presupposes that human beings are, by nature, isolated individuals, and so have a prepolitical and brutish beginning. But Strauss adds that Rousseau's account of the state of nature was a correction or perfection of Hobbes's radically individualistic and brutish premises. The discovery that humans are historical—as opposed to merely natural—beings depends on Rousseau's elaboration of all that is implied by the idea that human beings are by nature asocial. An asocial being must be simply an animal, wholly determined and unconscious. Prehistorical man had no distinctively human qualities at all.

Kojève makes the distinction between human beings and the other animals at the beginning of his introduction to Hegel's *Phenomenology of Spirit*. Human beings are self-conscious, conscious of the reality and dignity of historical freedom. That consciousness is social, the creation of uniquely interdependent beings. It makes humans "essentially different from the animals, which do not go beyond the level of simple Sentiment of self."[17] This simple, "sweet" sentiment is what Rousseau calls natural goodness, which is obscured, and finally obliterated, by history.[18]

The natural condition of man, Hobbes says, is war. But for Rousseau, what Hobbes called natural is really historical. For Kojève, the core of history is war, or the human willingness to fight and risk one's life for "pure prestige."[19] Kojève agrees with Rousseau, not Hobbes, on what is natural and what is historical.

Rousseau also anticipates Kojève's conclusion that the end of history is a return to humanity's beginning, that history is a circle. Near the end of his account of man's historical development in his *Discourse on Inequality,* Rousseau describes "the extreme point which closes the circle and touches the point from which we started. Here all individuals become equals again because they are nothing."[20] From a human perspective, all members of our species are equally "nothing" or ahistorical in the state of nature. The return to equality is the end of history.

Rousseau only suggests that this end of history is somehow a return to humanity's prehistorical beginning. The great merit of Kojève's wonderfully consistent Hegelianism is to allow him to see the necessity of this return unequivocally. Kojève allows us to see that Hegel must be understood to have completed the work Rousseau began.

One reason the connection between Kojève and Rousseau is missed is that Kojève himself does not make it. His view is that Immanuel Kant was the first thinker to distinguish between freedom and nature, to articulate a dualistic ontology.[21] But, as Strauss showed, Kant did so on Rousseau's foundation. Rousseau's distinction, more clearly than Kant's, is between history and nature, and so he comes much closer to Kojève's conclusion that any dualistic ontology must be temporary. It is replaced by a scientific, coherent monism at history's end. Rousseau, in fact, is closer to Kojève than Hegel himself. Hegel, Kojève observes, erroneously attempted to give a "dialectical" account of nature as part of a monistic account of *"everything,"* including history.[22]

For Rousseau, man's natural condition is good because it is solitary. In his *Discourse on Inequality,* he uses the adjective "sociable" three times. Sociability makes man a slave, evil, and only able to live in light of the opinion of others. The dependence on others deprives him of his natural self-sufficiency, goodness, and equality.[23]

Because natural human beings are not sociable, they have no language. Without language, the mind, reason, remains an undeveloped potential. Natural man has no consciousness of death, no idea of God, no imagination, and no consciousness of morality or duty. Individuals are good because they cannot know and have no use for the distinction between good and evil. All they have are purely animal functions.

Their needs are simply physical, because they owe nothing to the imagination. They are not inflamed by love or the desire for recognition, both of which require society to develop. Their wholly natural needs are very limited and easily satisfied. Natural beings are healthy. The "strong and robust" flourish; the weak do not survive.[24] Despite natural or physical differences, there are two reasons that human beings remain naturally equal: They are equally independent or self-sufficient, and they are equally determined by the universal laws of nature.

By nature, human beings, like the rest of nature, are well ordered. Through historical development, they become to some extent nonanimals, or disordered. The development of sociability is, as Hegel would say, the progress of "the dialectic of domination and servitude—in the relation of man to nature as well of that of man to man."[25] Human beings conquer nature and oppress each other in pursuit of the satisfaction of their growing or more social or historical needs. This capacity for development, which Rousseau ironically calls *perfectibility,* is actually a movement away from man's natural perfection.[26]

As human beings move away from nature, they become more self-conscious. They become more self-made, and conscious of what they have made. Almost the first moment in this development is the awareness of one's mortality or consciousness of time. As time passes, human beings become progressively more characterized by consciousness of time, more self-conscious. They become essentially historical and so temporal beings—beings with time in them.

Kojève echoes a suggestion of Rousseau by placing death at the center of history or human uniqueness. The human being, alone among the animals, dies. "He dies," the Kojèvian Tom Darby explains, "simply because he knows he will die." Each human being knows that today or tomorrow—sometime soon— he will die. But for the other animals, there is no "tomorrow." They have no extended time horizon, no idea of the future. So they have no idea of the inevitable culmination of their future. Death will come, the human being knows, and it will be his own. That fact is the core of human individuality. It divides human life into past, present, future, whereas the other animals, including natural man, have only the present. They are restful and content. We are restlessly discontent, unable to live in the present.[27]

"Man," Kojève says, "'appears' as a being who is always conscious of death."[28] That consciousness is at the foundation of human or historical existence. Its disappearance is the disappearance of human distinctiveness. So Hegel's "anthropological philosophy . . . is in the final analysis a *philosophy* of death." To give a complete account of human existence "is to accept without flinching the fact of death, and to describe . . . its significance and importance." To describe a human being is to describe what "*is* finite and mortal."[29]

Historical progress makes human beings essentially mortal. It does so by leading them to see that is what they are. It deprives them of both contentment with the present and illusions about eternity. Their free conquest of nature is making what is essentially infinite (nature) finite (human). Human freedom is what is not infinite or natural. Finite beings are historical and mortal. History is the record of human freedom from the infinity or givenness of nature. Consciousness of one's freedom must include awareness of one's mortality as a condition of one's humanity. So to be free, as Kojève explains, is to be willing to risk one's life for one's freedom, to overcome self-consciously one's natural instinct for self-preservation.[30]

According to Rousseau, historical development, which includes the risk of life for no (natural) reason, is in response to human discontent. Natural man is content. Over time, human beings make themselves more discontent in response to their discontent. They become more conscious of time, perhaps the source of all distinctively human misery. That misery, in turn, is the source of all human disorder: poverty, disease, inequality, hatred, love, vanity, war, and so forth. History is the record of the interplay of human misery and disorder. According to Kojève, the capacity to risk one's life and to even kill oneself "without a valid reason" is this animal's "mortal sickness." Human liberty is, from nature's perspective, a disease.[31]

Human beings, Rousseau contends, cannot be understood to have aimed to make themselves progressively more discontent. Historical development must be accidental. For no good reason, human beings move away from the health and contentment given them by nature. History is a misery-producing accident, above all, because human beings would be better off if they did not know that they are going to die.

So the lesson of history—which can be known for certain only at history's end—is that history is an error. Human beings ought to live according to nature, which means they ought to surrender what is uniquely human or disordered about their existence. Perfectly self-conscious mortals reject that self-consciousness. They may, for a moment, prefer their human misery in their pride. They have made themselves free, after all, even if they have made themselves miserable. They can take pride in their misery. But they cannot help but also see that all pride is vanity, because everything human is accidental. To be human, as we often see so clearly today, is to be a victim of one's place in history, to be deserving of compassion, not pride.

Tocqueville, also following Rousseau's lead, suggests that the history of democracy is the theoretical and practical movement toward the conclusion that human liberty is an error. He says the democratic movement begins in prideful self-confidence, but its more enduring effect is to make individuals feel weak, insignificant, and utterly contingent. That feeling grows with the decay of the illusions of the aristocratic imagination. Human beings are detached from one another and from God, making eternity or immortality seem incredible and making them progressively more aware of time and mortality. Tocqueville shows that the movement of democracy, unmoderated, culminates in individualism, an apathetic, asocial existence without love and hate.

Individualism, Tocqueville indicates, is the result of the judgment that human beings would be better off without human passion, particularly love and hate, which cause dependence and misery. Consistently articulated, individualism seems to be a judgment in favor of the brutish self-sufficiency of Rousseau's state of nature. Love of equality, Tocqueville shows, opposes itself to every other form of human love, love of a particular being or beings. It brings into existence a universal and homogeneous society of animals who are not ruled but administered, because they are without the human passions that make government necessary. Tocqueville even suggests that democracy, as the impersonal rule of nobody, points in the direction of the automatic rule of automatons.[32]

Fukuyama acknowledges that "Rousseau understood before Hegel the essential historicity of the human experience, and how human nature had been modified over time." Rousseau, he adds, was also "the first philosopher to question the goodness of historical 'progress.'" History had made human beings progressively more unhappy, because of "the gap that continually arises between new wants and their fulfillment." Rousseau's critique of "economic modernization," Fukuyma goes on, leads to "a highly radicalized environmentalism."[33]

That environmentalism is simply the view that everything distinctively human is bad for the environment, a category that includes human bodies. Fukuyama follows Tocqueville in rejecting this view. Tocqueville affirms human liberty despite its disorder and misery, and he worked consciously against history's end, which he thought to be possible but not certainly inevitable. It is not clear why Fukuyama is not a radical environmentalist at history's end. In a note, he makes the Rousseauean claim that "We must not for now assume the goodness of modern natural science or the economic development it has brought in its train." But his whole presentation of the human freedom and dignity at history's end seems to depend on that assumption. He calls attention to the pessimistic view that "modern science has not served to make men happier," without refuting it. He also calls attention to the view of the "classical political philosophers" that the coming of some "cataclysm" would actually show the "benevolence of nature," apparently through its destruction of too civilized or historical a world.[34] The classical view, ironically, is close to Kojève's.

But for him, history accomplished what nature could not on nature's behalf, and without the need for a natural cataclysm.

The Christian philosopher-novelist Walker Percy can explain why we should not fear but perhaps almost welcome some cataclysm. The existing civilization has become too disordered or loony for human beings to live well. But the contemporary Hegelian must attempt to show that the disorder that seemed to make nuclear devastation likely has disappeared. A world full of liberal democracies, Fukuyama says, is a world without war. Percy holds that dangerous disorder will always be present whenever or wherever one finds human beings. The Kojèvian-Hegelian agrees, but denies that human beings exist anymore. Kojève shows that Fukuyama is wrong to reject radical environmentalism. He shows instead that its goal has already been achieved in principle, affirming the Rousseauean experience of natural goodness that is at the core of all radical environmentalism.

But it seems that no Hegelian, not even Kojève, can agree with Rousseau that all human pride is simply vanity. At the end of history, the total independence of historical motion or action from the givenness of nature is proof of the existence of human freedom. Human beings become perfectly conscious of their freedom. So they are perfectly wise and perfectly proud.

Hegelians know that what one perceives about one's own freedom is true. They have historical—the only genuinely verifiable—evidence. Human action over time has culminated in the universal and homogeneous state. There everyone's freedom is recognized by equally free beings. Human self-consciousness is essentially social and therefore reciprocal. Without such intersubjective, universal recognition there is no way of distinguishing genuine consciousness of freedom from vanity or madness. The absolute freedom, or self-sufficiency, of each particular being can only be recognized in the social and political setting of the universal and homogeneous state. So that state is the end of all human or historical action.

But Kojève still distinguishes himself among the Hegelians by making clear that this reciprocal recognition of freedom and dignity occurs only for a moment. It occurs, more precisely, in the universal and homogeneous state that has been established only in principle or is imperfectly actualized. Kojève wrote that the state first established by Napoleon "was not yet actually realized in its perfection." What Hegel himself affirmed was the existence of "the germ of this State and the existence of the necessary and sufficient conditions of its flowering."[35] After that state perfects itself, human freedom, or idealism, and presumably the state itself withers away. Kojève, unlike Fukuyama, does not worry himself about the conditions for that state's perpetuation. He thinks it is impossible. The end of history, a place where human beings are perfectly satisfied or content, must also be the end of humanity.[36]

At the end of history, human beings cannot remain citizens, beings capable of historical action. Citizenship is the risk of life for an ideal. But in the perfected universal and homogeneous state there is no need for such risk. Fukuyama himself actually describes the process by which human beings, for a while, still continue to assert their dignity, but the foundation of such assertions becomes progressively more arbitrary and trivial. This "contradiction" of groundless dignity has become ludicrous, Fukuyama observes, in today's self-esteem movement. The premise is that one has dignity simply because one is a human being, but now it is completely unclear what a human being is. For Kojève, dignity for human beings must be won through action. As Fukuyama properly complains, "Self-respect must be related to some degree of accomplishment."[37] Without some standard to recognize or judge human accomplishment, the idea of human dignity withers away.

Fukuyama even shows, despite himself, another way in which the wisdom found at the end of history manifests itself in our time. It is easy to see the various forms of "postmaterialism," especially the ecological or New Age injunctions to live in harmony with nature. This pantheistic idealism, with the view that both capitalism and socialism are nature-threatening disorders, is obviously more posthistorical than either socialism or capitalism. Postmaterialism, most radically, opposes the disorder that results from the mixing of material desire with self-consciousness. It is actually *the* consistent materialism.

This posthistorical awareness, Fukuyama says, can be explained by the working out over time of the consequences of modern science, which cannot distinguish between human and nonhuman being. It denies the genuine existence of human liberty or "moral choice." More precisely, modern science denies the existence of history, the realm of human existence free from material determination. Modern science, until history ends, is clearly empirically incorrect for the Hegelian. But at history's end, it makes sense to say it has become completely true. There can be no more human choices or action. What distinguishes human existence no longer exists.

Fukuyama concludes that if there is no longer "any basis for saying that man has a superior dignity," then there is no longer any basis for man's conquest of or opposition to nature. This desire for consistency is what Fukuyama, following Tocqueville, calls "The egalitarian passion that denies the existence of significant differences between human beings." He says it "can be extended to a denial of significant difference between man and the higher animals." At the end of history, human distinctiveness is negated. The laughably incoherent "animal rights" movement exists for a moment before the nonexistence of rights.[38]

Kojève might add, to make this conclusion more clear, that this posthistorical wisdom is that the social being can never be a completely self-sufficient one. The desire for recognition, as the Christians see, is really for full and complete recognition, for a being who sees you as you really are. Social recognition, obviously, will always be partial. As Marx asserted in opposition to Hegel, modern human beings do not experience themselves most fundamentally as citizens. So their spirited desire to be recognized in their uniqueness will never be satisfied completely through social or political reform. Fukuyama says, quite rightly, that some will remain dissatisfied by merely receiving the recognition received equally by all. I think that no human beings would be fully satisfied. The awareness that one's freedom depends upon intersubjective freedom is as much a recognition of dependence as of independence.

So Kojève worked his way to the view that the Rousseauean and Hegelian conclusions are, in the decisive respects, indistinguishable. Humans are historical beings. History is time. Man is the being with time in him. If he is historical, his existence must be temporary. This conclusion applies not only to individual human beings but to historical existence as such. Human beings come into existence and pass away in a cosmos indifferent to their existence. Their disappearance was, in retrospect, inevitable, and no cosmic catastrophe. The cosmos, in fact, becomes well ordered, a cosmos, once again.[39]

THE DEATH OF MAN

The species *Homo sapiens* lives on in harmony with nature. What disappears is history, man properly so-called. So, as Kojève says, "The end of history is the *death* of man" as spirit. It is the death of death, meaning the experience of death. Man lives on after death as a body — matter without spirit, without consciousness of time or the desire and capacity to oppose matter or nature. Being without death, he no longer has any reason to be dissatisfied with nature. The end of history is, of course, good for nature. The disorder of human or historical existence, as the ecologists say, mixes with, corrupts, and threatens all natural order. The death of spirit is especially good for the health of particular members of the species *Homo sapiens*.[40]

Kojève claims that his wisdom at history's end is the acceptance, without flinching, of all that is implied by man's mortality. He sees that not only particular human beings but humanity itself are temporary. Human existence is finite; it must end. Wise persons are completely resigned not only to their own deaths but to the disappearance of all that is distinctively human. They do and must prefer wisdom to human liberty. According to Kojève, the philosophers before Hegel flinched at the fact of death to some extent. They were unable to render an account of all that it implies.[41]

The perception and acceptance of the death of man is the precondition for wisdom. At the end of history "specifically human error is finally transformed into the truth of absolute Science." Man disappears "in favor of static Being (that is, Space, that is, Nature)." Man, it turns out, "is perhaps the only error of Nature that 'by chance' (freedom?) was not immediately eliminated." That error, the accident of human freedom, had to be eliminated over time, or historically.[42] The truth is that history is an error. Only life according to nature is rational or without disorder.

Kojève came to see he was mistaken when he, for a time, repeated Marx's and anticipated Fukuyama's error that human beings might retain some specifically human qualities, such as art, love, philosophy, or play, at history's end. He had not yet articulated coherently all that wisdom about death implies. He finally concluded that *everything* human "must . . . become purely 'natural' again." Being wholly natural beings, "men would construct their edifices and works of arts as birds build their nests and spiders spin their webs, would perform musical concerts after the fashion of frogs and cicadas, would play like young animals, and indulge in love like adult beasts." They would be completely determined by instinct.[43]

Following Rousseau, Kojève calls posthistorical man *content* rather than happy.[44] His enjoyment could not be human. It would be the sweet sentiment of existence unburdened by time, worry, and anxious anticipation.

Language, human discourse, would of course also disappear. As Rousseau said, language is a historical acquisition. At history's end, there would no longer be the human or historical needs that brought it into existence. So "discursive wisdom," Kojève contends, "man's discursive understanding of the World and of Self" must also disappear.[45] Human beings no longer would desire or understand some of the truth about their mortality. The condition of wisdom, paradoxically, is that it not be perceived by human beings or articulated in human discourse, except for a moment.

Man properly so-called disappears once he recognizes his complete independence, or freedom from nature. He recognizes his self-consciousness as "nothing" and so negates it. When he recognizes his freedom, he also recognizes his radical contingency. There is no support for his negations in nature. The empty pride of the citizen is not adequate compensation for the deeper, miserable perception of his contingency. His satisfaction, as Marx says, is too obviously abstract or unnatural. The Rousseauean affirmation of the life according to nature triumphs over the spirited affirmation of freedom and dignity. Kojève's Rousseauean wisdom is that the historical view of human existence, beginning in and presupposing the asocial state of nature, must finally return there.

How could self-conscious mortals, the beings with time in them and nothing more, really be satisfied with the political recognition of their freedom? Fukuyama's attempt to defend this possibility from obvious and overwhelming criticism from all quarters is halfhearted and unconvincing. The remaining contradictions between the principles of universality and homogeneity and actual human life are far too clear for us, perhaps more clear than ever before. As Marx says (in "On the Jewish Question"), the articulation of political heaven only makes more clear our real hell. The coming of the universal and homogeneous state, renamed by Fukuyama liberal democracy, the state with no credible opposition left in the world, may have made clearer than ever that there is no social solution to the problem of human individuality.

PRAGMATISM, EXISTENTIALISM, AND WISDOM

Kojève understood pragmatism and existentialism to be the dominant forms of contemporary thought, and his wisdom, from one perspective, is recognizing the mixture of truth and error in each. Hegelian wisdom, he contends, combines Marx's pragmatism, with its emphasis on historical struggle and work, with Martin Heidegger's existentialism, the analysis of the experiences of the self-conscious mortal. Marx neglects death, "while admitting that man is mortal." So Kojève holds, with Heidegger, that Marxism is "vulgar," a turning away from one's consciousness of death through immersion in the everydayness of ordinary life. Marx shared, to some extent, the ordinary person's uncourageous avoidance of what he really knows.

Heidegger neglects history, man's free development through work toward wisdom or all that is implied in self-conscious mortality. He does not make thematic enough the fact that his almost radically atheistic book *Being and Time* could only have been written at or near history's end. He does not make clear that the identification of being with time signals history's end and humanity's disappearance. Heidegger, like Marx, does not accept all that is implied in an anthropological philosophy of death.[46]

Fukuyama, in the decisive sense, is a pragmatist, or Marxist. His book is vulgar because it neglects death, and so the best reason why human beings might remain dissatisfied in the universal and homogeneous state. But with the fall of communism, existentialism has become still more credible than pragmatism. Many fewer human beings now hope or work for a historical negation of the miserably human experience of individuality, and fewer still hold that they have become satisfied or content. More common is the Tocquevillian suspicion or fear that pragmatism or history culminates in existentialism, understood as fatalistic and apathetic individualism. That individualism is not the same, surely, as the unselfconscious play of healthy animals.

Maybe the most telling piece of evidence that Fukuyama flinches in the face of death is his view that human beings could remain spirited at history's end. He misunderstands a crucial part of Socrates' articulation on the nature of spiritedness in book 4 of the *Republic* (439e-440a). There Socrates tells the story of Leontius of Aglaion, whose spiritedness was the source of his resistance to his desire to look at dead corpses. Finally, his desire overpowers his spirit, and he looks.

The desire, clearly, is the natural curiosity that causes human beings to pursue wisdom. Leontius is on the way up from the Piraeus, ascending toward wisdom. The great opponent of wisdom is spiritedness. It resists, in the name of human dignity, the fact that we are all, in the end, dead bodies. Socrates seems to agree with Kojève that wisdom consists of not flinching at that fact. Kojève would add that Socrates—by not seeing humans as essentially historical beings—himself flinches in some subtle but fundamental sense.

But Fukuyama's interpretation of the story is different and muddled. He refers to "natural disgust at viewing a dead body." He says that spirited anger is "an ally of wisdom," neglecting its opposition to what genuinely human or historical wisdom is. Fukuyama does not see at all that wisdom or nature finally triumphs over spirited resistance or history.[47]

Kojève would say that Fukuyama is not wise because he does not accept what man is. He flinches at the fact of death. Leo Strauss, Aristotle, or some Christian might say, in Fukuyama's defense, that the most terrible account of human nature is not necessarily the truest. But if the truth is not absolutely terrible, the dispelling of all human hope or illusion, there is no reason why either wisdom or its absence would bring history to an end. By not flinching, Kojève shows us the misanthropy of Rousseau's radically modern discovery of the distinction between nature and history. He shows us what the modern view of wisdom really is.

CHRISTIANITY AND HISTORY: THE DEATH OF GOD AS THE END OF MAN

The wise man sees that Christian theology must be recognized as untrue for human beings to be satisfied with history's end. As long as human beings believe in the Christian God, they cannot experience the satisfaction that comes through recognition of one's own wisdom and freedom. Christians are called to compare themselves with God, and they inevitably suffer from the comparison. His wisdom and freedom are perfect; theirs are not. The Christian God, Kojève adds, even "made himself man in order to facilitate the comparison." Christians have "an inferiority complex pure and simple," as each Christian "tries in vain" to imitate Christ.[48]

Man will always tend toward some such belief in God as long as he is dissatisfied, or not totally at home in this world, in the here and now. Only by becoming totally at home here can he really free himself, as Strauss puts it, from "the thrall of religion."[49] As long as he can imagine as real the distinction between himself and God, or this world and another, he is not at home. He cannot help but criticize this world with an image of divine perfection in mind. God must die before man can become all that he imagined God to be. The distinction between divine and human freedom must disappear, because the Kingdom of God has realized itself through human effort in this world. "God must be killed," as Barry Cooper says, "before man could be at home in the world and recognized properly speaking."[50]

But Kojève also recognizes that at history's end Christian theology has become true, but not as theology. It has become rational and real. It was a "slave ideology," that is, "an ideal that can become true through struggle and work if it is secularized or made realizable."[51] The "history of the Christian world" was nothing but making the world conform to that ideal.[52] Christianity originally achieved equality by viewing the real world as a "mirage." But equality has been made real historically or politically.[53]

Christianity began as an imaginary way for slaves to reconcile the "ideal of liberty with the fact of slavery." It achieved this goal by denying the reality of the distinctions that constitute the historical world. "Equality is transposed into the beyond," where all men are brothers. But from another perspective, Kojève notes, the Christian imagination makes all men equally slaves to an "absolute Master."[54] Christianity could give neither a real nor a coherent account of human liberty.

But Kojève recognizes that the Christians do tell the truth when they said that all human beings want divine recognition for their uniqueness, or their particular, personal value.[55] So they believe in the empirically unverifiable existence of a God who sees clearly into men's hearts and judges them according to their intentions. Each Christian believes that he or she is recognized by God as unique, free, and infinitely valuable.

But the truth is there is no way to judge human beings according to their intentions, but only according to their deeds. At the end of history, they really do receive such recognition from each other. Man creates himself out of nothing. His infinite pride is satisfied by the fact that his freedom is not dependent on nature or God. In the universal and homogeneous state, "the strictly personal, political value of each is recognized as such . . . by all." What is recognized is the freedom of the "I" who exists independently not only of God and nature but of family, gender, race, social class, and nation.[56]

Evidence for the superiority of the Christian to the pagan conception of man, according to Kojève, is that it is impossible and undesirable "for a European of the twentieth century" to be a pagan. History's end is evidence of the truth of the Christian (or Augustinian) criticisms of pagan theology. The serious theologies of the Greeks and Romans were natural and civil. Natural theology is untrue because it understands human beings as merely part of nature, when in fact they are more. Kojève says he knows he is "not determined once and for all by innate nature." He knows he is free.[57]

Civil theology understands the human being as essentially a citizen of a particular political community. But human beings know that they are not, most fundamentally, citizens of this or that city but of the same City of God. So for the Christian, natural and civil theology are superficial or reductionistic. They miss the person's true freedom and dignity as an insistently particular being. The Christians were the first to see the significance of the person's consciousness of his particular existence.

Kojève views Christian anthropology as on the way to radical Hegelian atheism. Judeo-Christianity "discovered" man's "spirituality" or "individuality."

"Man differs *essentially* from nature" and not only in thought but "by his very activity." The Christian calls living according to nature "sin." The Christian injunction is that man "can and must *oppose* himself to and *negate* it in himself." That negation is human freedom. Man lives "in nature," but "he does not submit to its laws." So the Christian lives "'as a stranger' in the natural world" by virtue of his spirituality. The Christian believes that he exists and acts in "the image and likeness of God," as "an infinite and eternal," or otherworldly, being.[58]

But, in truth, one cannot be both free and eternal. "Christian thought," Kojève says, "subordinated immortal Man to his eternal infinite transcendent God." More fundamentally, the eternal God could not be free. Freedom requires dissatisfaction with, because it is active negation of, the given. It is the characteristic of neither animals (unconscious, wholly determined beings) nor God, but of self-conscious mortals.

Kojève shows that the Christian conception of the eternal, or infinite, Creator is incoherent. If God is eternal, he is satisfied and so would not create. Man must create himself out of nothing, or in response to his nothingness. Only man, never God, could act capriciously or gratuitously. In one Kojèvian formulation, man is the being who can actually or potentially commit suicide. God, of course, cannot (unless He becomes man).[59]

Hegel concludes, Kojève says, that the free individual must be a historical and self-conscious being, "finite in time and conscious of his finitude." "And having understood that," Kojève goes on, "Hegel denied man's survival."[60] That denial of man's immortality is required to recognize his genuine or historical freedom. The Christians are right to say that God had to become man to manifest His freedom. The word became flesh, then died or disappeared. The stranger disappeared from the otherwise wholly natural world. The denial of survival and the affirmation of suicide are the preconditions of wisdom.

THE PARADOX OF KOJÈVE

The modern view of wisdom as the acceptance without flinching of all that is implied in self-conscious mortality is not without its paradoxes or problems. Kojève's most comprehensive observation is his deepest paradox. In Stanley Rosen's words, "the pursuit of self-consciousness, wisdom, and happiness terminates in unconsciousness, silence, and subhuman contentment."[61] Self-consciousness is an error. It is characteristic only of unnatural beings, and it produces unnatural behavior or "action." In the name of wisdom, the genuinely self-conscious being must render himself unconscious. True wisdom is silence.

Language, Kojève echoes Rousseau, is unnatural, a historical acquisition. "Language," Kojève says, "is born of discontent. Man speaks of the nature that kills him and makes him suffer."[62] The being who speaks opposes himself to nature, and his speech both reflects and causes his discontent. Satisfied or contented beings do not speak. Only a world without speakers is without contradiction, a system. Kojève, by continuing to speak at history's end, contradicted himself. To be fair, he knew he contradicted himself.

Kojève sometimes seems to say that the human distinction between philosophers and nonphilosophers will continue to exist at the end of history. He defines the philosophers as those who are dissatisfied with the unconscious contentment generally enjoyed. They have not become either unconscious or content. They are "sick," because their lives are unnatural. But they have therapy available. They can pursue wisdom through "contemplation," the passive recollection of human reality or history.[63]

But what happens when they become wise? Wisdom is boring, as even Fukuyama can see, for beings with time in them. They need, as Blaise Pascal observed, diverse diversions, such as wisdom's pursuit. Kojève, by continuing to think, speak, and even act after having become wise, showed his discontent with his wisdom and his boredom. As long as human beings exist, they will always be potentially dissatisfied with the boring uniformity of universal and homogeneous life.

Fukuyama laughably claims that this potential dissatisfaction "is the 'contradiction' that liberal democracy has not yet resolved."[64] How could it resolve it? We might say, with Pascal, that the existence of boredom at history's end is evidence that human beings have religious longings that elude historical satisfaction. But Kojève does not say that. He is too reasonable to consider any human longing as essentially religious. There is, he saw, only one resolution to the contradiction of boredom. The capacity to be bored must disappear. When there is nothing to do, human beings are bored. But dogs and other contented animals go to sleep.[65]

So Kojève knew he contradicted himself when he said that philosophers could exist at history's end. When the philosopher becomes a wise man, he sees that means the end of philosophizing and so the end of philosophers. He perceives the rational self-destruction of the oxymoron human reason. Kojève's practice may have contradicted his theory, and that contradiction was a source of personal irony. But he knew it could not last for long.[66]

At the end of history, moral contradictions, based on the distinction between good and evil, or "ethics," will disappear. Moral distinctions are evidence of human disorder, or history. The only distinction remaining will be sickness and health, and Rousseau shows that even that distinction is suspiciously unnatural. Animals, by nature, are healthy.[67]

Kojève actually says that the distinction between sickness and health will remain, for a while, somewhat complex or unnatural. Sick animals will "get locked up."[68] The illness to which he refers is not physical but mental. The state or police or psychiatric prison remains only to control and cure the mentally ill. Kojève's reference to locking up the mentally ill is, of course, to the coercive utopianism of the Soviet Union. The purpose of the Gulag camps, as Solzhenitsyn explained, was to perfect Soviet society's universality and homogeneity. The main reason for being sent to a camp was manifesting the symptoms of the disorder of individuality—anxiety, loneliness, alienation, and so forth. But the regime of coercion and terror did not, in fact, experience much success. It did not extinguish the disorder of individuality in the camps, much less in Soviet society as a whole. Most everyone, Solzhenitsyn reports, continued to view the Soviet state's articulation of its principles as a lie. We also know how much pent-up disorder was released in Russia with communism's collapse. We might want to say, on the basis of the Soviet failure, that the historical perfection of the universal and homogeneous state is impossible because contrary to human nature.[69]

But Nietzsche writes of the voluntary surrendering of one's individuality. He and Tocqueville both thought the great threat to human liberty was therapeutic evolution more than political revolution. Human beings become "last men" in the name of "wretched contentment." They choose to live immersed thoughtlessly in the present, and so they consent to be drugged to avoid the mental and physical pain of impending death. Those who cannot so consent, Nietzsche predicts, will go voluntarily to a madhouse and submit to whatever therapy is available there. As Walker Percy observes, Americans today seem to want to surrender their personal sovereignty to scientific experts. They want to hear from experts that their experiences of individuality can be cured, that psychotherapy can remove self-conscious mortality as a painful problem.[70]

Leon Kass explains that the goal of contemporary technology has moved from the conquest of physical nature to the management of human existence. Psychotherapy narrowly understood, behavior modification, psychopharmacology, neurochemistry, genetic engineering, and the techniques of propaganda, social organization, and so forth all aim to order human experience in terms of easy, predictable contentment. Kass sees that what must be brought under control above all are human perceptions of death and dying.[71] Psychotherapy may in certain respects deny the Rousseauean distinction between nature and history, because its efforts are often to alter the natural functioning of human beings. But the goal is still Rousseau's: to reduce human experience to that of Rousseau's state of nature. The Soviet efforts depended on the thought that human perversity, or mental illness, could be overcome through political revolution. The psychotherapists disagree on whether the human aberration is a historical illusion or a natural fact, but they agree on the desirability and possibility of a scientific, therapeutic cure.

According to Kojève, the mixture of nature and history that is the particular human being disappears at history's end. It is replaced by a wholly natural existence. That existence will mean the withering away of political life and so the end of liberal democracy. Perhaps Kojève is wrong about nature, and human beings are diseased and discontented by nature. Still, contemporary technology or psychotherapy accepts his Rousseauean view that what separates human beings from the rest of natural existence ought to be eradicated in the name of health and contentment.

That psychotherapy has not withered away in the wake of communism's fall suggests that human beings remain miserable and that they are still working to return themselves to animality. They are working to eradicate the contradiction and so the bundle of paradoxes that is their distinctive existence or liberty. Contemporary ethics, or at least scientific ethics, is arguably still largely Kojève's Hegelian ethics. The moral injunction is to work toward a world without ethics.

Perhaps what we are witnessing today is the intellectual self-destruction of the universal and homogeneous state. Rousseau, as Kojève implicitly predicted, is overwhelming Hegel. Compassion is overwhelming pride. We would rather not know the truth about our contingency and mortality, because it makes us miserable. Rather than think of ourselves as worthless accidents, we surrender our self-consciousness. The "multicultural" challenge to political universalism may be a prelude to a more homogeneous universalism. The postmaterialistic pantheism of New Age ecologists, psychotherapy, the denial of human uniqueness by contemporary science, and the compassionate suppression of the truth by the politically correct all point in the same direction. Fukuyama opposes all these movements on behalf of human liberty and dignity, showing again his lack of historical wisdom.[72]

NOTES

1. See my "The Dissident Criticism of America," in *The American Experiment: Essays on the Theory and Practice of Liberty,* ed. P. Lawler and R. Schaefer (Lanham, Md.: Rowman & Littlefield, 1994).

2. Francis Fukuyama, *The End of History and the Last Man* (New York: Free Press, 1992).

3. Alexandre Kojève, *Introduction to the Reading of Hegel,* trans. J. H. Nichols and ed. A. Bloom (Ithaca, N.Y.: Cornell, 1968). This translation contains less than half of the French original.

4. Fukuyama, 216.

5. Kojève, 161n6.

6. See Barry Cooper, *The End of History: An Essay on Modern Hegelianism* (Toronto: University of Toronto Press, 1984), 378n55: "The principles of Soviet fundamental law are, in effect, those of a Hegelian state."

7. See Kojève's letter to Strauss (19 September 1950), in *On Tyranny: Including the Strauss-Kojève Correspondence,* ed. V. Gourevitch and M. Roth (New York: Free Press, 1991), 255–256.

8. Fukuyama, 166–169.

9. See Václav Havel, Address to the U.S. Congress (21 February 1990), in *The Art of the Possible,* ed. P. Wilson (New York: Knopf, 1996), with "Politics and Conscience," *Open Letters,* ed. P. Wilson (New York: Knopf, 1990).

10. See the recent speeches collected in *The Art of the Possible.*

11. Fukuyama, chapter 21.

12. Ibid., 138–139, 145–152, 162–165.

13. Ibid., 138n7.

14. See Kojève, *Essai d'une histoire raisonée de la philosophie païenne* (Paris: Gallimard, 1972), volume 2, 204, 224, 320–325. I am indebted to Patrick Riley's "Introduction to the Reading of Alexandre Kojève," *Political Theory* 9 (February 1981) for calling these passages on Aristotle to my attention.

15. Fukuyama, 264n8, citing Strauss's letter to Kojève (22 August 1948).

16. The Strauss-discovered relationship between Hobbes and Hegel, especially Kojève's Hegel, is ably explored by Cooper, chapter 1, and that relationship informs his fine book as a whole. Cooper relies on Strauss's early book on Hobbes (*The Political Philosophy of Hobbes: Its Basis and Genesis* [Chicago: University of Chicago Press, 1952; first published in 1936]). He calls attention to Strauss's note stating his intention to study in depth the relationship of Hobbes and Hegel with Kojève (354n26). No such study ever appeared in print. But for some reason, Cooper ignores Strauss's own later work, where he highlights Rousseau's correction of Hobbes as the foundation for the philosophy of history (*Natural Right and History* [Chicago: University of Chicago Press, 1953]).

17. Kojève, *Introduction,* 3.

18. Jean-Jacques Rousseau, *Discourse on the Origin and Foundations of Inequality among Men,* in *The First and Second Discourses,* trans. R. and J. Masters and ed. R.

Masters (New York: St. Martin's Press, 1964), 91, 115–116. All the discussion of Rousseau in this chapter is a commentary on this *Discourse on Inequality*.

19. Kojève, *Introduction*, 226–227.

20. Rousseau, 177.

21. See Shadia Drury, *Alexandre Kojève* (New York: St. Martin's Press, 1994), with Kojève, *Kant* (Paris: Gallimard, 1973).

22. Kojève, "The Idea of Death in the Philosophy of Hegel," in *Interpretation* 3 (1973), 124. This article was an appendix to the original, French edition to Kojève's *Introduction*.

23. Heinrich Meier, *"The Discourse on the Origins and Foundation of Equality among Men:* On the Intention of Rousseau's Most Philosophic Work," *Interpretation* 16 (1988–1989), 211–215.

24. Rousseau, 106, 117, 134.

25. Meier, 223.

26. Rousseau, 215.

27. Tom Darby, *The Feast: Meditations on Politics and Time* (Toronto: University of Toronto Press, 1990), 223.

28. Kojève, "The Idea of Death," 124.

29. Ibid., 132.

30. Kojève, *Introduction*, 226–227.

31. Kojève, "The Idea of Death," 137, 140.

32. This is a quick summary of a theme found in volume 2 of *Democracy in America*.

33. Fukuyama, 83–84.

34. Ibid. 356n44.

35. Kojève, "Hegel, Marx, and Christianity," *Interpretation* 1 (1970), 21–51.

36. Kojève, *Introduction*, 158n6.

37. Fukuyama, 302–303.

38. Ibid., 297–298.

39. Kojève, *Introduction*, 158n6.

40. Ibid., 158–164.

41. Kojève, "The Idea of Death," 124, 132.

42. Kojève, *Introduction*, 156.

43. Ibid., 158–159n6.

44. Ibid., 159n6. Kojève puts *content* in italics.

45. Ibid., 160n6.

46. Kojève, "The Idea of Death," 156n9.

47. Fukuyama, 133–134.

48. Kojève, "Tyranny and Wisdom," in *On Tyranny*, 152–153.

49. Strauss, Letter to Kojève (22 August 1948), in *On Tyranny*, 238.

50. Cooper, 188.

51. Kojève, *Introduction*, 55, 64, 69.

52. Ibid., 55, 64.

53. Ibid., 55–56.

54. Ibid.

55. Ibid., chapter 3.

56. Kojève, *Introduction à la Lecture du Hegel: Leçons sur La Phenomenologie de L'Esprit* (Paris: Gallimard, 1947), 145–146.

57. Kojève, Letter to Gaston Fessard (21 June 1956), in "Kojève-Fessard Documents," ed. H. Gillis, *Interpretation* 19 (Winter 1991–1992), 184–185.

58. Kojève, "The Idea of Death," 120–121.

59. Ibid., 152.

60. Ibid., 121–122.

61. Stanley Rosen, *Hermeneutics as Politics* (New Haven, Conn.: Yale University Press, 1987), 10.

62. Kojève, as quoted by Rosen, 106.

63. Kojève, letter to Strauss (19 September 1950), in *On Tyranny,* 255.

64. Fukuyama, 314.

65. Ibid., 306.

66. See Hugh Gillis, "Anthropology, Dialectic, and Atheism in Kojève's Thought," *Graduate Faculty Philosophy Journal* 18 (1995), 103.

67. Kojève, letter to Strauss (29 October 1953), in *On Tyranny,* 262.

68. Kojève, letter to Strauss (19 September 1950), in *On Tyranny,* 255.

69. See Cooper, pp. 303–318 for an interpretation of the Gulag as described by Solzhenitsyn as the end of history. But see p. 343, where Cooper adds that Solzhenitsyn observes that the lie of ideology had to be enforced by violence. What was achieved was only external obedience, not genuine belief or uniformity.

70. See Nietzsche, *Thus Spoke Zarathustra,* "Prologue," with the incisive commentary by Laurence Lampert, *Nietzsche's Teaching: An Interpretation of "Thus Spoke Zarathustra"* (New Haven, Conn.: Yale University Press, 1988), especially pp. 22–26. Also, Walker Percy, *Signposts in a Strange Land* (New York: Farrar, Straus, and Giroux, 1991), especially pp. 251–262.

71. Leon Kass, "Introduction: The Problem of Technology," in *Technology in the Western Political Tradition,* ed. A. Melzer, J. Weinberger, and R. Zinman (Ithaca, N.Y.: Cornell University Press, 1995), 4, 19–20.

72. Fukuyama, 297–298.

2

ALLAN BLOOM'S INEFFECTUAL RESPONSE TO RICHARD RORTY: PRAGMATISM, EXISTENTIALISM, AND AMERICAN POLITICAL THOUGHT TODAY

P ragmatism, the dominant form of thought in America today, has significant opposition. America's leading professor of philosophy, Richard
Rorty, is also the nation's most clever, subtle, and witty pragmatist. Contemporary America's most formidable opponent of pragmatism may have been Allan Bloom, the author of the philosophical best-seller *The Closing of the American Mind*. Rorty teaches that human beings should view as true whatever they
find useful in satisfying their desires. So the experience of one's own mortality
is neither useful nor true. He attempts to persuade us not to be moved by death.
Bloom trumpets the existential truth that Rorty tries to hide about the limits to
all pragmatic effort.

But Bloom may concede too much to Rorty to have his view of the truth
prevail. He concedes too much to the Rousseauean view of nature Rorty as-
sumes to be true, and so he is too open to the possibility that pragmatism has
actually conquered death. The extent of Bloom's and Rorty's agreement on the
condition of contemporary Americans should be troubling for those who hold
or hope that history has not come to an end. After socialism's collapse, they
may present the two fundamental alternatives in American thought today.

Pragmatism might be defined in large measure as the denial of death. Karl
Marx, John Dewey, and Richard Rorty never discuss the experience of one's
awareness of one's own mortality. Marx does say that human misery is caused
by the experience of individuality, but he explains that experience of nothingness as essentially economic. It can be transformed by a change in the economic
system. Dewey, despite his many elegant accounts of human experience in
terms of growth and decay, never discusses the experience of dying alone. He

41

writes of the courageous denial of certainty, but only abstractly. He does not come to terms with the only certainty we have about personal change, the one from life to death. With amazing consistency, Dewey describes all of life in terms of what Martin Heidegger called "average everydayness," a death- or self-avoiding immersion in life's ordinary details. Perhaps Dewey really does describe what a perfectly pragmatic life would be.[1]

My view is that the relationship between Rorty's and Bloom's thought may have been best expressed in advance by the great Hegelian Alexandre Kojève. The Hegelian wisdom possible at history's end combines the two dominant forms of contemporary thought, pragmatism and existentialism. Marx (Kojève's pragmatist) says that human beings gain their freedom and self-consciousness through historical struggle. But he vulgarly, or uncourageously, does not say what that self-consciousness is. The pragmatist cannot face without flinching what he really knows about his own existence, and so he writes to suppress it.[2]

Heidegger (Kojève's existentialist) says that human self-consciousness, what distinguishes human beings, is consciousness of one's own death. But Heidegger and Bloom do not make clear how human beings acquire that self-consciousness, not through passive contemplation of the human condition but through historical action. Bloom and Heidegger do not make clear that the identification of being with time could only have been made at or near history's end. Ironically, the final moment of the pragmatic struggle is coming to terms with the truth it was attempting to suppress, the natural limit of human existence and human satisfaction.

But the existentialist's victory over pragmatism lasts only for a moment. The perception of the truth about one's own mortality does nothing but make one miserable, and it reveals human distinctiveness to be nothing but a wholly contingent error. So that perception quickly disappears in the name of truth and contentment. What disappears is the truth of existentialism, the truth of the self-conscious mortal, what Bloom calls the philosophic experience. Then, in a way, pragmatism achieves complete success. Human beings finally can readily satisfy their desires through their own effort, because those desires have contracted to a subhuman level, that of Rousseau's brutish state of nature.

RORTY'S PRAGMATISM

Rorty follows Dewey most of all in feigning indifference to the existential questions. Rorty insists that some people think about death, others money, and

still others sex. There is no object of thought that "is more philosophical by nature than any other."[3] Rorty's denial of the obvious seems too dense to be credible. We can say nothing about the human desires for money and power without speaking of the connection between the desire to acquire and fear and
anxiety about one's contingency and mortality. Nor can we discuss human sexual desire without acknowledging what Allan Bloom calls the twinship between love and death.

Rorty writes essay after essay on Heidegger. But never does he discuss the
existentialist's theme of anxiety in the face of death and one's resolute or courageous response to it. In his hands, the founder of existentialism becomes re-
markably unconcerned with death. When properly understood, Heidegger's
concern with finitude is merely with the fact that we cannot acquire intellectual
certainty or transhistorical truth. Rorty does say, on occasion, that there is no
chance of surviving death. But he does not add that human beings are necessarily moved or even bothered by that fact. Rorty's Heidegger is really a pragmatist, as banal as Dewey.[4]

Rorty cheerfully admits that his Heidegger would have repulsed the historical Heidegger. For the latter, Dewey's or Rorty's pragmatism is "the most
degraded form of nihilism in which metaphysics culminates."[5] Rorty's aim is
"to stand Heidegger on his head, to cherish what he loathed."[6] What Heidegger
loathed, perhaps most of all, is the specter of human beings unmoved by death
and so the mystery of Being, the surrender of their authentic point of distinction.

Rorty agrees with Heidegger's proclamation of "the end of metaphysics."
But he disagrees that that end "was a matter of despair or nihilism."[7] He mainly
expresses his rejection of Heidegger's concern about the nihilism of our age
through silence. But he does assert, outlandishly, that "the word Being was
inessential to Heidegger's thought."[8] He creates the impression that Heidegger
had a good insight and a bad mood. "Heidegger," Rorty reminds us rather seriously, "was not the first philosopher to have taken his own idiosyncratic spiritual situation for the essence of what it means to be a human being."[9] Heidegger's concern for Being and human being was really a quirk of his own
psychological disorder, which caused him to view himself spiritually and to
take his political situation seriously. He was, at his best, an antiessentialist, but
at times he was part of the Platonic tradition of essentialist tyranny.

Rorty gives another argument against taking death seriously, in criticism
of a poem about death and dying by Philip Larkin. Rorty says that " 'Death'
and 'nothing' are equally resounding, equally empty terms." Fear is of something concrete, and so one cannot fear nothing or one's obliteration. For Rorty,

analytical philosopher Rudolf Carnap's satire of Heidegger's desire to talk about nothing is decisive. After that criticism, Rorty suggests, nothing disappears as a philosophical category, even from Heidegger's writing. Rorty adds that "the word 'I' is as hollow as the word 'death.'" Because I do not really exist, neither does my death.[10]

Rorty goes on to deconstruct a noteworthy quote from Harold Bloom, one that resonates from the philosophical and poetic traditions: "every poet begins (however 'unconsciously') by rebelling more strongly against the fear of death than all other men and women do." Bloom appears to mean that all men fear death and rebel against it. But poets, or great creators, rebel with special intensity. Rorty gives a different view: "Such people [poets] are . . . to be thought of as rebelling against 'death'—that is, against the failure to have created—more strongly than most of us." They do not really rebel against the inevitable end of one's life or existence. "Death," for the great creator, really means "not having impressed one's mark on the language," not having distinguished oneself through creative transformation. So the only "anxiety" felt by human beings and especially poets is that of not having any influence.[11]

The most astute of Rorty's sympathetic critics, René Arcilla, explains that his goal in redescribing Larkin's and Bloom's concerns is to cure human beings of their fear of death. In an early book, Rorty, with uncharacteristic candor, calls attention to the fact that people have that fear as part of the "problem of personhood," which originates in the "pre-philosophical craving for immortality." The philosophic and poetic approaches to the problem have been ways of "expressing our claim to be more than the beasts that perish."[12] The various poetic and metaphysical attempts to justify that claim have been failures. So Rorty "puts his money" on his "redescriptive powers" to eradicate that unique human need to make that futile claim about uniqueness. Arcilla interprets Rorty's redescription as a victory of the self as mind over the self as body, but it really aims to be a victory of the imagination over what the mind can really know about beings with bodies. Rorty is trying to describe away the desire to be a person, not a beast, and so we can say that his victory would be that of the body over the mind or soul.[13]

The distinguished professor of philosophy Charles Hartshorne attempted to get Rorty to consider seriously why human beings alone among the animals raise metaphysical questions? Metaphysical concern is not primarily epistemological, as Rorty would have us believe. It comes, Hartshorne says, from the one great "certainty," that of "our own eventual death." Metaphysics is not so much an inauthentic quest for certainty as a way of coming to terms with certainty. Generally, Hartshorne observes, Rorty "is overconcerned about problems invented by philosophers and too little concerned about problems of human beings, who are aware, unlike other animals, of their mortality." Pragmatists, by denying with obvious untruth that anything is certain, avoid confrontation with the really enduring philosophic issues. Pragmatism, despite its name, seems actually to be an escape from both theoretical and practical reflection on distinctively human life to a realm of empty abstraction.[14]

In response to Hartshorne, Rorty identifies the view that the concern with one's own mortality is the source of the metaphysical impulse of human beings with the early Heidegger. Rorty, usually silent on this core of Heidegger's thought, does not comment on the correctness of the identification of death with metaphysics. He just goes on to say that the later Heidegger concluded that poetry was a better way than metaphysics for expressing that concern. Hartshorne errs by wanting to back up the poet's, say, William Wordsworth's, concern with mortality with metaphysics. Rorty's view is that we should not ask whether any poetic description of reality is actually true, implying that he would criticize Wordsworth the way he did Larkin. Rorty ends up a long distance from Heidegger and Hartshorne: We cannot say that the poetic response to the inevitability of death is really a response to the truth. Again, we cannot say that "death" corresponds to death.

Rorty then quickly asserts the priority of a "poeticized culture," contending that all human awareness is a "linguistic affair." *All* of our experiences are a linguistic or poetic creation. We cannot say that they mirror any aspect of reality at all. So human beings can be moved through the linguistic manipulation of the imagination to say that "eternity" or "the silence of infinite spaces" do not matter, toward a world where religion, science, and metaphysics all seem like superfluous nonsense.[15]

Rorty's "philosophical therapy" aims to assure us that the poets created and can cure us of our concern with death.[16] He reads the poet Percy Shelley as saying "we should just forget about the relation between eternity and time."[17] Death need not seem essential or even important for human beings. It may seem, at first, inconceivable that we could lose such concern. But Rorty contends "we do not yet have any idea what is and what is not a conceivable experience." Language seems to have "no transcendental limits," and so Rorty conceives "of experience as potentially infinitely enrichable." There are no limits to how human beings might redescribe and so remake themselves. They should, of course, describe away the misery of self-conscious mortality. Rorty's approach to Hartshorne is condescending: He explains patiently that he solved in principle the problem that moved the philosophers to metaphysical reflection. Soon his solution will be implemented.[18]

Arcilla, one of Rorty's most sympathetic critics, complains that "Even as Rorty attacks positivism, his works seem prone to a positivistic impatience with existential mystery. It often summarily discounts any practical need we have to cope with the ineliminability of such mystery, thereby reducing the scope of what can count as pragmatic thinking."[19] Arcilla holds that a genuine pragmatism would help human beings live well with such experiences, and he reasonably aims to enlarge Rorty's pragmatism with that end in view. But Rorty questions the goodness of those experiences and the metaphysical dogma that they cannot be eliminated. Pragmatism uses language not to articulate but to correct human experience. Rorty actually works to make the impersonal science of the positivists as true as they believe it is.

Rorty does at one point criticize the scientific or philosophic "desire for objectivity" as "a disguised form of the fear of death of community" but not fear of one's own death. The philosophic tradition as a whole has been "an attempt . . . to escape from time and chance." But Rorty does not favor facing up to one's own scarcity of time. He wants to eradicate the experience that causes one to rebel against time and contingency. The personal pursuit of objectivity — one's desire to overcome time through thought — will disappear as impersonal or objective science finally becomes true.[20]

By depriving human death of its weight, Rorty does the same for God and His death. The end of essentialism and logocentrism described by Heidegger are events of no great significance. They are merely parts of a gradual and salutary linguistic transformation of the world. They do not "entail . . . existentialist, Sartrean conclusions."[21] Rebellions against death, the abyss, meaninglessness, and so forth, as the personal examples of Martin Heidegger and Jean-Paul Sartre show, are theoretical misperceptions rooted in personal obsessions that produce tyrannical politics. In what might be his finest and intellectually unfashionable moment, Rorty says that Raymond Aron was right to call Marxism "the opium of the intellectuals," knowing that Aron was writing mainly against Sartre's Marxist existentialism.[22]

Rorty calls the project of secularizing the world the Enlightenment, which culminates politically in liberal democracy. He claims to be satisfied with liberal secularism. He has no personal experience that would cause him to rebel against it. He has no reason to sneer at the material satisfactions and personal freedoms that its success has brought ordinary people. Rorty also denies that the death of God, or the near disappearance of religious faith in the sophisticated, contemporary West, has been morally or socially corrosive. People simply stopped aiming at personal salvation and started working for their grandchildren. The desire for personal immortality was transformed into a genuinely pragmatic goal for the future.[23]

For Rorty, pragmatism is really a therapeutic doctrine designed to ensure the success of modern technology. He agrees with Dewey that poets and philosophers are really linguistic social or political engineers.[24] He says his task is to complete the Enlightenment project begun by Francis Bacon and René Descartes to remove metaphysical and theological discourse — the results of the capacity to be moved by self-conscious mortality — from respectable human conversation. Rorty observes that theology is already obsolete. All that remains is to do to the metaphysical assumptions still present in some intellectual discourse what Thomas Jefferson did to references to the supernatural in the Bible. Rorty takes Jefferson's avoidance of theology one step further. He aims to make all human thought merely useful or superficial, completing the secularization of thought and life.[25]

For Rorty, the truth of pragmatism is that human beings are completely self-created. All their experiences are shaped by and depend upon language. His true debt to Heidegger is the thought that "language speaks man," which he interprets to mean that what human beings view as good or bad or true or false depends entirely on linguistic manipulation, description and redescription.[26] There are no "truths independent of language."[27] If the words that articulate a particular experience disappear, then the experience will too. Pragmatism succeeds by describing the experience that produces existentialism out of existence. The truth of pragmatism is that language is more fundamental than experience.[28]

RORTY'S CHOICE

Rorty's pragmatic choice against the truth about death is a choice for the perfection of the modern or liberal utopia. He affirms the Enlightenment's goal of a more cosmopolitan, just, free, happy, secular, and well-ordered world. Rorty sometimes claims to be postmodern epistemologically, rejecting the foundationalism of the modern philosophers and affirming the radical contingency of all things human. But he also is perfectly aware that his moral and political choices are modern. Given the antifoundational priority of politics or democracy to philosophy, Rorty knows he remains decisively modern or "bourgeois."[29] He may well be in every respect radically modern. He follows Niccolò Machiavelli and Karl Marx in aiming to make his view of the truth prevail in freedom from all illusions about the human dependence on nature and God. Like Machiavelli and Marx, he exaggerates how innovative his pragmatic antifoundationalism is.

Rorty rejects the genuinely postmodern view expressed by Martin Heidegger and Aleksandr Solzhenitsyn that if human beings were born only to be happy they would not be born to die. The beginning of postmodernism, in this view, is the recognition of death as the ineradicable limit to the modern project's success. For Rorty, human beings were not born to die or anything else, and so there are no ineradicable limits to their possibilities for happiness.

Rorty criticizes the postmodern moodiness of the cultural historian Christopher Lasch, who came to be "almost as dubious about the pursuit of happiness as Heidegger was." Lasch discovered the paradox that "the secret of happiness lies in renouncing the right to be happy." Rorty, suspicious of paradoxes if not of irony, holds that that discovery put Lasch in the camp of the religious fanatic Jonathan Edwards, away from the American democratic pursuers of happiness such as Thomas Jefferson, Ralph Waldo Emerson, and Walt Whitman.

Lasch rejected as an illusion the modern project's effort to conquer nature, one that has culminated in a spiritual crisis, "a dark night of the soul." For Rorty, the only sound reason for renouncing the effort to transform the human condition in the pursuit of happiness is the possibility of "supernatural redemption," and nothing is more illusory than that. He sees no reason to not cheerfully "persist in believing that a merely material and secular goal suffices: mortal life as it might be lived in the sunlit uplands of global democracy and abundance." The Enlightenment goal is more reasonable than ever. We linguistic engineers know that our happiness or unconstrained material enjoyment need not be disturbed by the fact that we have not really conquered death.[30]

PRAGMATISM AND JUSTICE

Rorty, for the record, begins with the antifoundationalist denial that there is "any neutral ground on which to stand and argue that either torture or kindness is preferable to the other."[31] But he quickly affirms the Enlightenment's choice of justice as "the first virtue," the foundation of human action.[32] Justice, Rorty explains, will be the result of the abolition of cruelty, the distinctively human aberration at the foundation of all injustice. Human beings unjustly inflict humiliation and suffering (Rorty even mentions killing)[33] upon one another. Sometimes Rorty denies the connection between cruelty and what is distinctively human by asserting that the pain inflicted by cruelty is prelinguistic, a merely animal feeling. But he adds that the other animals do not inflict cruelty on one another and that cruelty includes verbal humiliation, the imposition of linguistic or "mental" or distinctively human pain.[34]

One source of cruelty, Rorty explains, is the "private pursuit of aesthetic bliss," personal obsessions (such as Heidegger's) that make one "incurious" about how such pursuit affects others. Rorty identifies this rare sort of cruelty with the "genius-monster." The liberal, Aronian Rorty diagnoses well the sort of "criminal," totalitarian cruelty George Orwell and Aleksandr Solzhenitsyn described. The communist theoreticians were genius-monsters.[35]

But the bourgeois Rorty also reports that most human beings are cruel because they are afraid. They strike out against pain and death by inflicting pain and death. If they no longer experienced such misery, they would no longer be cruel. They would become "nice," not "piggy," not selfishly insensitive to the suffering of others. They would never be angry. The philosopher, the novelist, and the journalist all contribute to the progress toward justice by using poetic narratives to manipulate the romantic or sentimental imagination to correct experience. We know no limits to the malleability of the human imagination, and so we reasonably can hope that human beings can be induced to move from fearful, selfish calculation for themselves, their family, tribe, or country, to feeling compassionate sentimentality for all other human beings. Rorty suggests that the choice, which he tends to endorse, to limit the imagination's expansion to include all other human beings is arbitrary. There really is no morally important difference between our species and some of the others, or there will not be once we are freed from fear.[36]

Rorty does not address the concern that Alexis de Tocqueville would raise about this sentimental education. Its cosmopolitan scope would undermine human love as it actually exists. Because our powers of knowing and loving are limited, we can really be moved only by a limited number of others. Rorty, rejecting the idea of fixed, natural limits (which brings death to mind), does not acknowledge the force of this objection. But he may accept it implicitly by usually seeing that his goal is universal niceness and not universal love. The reduction of the passionate intensity might be the price to be paid for secularizing Christianity and so dispensing with the omnipotent and omniscient God of love. Maybe it is a price well worth paying: Love in the strong sense is inconceivable without hatred and cruelty, and we are better off without it.

Rorty does not emphasize the extent to which he would truncate love by disconnecting it from death. What would be left, his positive message goes, would not be destructive of ourselves or of others. Rorty does write of the "solidarity" that would include all others indiscriminately. He even calls Dewey's pragmatism "power in the service of love," but he means a vague "Whitmanesque" love of "democratic community." The pragmatic sentiment is a cosmopolitan love for humankind, not the love of particular self-conscious mortals or citizenship in some strong, positive sense.[37] But we can wonder whether the achievement of a cruelty-free existence would erode even the nice sentimentality of global community. It is my compassion, or revulsion against cruelty, that extends my imagination to others. If the liberal utopia abolishes cruel suffering, then surely it also abolishes compassion.

Part of Rorty's optimism about the prospects for sentimental education is the astounding progress it has already made in America, due to the fortunate combination of Enlightenment propaganda and economic prosperity. He reports that the American students' sentiments are now quite easy to manipulate. They are "already so nice that they are eager to define their identity in nonexclusionary terms." They are nice to everyone but those "they consider irrational—the religious fundamentalist, the smirking rapist, or the swaggering skinhead."[38] Rorty, of course, helps them expand that category to include metaphysical philosophers, theologians, and so forth. The students make that connection with little prodding, having already divided the world into the nice and the not nice. For Rorty, all that is required to complete the actualization of the Enlightenment utopia is to make the whole world as nice, secure, and well off as American students already are. His long-term goal is to universalize "an agreeable cultural cosmpolitanism," the easygoing, sentimental, "nice" culture of sophisticated Americans.[39]

Rorty finally tells students to abandon the distinctions between justice and injustice, good and evil, rational and irrational. Those who have been called bad, the cruel or not nice, are better called deprived. They are not deprived, as Platonists say, of truth or moral knowledge. What they lack is a "risk-free" life, one freed from fear. Only with such security can human beings "relax" enough to be affected by Rorty's "sentimental education." That sort of life is possible with modern technology's conquest of scarcity, but it requires more. Sentimental education and living a risk-free life are interdependent.[40]

Rorty's astute diagnosis is surely better expressed existentially. He almost never says, because he knows so well, that human beings are distinguished from the other animals by their self-conscious mortality. That consciousness's most potent effect is to make them miserable in a way other animals never are. Its existence seems an unfortunate, monstrous, cruel aberration from natural order. As Rousseau explained, it can hardly be understood to be good for one's own or the species' self-preservation. As the pragmatist says, it is not useful.

We cannot, as the Christians do, understand self-consciousness as a gift from a benevolent God Who made us in His image. If it came from God, we would have to blame Him for His cruelty. If we act in His image, we act cruelly. Human beings are cruel because their very existence is cruel. The worst form of misery is not what they do to each other but what has been inexplicably done to each of them. Until that cruel experience is eradicated by some therapy, until human beings stop being moved by knowledge of their deaths, they will not stop being cruel to each other. If justice is the abolition of cruelty, then it is the abolition of self-conscious mortality. God promises us eternal life, but it is now easy to know that promise is an illusion. Modern technology will never actually conquer nature in the decisive sense: Death will remain inevitable for all beings with bodies. The pragmatist promises not to free us from death's inevitability but to free us from being bothered in any way by it.

PRAGMATISM, HISTORY, AND WISDOM

The relationship between Rorty's pragmatism and the truth about human existence turns out to be rather ambivalent. The core of pragmatism, at first glance, is antiphilosophic or antiscientific. Its goal is to get human beings to view arguments about the truth about nature, God, and oneself with indifference.[41] "Metaphysicians think that human beings by nature desire to know," and they are wrong.[42] Rorty contends we have neither access to nor desire for the truth, and there is nothing privileged about the philosopher's perspective. No one has any standpoint by which to criticize the morality that happens to guide one's society. This affirmation of the conservative side of antifoundationalism makes Rorty the enemy of leftists, but only because they do not share Rorty's observation that the Left has already won.[43]

Rorty learned what the Hegelian Francis Fukuyama, Kojève's disciple, learned from the fall of communism. It is now impossible even for philosophers to imagine a plausible alternative for the future to liberal democracy, the just, universal, egalitarian political order. All that remains to be done is to attend to the details of its implementation. One argument Rorty gives for his views about language, selfhood, and so forth is that they "cohere better with the institutions of liberal democracy than available alternatives do."[44]

Rorty also says that he *knows* that to be human is to be finite or contingent or historical all the way down. What he refuses to say about one's own existence he says about all things human. There is one great certainty after all. Rorty actually suggests that our time is somehow privileged, because it has become unprecedentedly easy to perceive the truth.[45] In spite of himself, Rorty approaches the Hegelian view that wisdom is the complete articulation of the only truth we can know for certain: Man is a completely historical or temporary and contingent being. So he also approaches the view that we are at history's end, because wisdom is becoming possible and common. He opposes Heidegger's "nostalgia" by saying that our century is a particularly good time for thinking about "the most elementary words of Being."[46] Conceding that he sometimes asserts that his defense of the principles of our time is merely groundless chauvinism, we notice that Rorty cannot help but oppose Martin Heidegger with G. W. F. Hegel.

Rorty, the Hegelian in spite of himself, says that we should understand our recent past as the gradual implementation of the principles of the French Revolution. That progress has not been the work of reason, but of the sentiments. He says he follows not Hegel the wise man, but Hegel the constructor of fantasies about the future. Hegel's true innovation was the substitution of "hope for knowledge." Today's pragmatist knows that progress comes from linguistic manipulation, not the pursuit of wisdom.[47] Rorty accepts in principle "Nietzsche's criticism of Hegel's attempt to escape finitude by losing himself in the drama of history," but he admits that some such escape is required if we are to know how to hope and act.[48]

Rorty says that descriptions of history, the past, present, and future, are never merely factual, but propaganda in pursuit of some purpose. He thinks he is following Hegel in telling a story of progress, one created in the service of promoting the characteristics of his time of which he approves.[49] That progress, finally, is toward freedom from cruelty. In Hegelian fashion, Rorty claims that "Christianity did not know" what we can know, "that its purpose was the alleviation of cruelty." Christianity had to be secularized in the form of sentimental niceness to achieve its purpose. For the Hegelian, the secularization of Christianity is almost the final moment in the progress of thought.[50]

In his most recent book, Rorty employs "The Hegelian idea of 'progressive evolution'" as the most useful way of viewing the West and America.[51] He claims that the most inspiring Americans, Whitman and Dewey, were in turn inspired by Hegel, the German philosopher. Whitman thought it "obvious . . . that Hegel had written a prelude to the America saga," and in his Hegelian eyes, "the American Declaration of Independence had been an Easter dawn." America "would be the place where the promise of the ages would first be realized."[52] The realization of this promise depends on the success of the difficult task of "forgetting about eternity." Hegel's denial of the reality of eternity through his assertion that "time and finitude," or history, is all there is flows from his inspirational choice of pragmatic hope over knowledge. And his anti-authoritarian denial of all reality but history helped Americans choose the class-less society as their history's end.[53]

Rorty differentiates his story from that of the Hegelian "metanarrative" only as an afterthought. He says that the Deweyan or Hegelian pragmatist "urge[s] us to think of ourselves as part of historical progress which will gradually encompass all of the human race." In that light, he is "willing to argue that the vocabulary of twentieth-century Western social democrats is the best vocabulary the race has come up with so far." It is certainly the one that best uses "modern technology." The progress directed by the combination of that technology with social or liberal democratic vocabulary aims at a global society with equal freedom and prosperity for all human beings. The society Rorty calls cosmopolitan and egalitarian and Kojève calls universal and homogeneous.

Rorty adds, striving not to forget his ironic recognition of contingency, that today's vocabulary "will be superseded," as all vocabularies eventually are.[54] But its victory still seems definitive. Rorty himself contends that it is impossible and undesirable to go backward, to return to an enchanted, unjust, and deluded world. It is equally impossible, after the collapse of socialism, to imagine how we could radically go forward. Rorty is stuck with the Hegelian "hunch . . . that Western social and political thought may have had the last *conceptual* revolution it needs."[55]

Our ideas—the product of long cultural or historical development—are worthy of pride, Rorty asserts, because they are "the best hope of our species." They are the ones that have and deserved to have triumphed throughout the world.[56] Surely we cannot take pride in what is accidental or arbitrary. Rorty even asserts that we human animals have, in some Darwinian fashion, become "clever enough to take charge of our future evolution," to free ourselves from the experience of contingency.[57] Rorty may say his account of history is propaganda, but he cannot help but conclude that the real has become the rational. His Hegelian hypermodernism triumphs over his attempts at postmodern ironism.

As a result of the controversy stirred up by Fukuyama's book, Rorty discovered Kojève and thought himself in disagreement with him. But this perception of disagreement is based on a misinterpretation. Rorty thinks Kojève's seeming admiration of the moral fervor that leads one to risk one's life to have one's freedom recognized is too serious. Rorty too quickly lumps Kojève with the antibourgeois thinkers, while siding himself with the bourgeois aversion to the gratuitous risk of life. For Rorty, bourgeois culture is distinguished by the anti-Socratic view that thought and action in response to one's self-conscious mortality is not important at all.

Rorty does not see that Kojève himself finally affirms existence without thought or action, the end of history. But Rorty does recognize that the culture he affirms is the one Kojève finds at history's end, the "nihilistic wasteland" of Martin Heidegger populated by Friedrich Nietzsche's "last men."[58] This culture, in the eyes of such serious philosophers, is not a culture at all: "Nietzsche thought that the happy, prosperous masses who would inhabit Dewey's social-democratic utopia were . . . worthless creatures incapable of greatness."[59]

Rorty, like Kojève, knows what is lost with the emergence of bourgeois, liberal society: serious philosophy, artistic excellence, and noble deeds. He cheerfully acknowledges that "the typical character types of liberal democracies are bland, calculating, petty, and unheroic."[60] Their lives are disenchanted. Disenchantment is "the price we pay for intellectual and private spiritual liberation."[61] We are liberated, above all, from the need to respond passionately to our mortality. We are better off, and more just, because we are unmoved. Liberal culture "aim[s] at curing us of our 'deep metaphysical need.' "[62] Depriving people of that need, or, as Allan Bloom says, flattening their souls, is the way to stabilize liberal freedom.[63]

SOCRATES, MARX, AND RORTY

The pragmatist Rorty agrees with Marx that the point of philosophy is to change the world, not to understand it.[64] There is no theoretical standpoint by which one can resist the requirements of historical success. But Marx and Marxists do not go far enough in the pragmatic direction. Marx connected changing and understanding. By working toward history's end and comprehending the results of the historical struggle theoretically, Marx aimed both to end the misery of the oppressed and to make himself wise. And Marx held his own intellectual satisfaction was at least as important as freeing the proletariat from its misery.

Rorty lumps together Karl Marx, Leo Strauss, Theodor Adorno, Martin Heidegger, Michel Foucault, Vladimir Lenin, and Mao Tse-tung as antibourgeois and antiliberal thinkers. The real enemy of these thinkers is a wasteland populated by last men, what they believe to be the unselfconscious, enjoyment-oriented culmination of bourgeois culture. This thoughtlessly vulgar way of life "is the contemporary counterpart of the culture that put Socrates to death,"[65] the contemporary excess of democracy. Antibourgeois or pro-Socratic ire is what produced "Nietzsche's occasional antidemocratic frothings, Heidegger's attempt to climb on Hitler's bandwagon, Sartre's period of mindless allegiance to Stalin, and Foucault's quasi-anarchism," the various intellectual justifications of cruel tyranny in our century.

Due to Marxism's influence, Rorty notes, "the term 'bourgeois culture' has become a way of lumping together anything and everything intellectuals despise," mainly the happy indifference of the "many" to their claims for wisdom.[66] Marxism has kept intellectuals from facing up to their intellectual prejudices. The Marxist-Leninist has imagined that the revolutionary destruction of "the present, degenerate bourgeois many will be replaced by a new sort of many—the emancipated working class."[67] This new class will somehow be both perfectly content and self-conscious or Socratic. So Marxist intellectuals claim not to have to choose between their own happiness and the happiness of the many.

But the experience of communist tyranny—Rorty actually echoes Ronald Reagan by calling the Soviet Union an evil empire—and the successful revolution against it in 1989 make it impossible for anyone to find Leninist hope credible anymore. So intellectuals now cannot avoid asking whether "we are more interested in alleviating misery or in creating a world fit for Socrates, and thus for ourselves." Intellectuals are now stuck with the sad thought that "we, the people who value self-consciousness, may be irrelevant to the fate of humanity. That Plato, Marx, and we ourselves may just be parasitical eccentrics."[68] The ironic pragmatist acknowledges that the pursuit of wisdom is an idiosyncratic, unachievable whim. The philosophers have no right to dominate others on its behalf, and they can no longer "hold on to the Platonic insistence that the principal duty of human beings is to *know*."[69] If intellectuals are to be judged useful or unparasitic, they must contribute to the alleviation of cruelty.

Rorty shares the Marxian or Hegelian goal of the achievement of a classless society, and all political reform, even prideful American nationalism, is useful if it contributes to that goal. But Rorty, like Kojève, claims to be free from cultural delusions about what that society will be like. He does not successfully explain why his pragmatism is not a more extreme form of modern Western rationalism than even Marxism. Rorty sides with Marx against "cultural" thinkers on both the Left and Right today in that human desire might be transformed to achieve complete human satisfaction and that there is nothing necessarily mysterious or elusive about human existence.[70] There will be nothing irrational—or cruelly, perversely contrary to human happiness—in the agreeably cosmopolitan life that the pragmatist hopes will eventually be possible for all human beings. But Rorty persists in asserting that the liberal or leftist America and then the world he is trying to construct "is neither more natural nor more rational than the cruel societies" of the past.[71]

This assertion is Rorty's answer to Nietzsche's "insinuation that the end of religion and metaphysics should be the end of our attempts not to be cruel."[72] Morality defined as egalitarian alleviation of cruelty, Nietzsche contended, was biblical, and its goodness depends on the biblical God's existence. If God is dead, biblical morality should be abandoned, because it is not self-evident or rational. Nietzsche's standard for this conclusion was "intellectual probity," or a truthful confrontation with the human condition.[73] But Rorty rejects what amounts to Nietzsche's rationalism. There is no reason why human beings should not secularize Christian morality and achieve for themselves what God allegedly promised.

As long as human beings remain self-conscious—or moved by the intractable limitations of their finite, death-defined existences—the promise cannot become true. Rorty talks away Nietzsche's objection to linguistic self-deception by saying that Nietzsche confused the Christian, existentialist self—the one miserably agonized by its awareness of the abyss that surrounds contingent human existence—with the true self. But there is no true self, as Nietzsche himself said in opposition to Socrates, and so no reason not to create a less miserable self.

In Rorty's hoped-for and worked-for future, the world of human beings will be agreeable and reasonable or predictably tranquil, because they will be largely unselfconscious. Socratics and Nietzscheans affirm the perpetuation of cruel and unreasonable inegalitarian political oppression as the precondition for the existence of rational, meaning self-conscious, individuals. Both the "last man" and Socrates live reasonably in his own way. But neither way of life is completely rational.

Rorty chooses the classless society of agreeably cosmpolitan last men by denying the very possibility of self-consciousness. But that pragmatic denial is not particularly convincing. He lectures Marx and Marxists for imagining that a classless society could be a Socratic one. He ironically presents that impossibility as the only limit reason or reality can place on the pragmatic imagination. The choice between Socratic or individual and historical or social rationalism has to be made, and neither is clearly more rational than the other. In this sense, Rorty cannot call his hopeful choice rational.

Still, Rorty suggests strongly what Kojève concludes explicitly: Liberal society is the product of wisdom or genuine self-consciousness. It is full of people who can be understood to have surrendered that consciousness as a miserable error. Paradoxically, they surrendered wisdom in the name of wisdom, the truth about history. History, or human self-consciousness, is nothing but a misery-producing error, a unique, aberrant exception to the reasonable order of nature or the cosmos. Bourgeois thinkers can be understood to have experienced all that is implied in being a self-conscious mortal, as thinking at history's end. The thinker who defends bourgeois society against its reactionary critics is really defending its residents against their miserable perception of the truth, while defending their existence at history's end as a genuine manifestation of the truth. Rorty says that the "chief virtue" of liberal society is "freedom as the recognition of contingency."[74] The virtue is really to recognize the truth, and then to win one's freedom from it by being indifferent to it.

CLEVER (POSTHISTORICAL) ANIMALS

Rorty is ambivalent about the distinctiveness of human beings in our time, and so about whether history has really come to an end. He may be saying that his self-contradictions are in the process of disappearing and that human beings will soon be qualitatively no different from the other animals. He asserts at one point that, properly understood, bourgeois society is not held together by some conception of human rights rooted in shared human nature. We are coming to recognize ourselves as "clever animals" and nothing more.

Rorty has always said that human nature, properly speaking, is an oxymoron. But his usual argument is that human beings are not natural but historical, accepting the Hegelian distinction between human, language-based freedom and animal, determined nature. Human beings are those who somehow oppose spirit to matter (or nature) or, as Rorty says, engage in self-creation expressed in language. Rorty's massive and obvious contradiction is to say that human beings are both wholly historical, or linguistically self-created, and wholly natural, or merely clever animals.

But much of that contradiction dissolves as he goes on to explain that defining human beings as clever animals is not "philosophical and pessimistic," but "political and hopeful." The hope is that "if we can work together, we can make ourselves into whatever we are clever and courageous enough to imagine ourselves becoming."[75] But if we are clever animals in what sense are we political, or concerned with justice and injustice? Hopeful? Courageous? Imaginative? Those qualities surely depend upon self-conscious mortality, on some qualitative distinction between human and other beings. Does not the desire that animates self-transformation rest upon that distinction?

The pragmatist has clever answers for most of these questions. If we are merely clever animals, we would not rebel against our mortality. We would not imagine ourselves becoming anything we cannot be. The imagination would contract itself to producing goals toward which we can actually work. We would be "courageous enough," because there would no longer be any particular need to be courageous at all. For Rorty, "political" means fitting the requirements of our bourgeois society. The pragmatist accepts as his political project whatever is useful for his society's flourishing. That does not include thought and action in response to self-conscious mortality, or history in Hegel's sense. Self-consciousness may even get in the way of our potential for cleverness. The anxious dislocation, brooding fear, and dark melancholy it produces can inhibit the brain's calculative functioning. It can also block memory and put us in unproductive moods. We pragmatists can say that the experience of self-conscious mortality is untrue. Without it, we are clever animals and nothing more.

Clever animals, Kojève says, are what human beings are at the end of history. As a result of having become completely historical, they become completely natural. Because they have "definitively mastered" nature, they have "harmonized" their existence with it.[76] They no longer have any reason to oppose nature with history; they are content. Clever animal is the definition of our species that would have to be true for pragmatism to succeed completely.

Rorty calls the definition of human beings as clever animals Darwinian. Like the other animals, all they do is try their best "to cope with their environment" and "to enjoy more pleasure and less pain." "Words," in a Darwinian light, "are among those tools which those clever animals have developed," and nothing more. So Rorty "repudiates the question of whether human minds are in touch with reality. . . . No organism, human or nonhuman, is ever more or less in touch with reality than any other organism."[77] If human beings are really as unconscious as the other animals, then, in the decisive sense, they exist in Rousseau's wholly brutish state of nature.[78]

Rorty's intention to make morality, a quality only found among self-conscious mortals, obsolete is clear in his Hegelian history of America. The Hegelian Whitman identified the progress of civilization with the end of the cruel repression of sexual eros and so with the growth of "the kind of casual, friendly copulation which is insouciant about the homosexual-heterosexual distinction." This vision began to become social and political reality in America with the "youth culture" of the 1960s. Prosperous young people became erotically and morally casual enough not to privilege one form of sexual activity over another and began to abandon their humiliation of homosexuals in particular.[79] And although a Deweyan pragmatist might be a bit uptight about innovative forms of liberation from cruelty, he must admit that sexual promiscuity, recreational drugs, and music to the beat of the mechanical rutting of animals are all signs that American students have become nicer and more devoted to the American idea of justice. The American Right wrongly believes that civilization was devastated by the sixties, because it connects civilization with the perpetuation of arbitrary standards of personal virtue.[80] But the leftist Rorty regards that connection as a failure of the imagination, coming from the illusion that human experience is shaped or limited by "sin," some cruel, ineradicable flaw.[81] For Rorty, all moral restraint is repressive cruelty unless it contributes to progress toward social justice, and so in a just society moral restraint itself will wither away.

Rorty agrees with Kojève that the common recognition that human beings are historical all the way down signals the coming of the world where they are not historical at all. Rorty's writing may be understood as propaganda for history's imminent end. He acknowledges implicitly by opposing radically the miserable truth about human or historical contingency. He aims to negate that truth in the name of the truth, the truth about the natural world in which clever animals are qualitatively no different from the other animals. Human beings will always be more than clever animals as long as Rorty writes. His incredible denials of the obvious, his contradictions, are evidence that he is troubled by his own self-conscious mortality. But he writes to eradicate that truthful perception of error, or history, on behalf of the prosperous, contented, and rational flourishing of our species, the true utopia of the Enlightenment.

LIBERAL IRONY

Rorty's irony is finally his recognition that his own human distinctiveness is without foundation, an error. His posthistorical wisdom contradicts his own existence as a philosopher. Rorty distinguishes between "liberal ironists" and most human beings even in his liberal utopia, the fully secularized society. In Jerry Weinberger's words, the liberal ironist "lives in the greatest possible awareness of the existential burden of irony."[82] The proper response to what he knows about his existence is irony or play. He is alienated even from his own social order, because he sees so radically how contingent and arbitrary all human creations are. Such radical irony is always an inherently private experience. Rorty admits he "cannot imagine a culture which socializes its youth in such a way as to make them continually dubious about their own process of socialization." Human beings cannot live well if they really recognize and reflect on their wholly historical existences.[83]

The ironist has the existential burden of recognizing how idiosyncratic, even ridiculous, his personal reflections are. He knows he should not find the death of God, the mediocrity of society without deep belief, or his own death to be sources of anger and anxiety. If he does have such feelings, he knows they are merely private fantasies. He experiences himself as more interesting and complex than others, but he knows he cannot credibly say why. All human beings have idiosyncratic fantasies, and there is no nonidiosyncratic way to rank their quality. That recognition is what makes the ironist liberal: All human beings should have the equal opportunity to fulfill their fantasies, as long as they are genuinely private or do not impinge on the fantasies of others. Contrary to Plato, Heidegger, and many philosophers in between, Rorty holds that healthy human life in no way depends on the efforts of great thinkers to create or pursue the truth. He ironically admits that he might find Nietzsche's and Foucault's fantasies to be particularly fascinating. But their intense personal obsessions are politically dangerous; they were not ironic or playful enough about the futility of attempts to make them more than idiosyncratic.[84]

The liberal ironist knows that it is pointlessly cruel for him to impose his obsessions on others politically. He may feel himself a genius, but he refuses to be a monster. He is both amused and repulsed by the cruel effects of political projects in response to theological, philosophical, existential, and other obsessions throughout history. He will leave other people alone or in peace. If he acts politically, it will be to expose the monstrous idiosyncrasy of the cruel impositions of others. His limited political goal is to free the world from the illiberal effects of anger and anxiety by discrediting the seriousness of thought and contributing to sentimental education.[85] That goal, of course, is really not so limited. It is nothing less than the completion of the actualization of the liberal or Enlightenment utopia. It is the creation of a world without cruelty and so without the experience of self-conscious mortality. It is, ironically, finally a world without liberal ironists.

Finally, the liberal ironist is ironic about his irony. He knows, as Rorty says, "there is no such thing as *inner* freedom," and there is no truth to "liberal individualism." He holds that "There is nothing to people except what has been socialized into them."[86] Irony, or any form of detached thought and feeling, is really impossible. The ironist cannot explain and so must deny that his irony is possible. Clever animals are not ironic. Kojève became an ironist once he was certain history had ended, aware that there is no way really to articulate credibly or seriously the impossible superfluity of his personal dissatisfaction.[87]

IRONY AND PRAGMATISM'S TRUTH

Perhaps the ironist, most of all, cannot purge himself of his awareness of pragmatism's vulgarity. He seems actually to privilege the ordinary person's unironic, antiphilosophical, and uncourageous aversion to the truth. Rorty says quite cheerfully that his goal is to make people more banal or ordinary, and so to purge the world of both geniuses and monsters. The pragmatist replaces personal efforts to search for the truth in the depth of one's soul with the indiscriminate construction of private fantasies. Rorty encourages, even in the case of great creators or "strong poets," the democratic tendency to shrink away from the depths.

If self-realization is a radically private matter, then Rorty cannot avoid saying that it is the question of "what should I do with my aloneness?"[88] Part of Rorty's answer is not to dwell on the fact that one is alone. One begins with the denial that the "I" is really an I, that there really is such a thing as personal experience.

But Rorty cannot make that denial consistently, which is why he cannot sustain the definition of man as a clever animal. He sometimes acknowledges that "every human being" acts out "consciously or unconsciously . . . an idiosyncratic fantasy." Fantasizing or imagining is what distinguishes human animals from the others. We are more than clever; we are imaginatively self-deceptive, and it is impossible to speak of self-deception without acknowledging somehow the self. Rorty claims that his definition of human distinctiveness follows Sigmund Freud, who democratized "genius" by reducing it to fantasy.[89]

Fantasies, Jean-Jacques Rousseau says, are imaginary reveries one employs to both fill and divert oneself from time.[90] What we call poetry and philosophy,

Rorty explains, are idiosyncrasies that "just happen to catch on with other people," that they just happen to find useful.[91] But people cannot help finding certain fantasies useful for diverting themselves from what they really know. Part of Rorty's irony is that people "just happen" to find his poetry useful.

Rorty's preference for the comfortable to the true is clear in his approval of Dewey's use of God and his appeal to the "religious attitude" in *A Common Faith*. Rorty praises Dewey's astute insight that "aggressive atheism" has "something in common with traditional supernaturalism." What they share is "the excessive preoccupation with man in isolation." Both the Christians and the existentialists dwell on the isolated individual's contingency and mortality, what Rorty would finally have to acknowledge to be the truth about the individual's existence. Dewey rightly corrects that preoccupation with the "religious attitude," which "connect[s] . . . man in the way of both dependence and support, with the world that the imagination feels is a universe." The human imagination opposes the truth, the miserable facts of contingency and isolation. Without such imaginary location, Dewey contends, man stands unprotected from the moods of "despair and defiance" that come with the perception of isolation.[92] Rorty acknowledges that we cannot live well in light of the truth and nothing but the truth, which is why to be human is to construct linguistic fantasies. The imagination's function is to protect us from the truth of existentialism, and its destructive excesses of fatalistic despair and aggressive defiance.

Rorty also defends solidarity as a comfortable lie. He admits, uncharacteristically, that it may be impossible to eradicate "the hope of surviving our individual deaths through some satisfying transfiguration." Pragmatism may not completely succeed, and human beings may not be deprived completely of their longing for immortality. So let them have some hopeful illusion about their community or species, but let that longing be as abstract or vague as possible. The key is that such "solidarity . . . be our *only* comfort, and to be seen not to require metaphysical support." Human hope should not require "a theory about the nature of man," which would include reflection on to what extent individuals or species are really immortal. Hope depends, as Hegel said, on forgetfulness of eternity. Rorty's hope is a baseless lie that provides comfort for beings who are not capable of strong longing or love.[93]

Rorty's easygoing, atheistic, hopeful defense of solidarity is present in the "thoroughgoing" secularism of his promotion of "civic religion."[94] The aggressively atheistic Left sees religion as "narrow-minded and obsolete nationalism."[95] But Rorty wants national devotion properly understood now to become the whole of human devotion. Following his inspirational American heroes Dewey and Whitman, he wants reform toward "the utopian America to replace God as the unconditional object of desire." So "the struggle for social justice" should become "the country's animating principle, the nation's soul."[96] Human longing in our country should be for nothing more or less than "a class-less and castless America."[97]

Rorty implies that a thoroughgoing secularist would not speak of the nation's soul. He does not mean, for now, to dispense with the religious "impulse to stand in awe of something greater than oneself."[98] That impulse, of course, is not permanent or natural. It was a social or linguistic construction, and it might be destroyed the same way. But a thoroughgoing atheist would be an apathetic, detached individual, without hope. He might be a person, like Socrates, who prefers knowledge or self-knowledge to doing what is possible to alleviate human misery. Without a hopeful awe for the nation's future, Americans will not act as citizens. So a pragmatist cannot work to end religious devotion now, because that would be the end of pragmatism.

The pragmatist concludes that both the aggressive atheist and the traditional supernaturalist are far too serious about the truth. In this sense, pragmatism is "a philosophy of solidarity rather than despair."[99] Rorty has no objection, finally, to using God and religion as tools until the need for them completely withers away, until we have constructed a still better fantasy. That fantasy is that we are nothing but clever animals, because we are unmoved by the facts of contingency and mortality. But if that fantasy, which will be, Rorty must acknowledge, a sort of shared idiosyncrasy, is as successful as we have reason to hope, then it will actually become true. The need for fantasy will wither away, as Marx first said, even if Rorty explains better what that withering would actually entail.

Rorty cannot help but know that pragmatism is a lie. He really means to say that we do well to live by useful lies, including the lie that we should judge truth by the criterion of utility. Lies that spare us cruelty lose their effectiveness if we dwell on their untruth. We should say we have no transcendent or trans-historical truth, no certainty, by which to compare them. That way, anyone who has such metaphysical or theological opinions about the truth can be excluded from discussion in a liberal democracy. They can rightly be labeled mad. Whatever threatens our society's conception of freedom and justice — our common, idiosyncratic fantasy — we can call untrue. We can prove such opinions untrue by simply saying they do us no good. Rorty says our view of moral community is sufficient reason to drop metaphysical and theological questions "and the vocabulary in which such questions are posed." The disappearance of the vocabulary means the end of the questions.[100] Our deepest social and political hope is to make pragmatism true.

AMERICAN NICENESS AND FLATNESS

The irony of pragmatism is the human effort to make a lie true. Rorty says we are well on the way to making ourselves clever animals and nothing more. The possibility that such a project could succeed offends common sense. Nobody believed Fukuyama and almost no one believed Kojève when they said history had come to an end. We still know we are mortals; we still make history.

But there is some striking evidence that Rorty is right: the similarity between his and Allan Bloom's descriptions of contemporary American students. We might suspect that is because Bloom is greatly indebted to the work of Kojève, even more than he acknowledged.[101] But Rorty did not read Kojève until his pragmatism was developed. Rorty did not learn much from Bloom, nor Bloom from Rorty. Nevertheless, they both describe American students as nice, and becoming more so.

Bloom describes the students he taught as having been formed by something very like Rorty's pragmatic, sentimental, officially relativistic pragmatism. Bloom sees clearly that such relativism is not really so relativistic, but a pragmatic, chauvinistic defense of bourgeois society. Relativism is a "moral postulate" that prevents students from being moved by critics of their society's egalitarian, pragmatic principles. It causes them to "worship . . . vulgar success," or vulgarly to regard antibourgeois criticism as not useful. Relativism supports "the only form of justice they know," and they "cannot even imagine" an alternative. They are taught not to extend their imagination to the past, when human beings were insanely cruel and unjust. As Rorty said, they have been deprived of antibourgeois words and so antibourgeois experiences.[102]

So today's students, according to Bloom, are unimaginative and unidealistic. They are nice, or pleasant, friendly, and inclusive, but "listless." Their niceness reflects their "lack of passion, of hope, of despair." They are untouched by "the sense of twinship between love and death." They are "competent specialists," or clever animals, and nothing more. Bloom himself finds their lack of passion "incomprehensible." The effort to understand and to come to terms with the twinship between love and death is what constitutes his distinctively human, but now quite idiosyncratic, life.[103]

Bloom reports that the eros of today's students is "lame" or one dimensional, because it is free from all illusion and so all distinctively human long-ing. Without such illusion, eros becomes simply sex, or mechanical rutting. The students' music is the rhythm of that rutting. "To strangers from another planet," Bloom explains, "what would be the most striking thing is that sexual passion no longer includes the illusion of eternity." *The* contemporary phe-nomenon is "the deeroticization of the world." The students have become just like the other animals, no longer beings with souls.[104]

Today's students experience nothing as permanent and so everything hu-man as contingent. They "are the first historical or historicized generation, not only in theory but in practice."[105] As Rorty observes, it is becoming commonly known that human beings are historical all the way through, and that fact in a way informs their whole lives. But they are not moved by restless longing to thought or action by it. They are satisfied with their finitude without any effort. Bloom cannot believe they are really self-conscious at all. But he describes them as without illusion concerning their finitude. They recognize the truth about both history and eternity.

Like Rorty, Bloom understands this unprecedented flatness of soul as the culmination of the Enlightenment in America. He makes general statements about that development of thought and its effects on practice that do not depend upon his personal knowledge of his students. What Marx claimed was possi-ble, Bloom insists the Americans have virtually achieved. They have freed hu-man life from tension or contradiction. They have freed it from definition by necessity's constraints, especially the necessity of death.

Bloom finds three stages to the development of the Enlightenment in America. He instructively adds psychological detail to Rorty's rather abstract narrative, but he tells basically the same story and certainly reaches the same conclusion. First, the Americans "slowly executed" God. He lost out to "the sa-cred," a euphemism for scientific atheism. Next, "love was put to death by psy-chologists," who replaced it with "sex and meaningful relationships." Poly-morphous and largely insatiable longing has been reduced to readily comprehensible and achievable satisfaction. The American pragmatic expert explains that God and love really contribute nothing to useful and productive lives.

The perfection of the pragmatic science of sex produced another "new sci-ence, thanatology, or death with dignity." This science "is on the way to putting death to death." The only way wholly to separate death from indignity, as Rorty says, is not to be bothered by it. "Death," Bloom reports, "isn't what it used to be." It no longer terrifies. So philosophy, "Socrates' long and arduous education, learning how to die," is largely obsolete.[106] Socrates' education began with the pain that comes with questioning all that one holds most dear and ends somehow with both intense pleasure and serene resignation. Today's student is incapable of feeling the pain that leads to that distinctively human pleasure. He has learned how to live comfortably with death and with what is left of love.

Professors Bloom and Rorty recognize that the flat-souled or unserious niceness of their students is evidence of the Enlightenment's success. Death no longer defines human existence. Bloom says he is not certain what will replace it. He does report "a divination of Engels," a most scientific Marxist. What comes next is "the classless society," which "would last, if not forever, a very long time." The death of death means the Marxian-Hegelian end of history is now here. Justice, universally and homogeneously defined, has triumphed, because we are clever animals and nothing more. Human beings have definitively conquered nature; they have, Bloom reports, made themselves "perfectly at home on earth." Only their experiences of having to come to terms with God, love, and death prevented them from being so.[107]

BLOOM VERSUS RORTY

Bloom and Rorty agree on their descriptions of contemporary American students, and on the psychological analysis about what is required for the Enlightenment project really to succeed. "All one has to do is forget about eternity," Bloom concludes, and "the most intractable of man's problems have been solved."[108] The pragmatic method of problem solving is forgetting through the manipulation or truncation of the imagination.

Bloom and Rorty do seem to differ radically on the level of evaluation. Rorty is all for effective problem solving. Bloom opposes the soul's flatness on behalf of "the deepest human experience," or "what is uniquely human, the very definition of man."[109] With the experience of the philosopher, Bloom claims to have a standpoint by which to criticize historical success. He asserts that "all the philosophers agreed that the fulfillment of humanity is the use of reason."[110] In the name of reason, Bloom shouts what he knows about the inevitability of his own and others' deaths, the truth Rorty unreasonably refuses to mention. Death, as Socrates said, is not a problem to be solved but a truth to be experienced. The experience of death, to be sure, is what makes much of our behavior unreasonable. But we have it, paradoxically, because we alone among the beings can reason, and it is unreasonable to deny that we have it.

The philosopher is the most complete human being because he is the least self-forgetful. "The essential difference," Bloom asserts, "between the philosopher and all other men is his facing of death or his relation to eternity." He neither flinches before nor feigns unconcern with the fact of his mortality; his "facing of death" is "intransigent." The "reality of death" infuses "every thought and deed" of the philosopher. The philosopher seems, in Kojève's sense, actually to be wise: "No other way of life than the philosophic can digest the truth about death."[111] Bloom contends that "Philosophy is the rational," and presumably true, "account of the whole," and not just the quest for that account.[112]

With that truth, the philosopher sees the groundlessness of all human hopes. They are always for one's salvation. The philosopher can only "dissolve" human aspirations, and so most human beings find his "somber" insight "intolerable." The philosopher himself experiences an "intense pleasure" in compensation for the insightful misery of his self-conscious morality. Without that pleasure, which very few share, he too would find life in light of the truth intolerable.[113]

But, for nonphilosophers, the truth is no clear guide for action. The social hopes for the future, for one's grandchildren, that Rorty encourages depend on forgetting that one will not likely be around to see them become reality. In any case, the achievement of such freedom and justice will not fundamentally transform one's existence. Hope for personal salvation is a more genuine, if illusory, response to the human longing. Bloom seems actually close to agreeing with Rorty that genuinely self-conscious mortality is useless. Most human beings cannot live well with it, and so would be better off without it. The radically different experience of the rare philosophers, Bloom's experience, seems too "idiosyncratic"[114] to *effectively* oppose this conclusion. But a complication is that Bloom says that today's students know the truth about death and certainly have no hope for salvation. They do not seem to find the truth intolerable, or even somber. In what way are they less reasonable than the philosopher?

Rorty agrees with almost every particular statement Bloom makes about human finitude and contingency. He does not hope to be saved from death. He would acknowledge that he will die alone. He regards all metaphysical and theological statements about immortality to be untrue. Unfeeling acceptance of the transience and contingency of all things human, Rorty agrees with Bloom, is becoming more and more the common sense of our secular, postmetaphysical, nice or unserious world.

Rorty joins the students against Bloom by denying that there is necessarily anything terrible about any of this. He never says he fears death or longs for immortality, and he adds that those who do have such fear and longing may well be cured by sentimental education. We have reason to disbelieve Rorty's ironic self-denial, but the nice students he and Bloom describe really are that easygoing. They do not love anything at all. Bloom actually presents better evidence than Rorty that Rorty's pragmatism is true. Pragmatists may have very little left to do. Bloom is at least not certain that to be moved passionately by love and death is a permanent part of the condition of our species. It is the point of human distinction, but it may be on the way to disappearing. Surely Bloom has no reason to disagree with Kojève or Rorty that it would be perverse to work to restore death if it really has been overcome. Bloom and Rorty both affirm the priority of the pragmatist's linguistic manipulation to the existentialist's truth, because they both agree that most human beings would be better off not knowing or being moved by the fact they are going to die.

BLOOM, NATURE, AND HISTORY

Bloom's agreement with Rorty and Kojève on death seems to contradict what Bloom says about the way of life of the philosopher as a natural perfection. But considering all that he has written, the least we can say is that Bloom is not certain about that relationship between philosophy and nature. He reports, for example, that the philosophers regarded fear of death as natural. But he also notes that Rousseau, a philosopher, "flatly denies that man . . . naturally fears death."[115] Had he ever written on Rorty, Bloom certainly would have said that Rorty's position—and the Hegelian distinction between nature and history it presupposes—was best expressed by Rousseau.

Rousseau and Rorty agree that awareness of death and so, in a way, death itself "is really a product of the imagination." By nature man enjoys an "idle and pleasure-loving life," one unconcerned with and so unresistant to death. So "men naturally know how to die," because they do it unconsciously. They naturally are "without the illusions about death that pervert life and require the Socratic effort." Death, and the corresponding human perversions, are historical, not natural, phenomena. The historical Socrates struggled to achieve imperfectly what natural man had easily and perfectly. Bloom shows that natural man, with Rousseau's help, is Socrates' best critic.[116]

Bloom reports that "the souls of young people [today] are in a condition like that of the first men in the state of nature." So it is not surprising that they are also Socrates' critics. They, like Rorty, use his method against him.

Socrates' critical inquiries dispelled the illusions that give weight to every way of life but his own. Why does the philosopher take death so seriously? What is his problem? Today's young, Bloom goes on, "are exaggerated versions of Plato's [Socrates'?] description of the young in democracies."[117] He suggests that democracy's perfection is philosophy's end, because it is the end of death or being animated by the perception of invincible necessity. From Bloom's perspective, Socrates rightly thought democracy's perfection to be undesirable, but he wrongly thought it to be impossible.

What Rousseau says about death, he also says about love. It too is an imaginary illusion. It certainly does not point human beings in the direction of the truth. Instead, it aids in covering up their unnatural, perverted knowledge of death. So Rousseau tries to take love seriously for the perverted, social beings who must employ the imagination to live well. "The enigma of Rousseau's whole undertaking," Bloom observes, "is how can one believe in what one knows to be the product of the imagination?" That enigma plagues the fantasizing Rorty. But finally, Bloom shows, there is no enigma. The effectual truth of Rousseau's teaching on love, against his intention, has been to destroy it. It produced Rorty's belief that the imagination can be manipulated to allow human beings to live in abundance and without cruelty, as did natural man.

Rousseau criticizes the "modern philosophers," and the uncruel Rorty is surely one, for their "notably unerotic teachings." Rousseau, against their efforts, tried to restore the poetry of love to the world. But his criticism of the modern philosophers includes the acknowledgment that they "see nature as it is," unerotically or unpoetically. Rousseau and Rorty agree that there is no natural or true foundation for poetry and love. Rorty and Bloom describe a world in which Rousseau's modern view of the truth defeated his poetic creativity or illusion. The oxymoron flat soul is the true soul.[118]

Rousseau's teaching about nature is the foundation of the science or wisdom Bloom finds present among the students who have nothing to learn from him at history's end. Psychotherapy (or thanatology) of various sorts, including that practiced by Rorty, is restoring man, mentally diseased by history, to natural health. This cure is for the "wounds inflicted by society," gratuitous suffering, or cruelty for which one has no responsibility.[119]

Bloom reminds us that Rousseau preceded Rorty in the abandonment of the moral language of virtue and vice. He replaced it with the medical language of health and disease. This reductionistic psychotherapy, Bloom claims, makes him the most modern of the moderns.[120] Kojève and Rorty do seem merely to follow his lead. The final goal of psychotherapy is euthanasia, the perfectly good death praised by the philosophers. The man who dies such a death is beyond the diseased realm of virtue or vice, or good and evil.

Bloom does say he has reason to disagree with Rousseau's diagnosis of the problem of human liberty and his proposal for a cure. *Love and Friendship* was written as "an attempt to recover the power, the danger, and the beauty of eros." The emphasis is not on restoring the capability of human beings to be moved by death, but on the Socratic foundation for opposing Rousseau and his successors on man's natural solitude. "The difference between Nietzsche and Socrates," Bloom asserts, "comes down to the possibility of that most ultimate form of community, mutual understanding." This "logocentric" friendship is between philosophers who share the truth about "being," as well as a love of that truth.[121] Perhaps if that friendship did not exist, then love really is an illusion. All that would remain are idiosyncratic fantasies or solitary reveries.

But philosophic friendship, Bloom acknowledges, is extremely rare. The example he gives is the one between Michel de Montaigne and Etienne de La Boétie, centuries ago. It seems mainly to have been the shared exhilaration of secret liberation from the religious illusions of their time. Could that exhilaration be experienced today, when the popularized religious indifference described by Bloom and Rorty has taken so much of the danger and the fun out of free thought? Is this philosophic friendship liberation from illusion for the truth about death? How can this truth, which would appear radically to isolate the individual, be the foundation of community?

Bloom may acknowledge that philosophic friendship is too rare and questionable really to be of human significance. He does say that friendship "in any sense intended by Montaigne" is virtually impossible in America today. Does he agree with Rorty that the possibility of philosophic friendship is too useless to be true? It seems to have no relevance to almost all human lives, especially lives today. Does Bloom really say or mean to say enough not to agree with Rorty that what Montaigne and La Boétie enjoyed was a private fantasy? In truth, were they so touched by each other that they were relatively untouched by death?[122]

CONCLUSION: RORTY AND BLOOM
AT THE END OF HISTORY

Bloom, like Kojève, says philosophy is acknowledging all that is implied in, without flinching about, one's death. That surely includes acknowledging that the very existence of human beings is historical or temporary. The end of history, of course, is the end of illusion, especially illusions about eternity that made human eros possible. Part of wisdom may be knowing that the human perception of it will pass away. Does Bloom acknowledge that philosophy has disappeared or is about to disappear? Does he share Rorty's or Kojève's ironic awareness of how idiosyncratic his personal experiences are?

Rorty thinks he disagrees with Bloom's portrayal of Americans uneasy in the midst of a "deep spiritual malaise." The pragmatist denies that "our problem is . . . internal hollowness." It is only the apparent intractability of certain "external" or social problems, ones that really can be overcome through the linguistic manipulation of the imagination.[123] But Rorty misreads Bloom; the students he describes suffer from no such malaise. A flat soul is not a hollow one. One can fill up a hollow soul, but perhaps nothing is to be done with a flat one. If Rorty had read Bloom more closely and sympathetically, he surely would have seen that Bloom is more convinced than Rorty that Rorty is right about America's future.

Rorty, the Hegelian in spite of his antirational pretensions, remains too charmed by the fundamentally undemocratic Socratic or rationalist tradition by agreeing with Bloom, in effect, that the choice must be made between Socratic self-consciousness and a classless society full of clever animals. The Socratics and pragmatists agree that most people cannot live well in light of the truth about death. And so the ironic philosophers or intellectuals give ordinary people linguistic therapy. Both Socratic and pragmatic thinkers and poets tell lies to talk away the truth in view of its cruelty, and they both use ordinary people to achieve their not wholly rational ends through civic religion.[124]

Rorty is in one way more democratic than Bloom by refusing to privilege the experience of Socrates. But in another way he is more elitist: His political or rhetorical struggle against the common perception of eternity and so the limits of human effort is more extreme. The Socratics, by perpetuating the distinction between man and God, mean to keep some intimation of the truth in human imagination, but Rorty claims that distinction was a failure of the imagination that the Americans have overcome. So for Rorty there are no limits to what political reform might and should achieve, and there are no human limits to the reach of government inspired by therapeutic intellectuals.

AN AFTERWORD ABOUT A LEFTOVER

There is a very fundamental contradiction in Bloom's book about America, and it would be misleading to ignore it. He says that children of divorce are different from his other students. Their niceness is really rigidity. For them, the principles of egalitarian relativism are really "desperate platitudes" with which they try and fail to make sense out of "the chaos of their experience."

The children of the divorced have been subjected to "therapy," provided by psychological experts and paid for by their parents. The therapy is linguistic. The psychologist speaks the platitudes about self-determination and the relationship between divorce and personal happiness. But the therapy usually fails because the "artificial language" about "artificial feelings" does not speak to the real longings within the soul of the child. The child may have nice manners and echo the expert's platitudes, but they are "a thin veneer over boundless seas of rage, doubt and fear." Bloom says that the children of the divorced are "victims" who deserve our "pity." For them, "their disarray in the cosmos" is the appropriate "theme of reflection and study."[125] They are, as Walker Percy says, lost in the cosmos, and their lives are not those of clever, contented animals at history's end.

But Bloom does not actually present children of the divorced as exceptions to the rule. They are "symbols of the intellectual-political problems of our time." One of the consequences of the Enlightenment in America is the desocialization that comes with the deeroticization of the world. All of life, including marriage, is redefined in terms of personal calculation. So the institution of marriage is failing, and no one knows what to do to save it. Divorce has become more pervasive, and even couples who stay together spend less time with and are less attached to their children. The children of the divorced "represent in extreme form the spiritual vortex set in motion by loss of contact with other human beings and with the natural world."[126]

It makes sense to say that the extreme experience will become more common, and so students will more commonly experience themselves in cosmic and personal disarray. Does not the resulting fear, rage, and doubt show they have souls? The pragmatic project to deeroticize the world is not really returning human beings to Rousseau's state of nature.

Does not this likely explosion of imperfectly repressed passion show that those who speak of the end of history only speak of a fragile and temporary surface of human reality? Why is the experience of "disarray in the cosmos" not closer to the truth than the self-avoidance of niceness? This line of inquiry could be Bloom's decisive refutation of Rorty, and we wonder why and are disappointed that he does not pursue it. Perhaps Bloom simply prefers not to say that human reality to some extent eludes reason.

NOTES

1. Harvey C. Mansfield Jr., "Dewey: All-Out Democrat," *Times Literary Supplement* (24 January 1992), 26.

2. Alexandre Kojève, "The Idea of Death in the Philosophy of Hegel," *Interpretation* 3 (1973).

3. Richard Rorty, "After Philosophy, Democracy," in *The American Philosopher,* ed. G. Borradori (Chicago: University of Chicago Press, 1994), 116.

4. Richard Rorty, *Contingency, Irony, and Solidarity* (Cambridge: Cambridge University Press, 1989), 150–158.

5. Ibid., 16.

6. Ibid., 113n15.

7. Ibid., 106.

8. Richard Rorty, *Objectivity, Relativism, and Truth* (Cambridge: Cambridge University Press, 1991), 71.

9. Rorty, *Contingency,* 110.

10. Ibid., 23, 71.

11. Ibid., 24, including the note.

12. Richard Rorty, *Philosophy and the Mirror of Nature* (Princeton, N.J.: Princeton University Press, 1979), 70.

13. René Vincente Arcilla, *For the Love of Perfection: Richard Rorty and Liberal Education* (New York: Routledge, 1995), 98–99.

14. Charles Hartshorne, "Rorty's Pragmatism and Farewell to the Age of Faith and Enlightenment," in *Rorty and Pragmatism: The Philosopher Responds to His Critics,* ed. C. Saatkamp (Nashville, Tenn.: Vanderbilt University Press, 1995), 21–22.

15. Rorty, "Response" [to Hartshorne], in Saatkamp, 31–34.

16. Ibid., 34.

17. Richard Rorty, "Expanding Our Culture," in *Debating the State of Philosophy,* ed. J. Nitzik and J. Sanders (Westport, Conn.: Praeger, 1996), 25.

18. Rorty, "Response," 35–36.

19. Arcilla, x.

20. Rorty, *Objectivity,* 32.

21. Richard Rorty, *Essays on Heidegger and Others* (Cambridge: Cambridge University Press, 1991), 13.

22. Ibid., 137.

23. Rorty, *Contingency,* 85.

24. Rorty, *Essays,* 24–25.

25. Rorty, *Objectivity,* 175–196.

26. Rorty, *Contingency,* 113, text and note 13.

27. Ibid., 173.

28. Richard Rorty, [Untitled Comments], in *Debating the State of Philosophy,* 114.

29. Rorty, *Objectivity,* 175–196.

30. Richard Rorty, "Two Cheers for Elitism," *New Yorker* 70 (30 January 1995), 88–89.

31. Rorty, *Contingency,* 173.

32. Rorty, *Objectivity,* 182.

33. See Rorty, *Contingency,* 40.

34. Ibid., 179.

35. Ibid., 146, 158, 161, 173, 182.

36. Richard Rorty, *Truth and Progress* (Cambridge: Cambridge University Press, 1998), 67–85.

37. Rorty, *Essays,* 48. Rorty's new book, *Achieving Our Country: Leftist Thought in Twentieth-Century America* (Cambridge, Mass.: Harvard University Press, 1998), in one sense opposes cosmopolitanism with nationalism. But Rorty's argument is that we must use nationalism today as the most effective means of achieving cosmopolitanism tomorrow. He is no Pat Buchanan.

38. Rorty, *Truth,* 179.

39. Rorty, *Achieving,* 85.

40. Rorty, *Truth,* 179–185.

41. Rorty, *Objectivity,* 182.

42. Rorty, *Contingency,* 35.

43. Rorty, *Essays,* 25.

44. Rorty, *Contingency,* 197.

45. Ibid., 46.

46. Rorty, *Essays,* 47.

47. Rorty, *Truth,* 176–177.

48. Rorty, *Contingency,* 73; Rorty *Essays,* 100.

49. Rorty's *Achieving* is a Hegelian history of America. It is, in other words, pragmatic, not "objective," history. It is a tale told to encourage political reform toward the classless society.

50. Rorty, *Contingency,* 55, 73.

51. Rorty, *Achieving,* 24.

52. Ibid., 21–22.

53. Ibid., 19, 30.

54. Rorty, *Contingency,* 219.

55. Ibid., 63.

56. Rorty, *Objectivity,* 208, 216.

57. Rorty, *Truth,* 173–174.

58. Ibid., 230–233.

59. Rorty, "Relativism—Finding and Making," in *Debating the State of Philosophy,* 43.

60. Rorty, *Objectivity,* 190.

61. Ibid., 194.

62. Rorty, *Contingency,* 46.

63. Rorty, *Objectivity,* 192.

64. Rorty, *Achieving,* 27.

65. Rorty, *Truth,* 230.

66. Ibid.

67. Ibid., 230–231.

68. Ibid., 231. On the evil empire, see *Achieving,* 66.

69. Ibid., 184.

70. This radical assertion about the truth of pragmatism is the theme of *Achieving Our Country.*

71. Rorty, *Achieving,* 30.

72. Rorty, *Contingency,* 196.

73. The phrase "intellectual probity" is not Rorty's. It is drawn from Leo Strauss's criticism of Nietzsche. See Peter Berkowitz, "The Reason of Revelation: The Jewish Thought of Leo Strauss," *The Weekly Standard* 3 (25 May 1998), 31–34.

74. Rorty, *Objectivity,* 192.

75. Rorty, *Truth,* 175.

76. Kojève, *Introduction,* 158–159, note 6.

77. Rorty, "Relativism," 38.

78. The intellectual Rorty, of course, cannot adhere to this position consistently: "But we of course go on to add that being an irrationalist . . . is not to be incapable of argument. We irrationalists do not . . . behave like animals" (Rorty, "Relativism," 34).

79. Rorty, *Achieving,* 25–26.

80. Ibid., 34.

81. Ibid., 32.

82. Jerry Weinberger, "Technology and the Problem of Liberal Democracy," in *Technology and the Western Political Tradition,* ed. A. Melzer, J. Weinberger, and R. Zinman (Ithaca, N.Y.: Cornell University Press, 1993), 264.

83. Rorty, *Contingency,* 87–89.

84. Rorty, *Objectivity,* 192; Rorty, *Contingency,* 53, 89.

85. See Weinberger, 262–265.

86. Rorty, *Contingency,* 177.

87. Hugh Gillis, "Anthropology, Dialectic and Atheism in Kojève's Thought," *Graduate Faculty Philosophy Journal* 18 (1995), 103.

88. Rorty, *Objectivity,* 13.

89. Rorty, *Contingency,* 26, 36–37.

90. Rousseau, *Reveries of a Solitary Walker,* Walk 5.

91. Rorty, *Contingency,* 37.

92. Rorty, *Objectivity,* 69–70.

93. Ibid., 32.

94. Rorty, *Achieving,* 15, 30.

95. Ibid., 15.

96. Ibid., 17.

97. Ibid., 30.

98. Ibid., 17.

99. Rorty, *Objectivity,* 33.

100. Ibid., 183, 186–187, 190.

101. See Allan Bloom, *Giants and Dwarfs* (New York: Simon and Schuster, 1990), 268–273.

102. Allan Bloom, *The Closing of the American Mind* (New York: Simon and Schuster, 1987), 25–26, 90.

103. Ibid., 123, 134.

104. Ibid., 68–81, 123, 132–133; Allan Bloom, *Love and Friendship* (New York: Simon and Schuster, 1992), 15.

105. Bloom, *Closing,* 106–108.

106. Ibid., 230.

107. Ibid.

108. Ibid.

109. Ibid., 273.

110. Ibid., 292.

111. Ibid., 277–285.

112. Ibid., 264.

113. Ibid., 277.

114. Ibid., 312.

115. Bloom, *Giants,* 185.

116. Ibid., 185–186.

117. Bloom, *Closing,* 87.

118. Bloom, *Giants,* 200.

119. Bloom, *Love and Friendship,* 44.

120. Ibid.

121. Ibid., 12, 542–543.

122. Ibid., 410–428.

123. Rorty, "Straussianism, Democracy, and Allan Bloom I: That Old Time Philosophy," in *Essays on the Closing of the American Mind,* ed. R. Stone (Chicago: Chicago Review Press, 1989), 103.

124. The idea of connecting Rorty's and the Socratics' pragmatic concerns came to me from Patrick Glynn, *God: The Evidence* (Rocklin, Calif.: Prima, 1997), 144–145.

125. Bloom, *Closing,* 121.

126. Ibid., 118–121.

3

WALKER PERCY'S
TWENTIETH-CENTURY THOMISM

W alker Percy was both a novelist and a philosopher or theorist about being and human being. He published philosophical essays before any of his novels, and he continued to write such essays his entire life. During his most productive years, he wrote fiction in the morning and theoretical essays in the afternoon.[1] He was, perhaps not without reason, unsure he was a great novelist.[2] He thought his work on "the nature of the semiotic process," of man as a languaged being, would be his "chief claim to be remembered 100 years from now."[3] He said his "BREAKTHROUGH" concerning the natural and unique foundation of human language "was much more important than making up novels."[4]

Percy wrote an explicitly theoretical book, *Lost in the Cosmos: The Last Self-Help Book,* which presents, in a complex variety of literary forms, his "New Science" of the self. This science is to replace the "Old," "Present Day" science, which can account pretty well for everything but the self.[5] *Contra Gentiles,* the book he was writing at the time of his death, was an explicitly Catholic, or Thomistic, defense of the natural foundation of the mystery of human language. But all of his work, especially his science, points in the direction of the truth of his faith. My purpose in this chapter is to take Percy seriously as a theorist or scientist.

Percy defends the "Scholastic view" that human beings "share certain characteristics with other creatures" but also "are capable of higher perfections peculiar to themselves."[6] For the Thomist, the human being is "distinguished from the beast in being endowed with soul, intellect, free will, reason, and the gift of language." The gift of language is *the* fundamental natural human capacity, the one responsible for the development of the others. With that gift, human beings can name things, think about them, convey thoughts with words that can be understood by others, come to know much of the truth about nature and something about themselves, and exercise their freedom well or badly.[7]

Man becomes man, Percy observes, by "breaking into the daylight of language."[8] Humans became human in the sense of the species becoming qualitatively distinct at some recent point in the evolutionary process. But in the natural development of the particular human creature, humans become human, or children acquire language, all the time. Percy observes that "the transformation of the responding organism into the languaged human . . . is undoubtedly the most extraordinary natural phenomenon in all of biological behavior, if not in the entire cosmos, and yet the most commonplace of events, one that occurs every day under our noses."[9] Percy wonders why we do not wonder more about what is genuinely extraordinary, the commonplace mystery of becoming and being human.

REALISM

Percy often connects his discovery of the capacity for language as distinguishing and defining human nature to C. S. Peirce, the most rational and joyful of American philosophers. Peirce said "there are Real things out there whose characters are independent of our opinion of them." Percy explains that Peirce "meant that there is a real world and it is possible in a degree to know it and talk about it and be understood."[10]

But too much should not be made of Percy's use of Peirce. He was "not a student" but "a thief of Peirce." He took what he wanted and "let the rest go, most of it," or ninety-nine percent of it. Percy was interested in Peirce only insofar as he could use "his attack on nominalism and his rehabilitation of Scholastic realism." He employed the thought and authority of Peirce to make realism credible as philosophy and science to contemporary scholarly audiences. Peirce, for Percy, is "the foundation" of "Catholic apologetic" for our time.

Percy was "massively uninterested" in Peirce's obsession with "formal logic," and he viewed his anti-Christian prejudices and his inability to see the distinctiveness and plausibility of the Christian claim for truth as "the silliest kind of nonsense." He knew his apologetic use of Peirce would send the philosopher "spinning in his grave."[11] Percy eventually said he "had quite enough from" Peirce, complaining that he never developed what "God knows he should have" on the basis of his scientific realism, an anthropology in the proper sense, "a scientific, i.e. rational, theory of man."[12]

But too little should not be made of the connection between Percy and Peirce. The attack on nominalism on behalf of realism, they both understood, is what is required to restore the ordinary common sense that makes science, a community of knowers, possible.[13] There really is a connection among things, words, and human knowledge. That connection is language, where both mind and matter and particular human beings intersect. Percy wrote that Peirce understood "exactly what language is about," and he predicted the emergence of "the Peirce-Percy theory of meaning."[14] But their theoretical breakthrough would actually be nothing but Thomism updated, and it was up to the Thomist Percy to supply the theory of man suggested by Peirce's theory of language or meaning.

Peirce "came up with . . . modern scientific confirmation of the ancient realism of Aristotle and the later realism of the medieval schoolmen who saw mental entities like ideas as part of the same reality as things and bodies." He rejected the incoherent, untenable dualism of René Descartes that produced "the regnant and diverging materialism and idealism of the Nineteenth Century." The materialists tried to explain everything "by the doctrine of matter in motion." The idealists, Immanuel Kant and G. W. F. Hegel, attempted to explain everything as subjectivity freed from matter. The question remained: What do matter and mind "have to do with each other?" Language, Peirce discovered, "the observable behavior of a speaking and listening human," is where mind and matter intersect. So language, from "the posture of a natural scientist," ought be the focus of investigation "of those traits which seem," to common sense and the Judeo-Christian tradition, "to set man apart from the other species."[15]

In the earlier and seemingly scientifically discredited Scholastic language, only angels can see things directly and communicate with one another without symbols. Human beings know things indirectly and imperfectly, through the medium of words or symbols. But know them they do, and the communication of that knowledge is a real foundation of human community.[16]

For Peirce and Percy, the human being is the being with language. Their scientific concern is with the *"phenomenon of language . . . as a natural phenomenon,"* not merely as a *"formal structure."*[17] For Percy, Peirce's thought was most interesting as the foundation of a "semiotic" as "a natural science of signs."[18] This account of nature shows that man is, by nature, a social being. Human self-consciousness must be experienced through symbolic interaction with others. Percy's science is opposed to all forms of post-Cartesian or post-Rousseauean analysis based on the premise that what distinguishes human beings is not natural, and so neither love nor man's openness to the truth has a natural foundation.[19] Percy and Peirce take the side of science against all those who deny that human beings have a natural capacity to know. Percy agrees with Aristotle and Saint Thomas that discovering the truth and communicating it to others may be the greatest of the human pleasures.[20] That pleasure "is a fundamental thing, going back to the origins of speech or consciousness." Its "very strong social dimension" is in "the delight [that] occurs in the transaction" of communication, of naming and understanding, from one person to another.[21]

Percy affirms what for Aristotle, Saint Thomas, and even Blaise Pascal is a scientific conclusion. The languaged being exists in between the well-ordered beings, as "more than an organism controlled by his environment, but not a detached, wholly objective angelic being."[22] But where man is located is for Percy, more than for Aristotle, ineradicably mysterious. He joins Pascal in emphasizing his strangeness and perversity, while remaining as devoted as Aristotle to the possibility of a science of human nature.

The languaged being's self-conscious imperfection distinguishes him from both angel or God and animal. The reason for this difference eludes science, which is why scientists often doubt realism's truth. The capacity for language cannot be understood the way other natural capacities can, as simply a tool for the preservation or adaption of the species. Language is the source of the many forms of self-destructive human perversity, of war, murder, suicide, anger and self-hatred, boredom, depression, anxious restlessness in the midst of prosperity, and so forth. Language also makes possible the unique human phenomenon of lying, both to oneself and to others.[23]

Alone among the animals, Percy explains, the human being "has the . . . capacity for making himself unhappy for no good reason, for existing as a lonely and fretful consciousness which never quite knows who he is or where he belongs."[24] His science, in part, is an account of why the human being is "the only alien creature, so far as we know, in the cosmos." The languaged, social being cannot be accounted for by a "dyadic" or stimulus-response explanation. Man experiences himself as an alien because he cannot, through language or thought, formulate or locate his own place in a cosmos that is otherwise dyadic. So he can experience or interpret his self-consciousness as a natural "catastrophe," "a genetic accident," or "a diabolical mutation."[25] He can hate, deny, or attempt to destroy what distinguishes human existence.[26]

But the human being can also enjoy the contemplation of the "comic mystery" of his own existence.[27] The openness language gives him to the truth, including some truthful self-consciousness, can be the source of both "cognitive" and "ontological" joys,[28] often ample compensation for the anxious misery one experiences in the face of what one can neither understand nor ignore.

The languaged being is capable of loving the pursuit and discovery of the truth, and sometimes preferring the truth to self-preservation. But he can also prefer self-preservation to the truth. Human beings can both love and hate what they perceive to be true and either embrace it or aim to negate it. Realism is both an awareness of the languaged being's openness to the truth about being and human being and an acknowledgment of the singular, mysterious elusiveness of that being.

Percy distinguishes himself among "postmodern" thinkers by not turning his back on philosophy and science. He holds that human beings can know, objectively, the truth about nature or the cosmos and even love that truth. But he also holds that the novelist and the Christian believer also possess genuine ways of knowing. He contends that "these sentences of art, poetry, and the novel ought to be taken very seriously indeed since these are the cognitive, scientific, if you will, statements that we have about what it is to be human."[29] They are capacities the languaged being has to communicate the truth about shared human experiences, and the mode of expression of the novelist is characteristically a genuinely scientific correction to the scientist's tendency to abstract from what is particularly human. Percy incessantly pursued a genuinely comprehensive science, one that would incorporate the true artistic and theological criticisms of the self-denial characteristic of science and scientists. He holds that the old quarrels between philosophy and poetry, and reason and revelation, depended for their intensity on an incomplete understanding of the character of science or human knowledge.[30]

AUTHENTICITY

Human beings are capable of experiencing, denying, and attempting to account for their mysterious natural distinctiveness in all sorts of ways. They can, for example, view their existence as pure chance, and so as good but mostly bad luck.[31] The Thomist's view is that language is a gift to be used responsibly by those created in God's image. But the Thomist adds that what human beings have been given uniquely by nature imposes on them certain responsibilities, whether or not the gift is from God. So "the standard of human existence" is "wholly different from that by which we judge the flora of Australia and the ape population of the Congo."[32]

The capacity for language, and so self-consciousness, introduces into nature, Percy says, "a value scale of rightness, authenticity; in short, a concept of human nature and what is proper to it."[33] That concept includes specifically human needs: "An organism is oriented toward the world according to its organismic needs, but a person is oriented in the mode of truth-untruth."[34] What distinguishes the person, the need for and the possibility of living authentically with the truth, is neither meaningless, arbitrary, illusory, nor futile.

The distinction between authenticity and inauthenticity, Martin Heidegger explains, is rooted in man's "primordial relation to language." Spoken language often degenerates into idle talk or gossip. The search for understanding readily becomes merely idle curiosity. Living in light of the "I," one's own, personal experiences, easily becomes deferring to "the anonymous *man* . . . what they say." In each case, the "fall" into inauthentic existence is movement of language away from its authentic purpose of articulating the truth about being and human being.[35]

Human beings are given needs and capabilities beyond merely biological existence. It is largely up to them whether or not they fulfill them. So it is possible to ask whether and in what way a man has betrayed his human destiny. But a dog is incapable of betraying his destiny as a dog. It is possible to say that a human being is alienated from the truth about being, particularly his own being, and so is living inauthentically or irresponsibly. But a dog, lacking the capacity for language, can neither be alienated from nor open to the truth. Human beings are capable of being better and worse than dogs, but not of reducing themselves to the amorality of doglike simplicity.[36] They cannot become posthistorical beings or return to nature in Jean-Jacques Rousseau's sense.

An inauthentic self is one that is self-deceived or diverted. This distinction between diverted and undiverted lives Percy calls Socratic.[37] But he finds it most plainly expressed by Pascal, who "spoke of the man who comes into this world knowing not whence he came nor whither he will go but only that he will for certain die, and who spends his life as though he were not the center of the supreme mystery but rather diverting himself (and, we might add, adjusting himself). Such a man . . . is worse than a fool."[38] The miserable foolishness of diversion is what, Percy says, "Heidegger calls "fall[ing] prey to everydayness."[39]

All animals die, that is for certain. But only human beings know that natural fact and its significance in one's own case. That miserable, anxious awareness is the price to be paid for the gift of language, for thinking about the mystery of human existence. Those who divert themselves from the mystery through the pursuit of material enjoyment, sexual pleasure, scientific theory that abstracts from what is particularly human, the "other directed" everydayness of daily life, or immersion as a detached spectator in newspapers, films, and television, really "forfeit the means for understanding themselves."[40]

THE LIMITED TRUTH OF EXISTENTIALISM

Percy sides with the existentialists against pragmatists from René Descartes through Karl Marx and John Dewey. The experience of human alienation is not a treatable symptom of one's maladjustment to one's environment or society. It is not the result of the capitalist economic system or modern technology. It is "the perennial condition of human existence."[41] The existentialist and "orthodox" Christian understanding of alienation is in a fundamental sense the same: "Man is alienated by the nature of his being here."[42]

So to aim to cure human beings completely of their anxious misery is actually to aim to deprive them of their humanity. All organisms are capable of fear or instinctive aversion to danger. But only a human being can be anxious or "afraid of nothing." One is uneasy about and terrified of what is evidently beyond one's comprehension and control, particularly the mystery of one's own being. Unlike fear, anxiety "serves no biological function." From a biological perspective, it is at best a superfluous and at worst a self-destructive mood.[43]

But the Thomist's agreement with the existentialist is limited. The existentialist holds that the human being's anxious experience of alienation is a sign of the "absurdity" of human life.[44] The existentialist is no realist; he sees no natural foundation for self-consciousness, and so no natural connection between language and things. He cannot explain why he knows anything about anything, himself or the world. His ungrounded introspection is bound to tend to become neurotic or fanatical.[45] The existentialist often seems stuck with the joyless burden of asserting his useless liberty against nature and without God.[46] But even Jean-Paul Sartre cannot help connecting the discovery of one's "nothingness" with the "elation" that comes with knowing something real.[47]

Percy makes the elementary realistic observation that Sartre's official, "atheistic existentialism" is self-contradictory. Its presumption is that "life and existence are without meaning." So "communication is impossible or at least unnecessary." But "Sartre's whole vocation is that of a writer: communicating—and communicating a lack of meaning to people meaningfully." If Sartre really experienced what he said to be true, "he should have shut up." But he enjoyed himself immensely writing almost endlessly about existence's absurdity and the misery of his characters.[48] Sartre's turn to Marxism was, from one perspective, away from the truth about one's own existence to angry, ideological scientism. But Percy also remarks that at least it made him "aware of a social dimension" to human existence, of an irreducible part of a being with language, and especially a writer.[49]

The true claim of Heideggerian existentialism is that human beings are open both to the elusive truth about being through language and capable of falling away from that truth. That claim's credibility depends, in Percy's view, on Thomism, on some realistic explanation of how a human being can know and take pleasure in the truth, and on why such experiences are the fulfillment of an individual's being. There is no existentialist decisionism and no historicization of Being in Percy's appreciation of Heidegger. The Thomist attempts to give a realistic account of the individual human experiences Heidegger often describes so well.[50]

NATURAL SCIENCE

Percy's realism, or science, attempts to overcome the division between American empiricism and European existentialism, both of which he criticizes for a "failure to make a unifying effort toward giving an account of all realities."[51] The existentialist gives an account of uniquely human existence. But he gives it in opposition to science and cannot show it to be more than a subjective perception. The empiricist rightly demands objective or scientific evidence, but he limits his investigation to sensations and ignores the rest of human existence.

Percy says his own position is closer to but even more empirical than the empiricists'. The unreasonable self-limitation of modern science is the reason for the apparent strength of the existentialist position. Today, because of the popularization of dogmatic, scientific atheism, most people dismiss talk about God and the soul. Those who use that outmoded, traditional language lose everyone but the believers. But empiricists or behaviorists such as B. F. Skinner say that everything man does can be explained by operant conditioning. They lose "every reader who knows there is more to it than that and Skinner has explained nothing."[52] The atheistic existentialists seem to say both religion and science are bankrupt, conceding too much to the claims of modern science. The self cannot sustain its sanity, or experience itself as good, if it sees no evidence for and cannot explain its undeniable existence. So one purpose of the Peirce/Percy science is to use "the ancient tradition of Anglo-Saxon empiricism" to administer "therapy to the European tendency to neurotic introspection."[53]

Percy differs from pragmatists, empiricists, and existentialists by being a

Christian theologically and a "Darwinian-naturalist" scientifically.[54] He sees the compatibility of theological and scientific truth. He seeks to show, in language accessible to contemporary scientists, why revelation completes, not opposes, reason. The existentialist's rebellion against the impersonal nature or cosmos described by modern scientists resembles the antievolutionist creationism of the fundamentalist.

The fundamentalist, like the existentialist, opposes faith and morality to reason and science. He actually understands human existence to be torn apart by incompatible goods, and so morality to be, in part, an angry denial of what human beings can really know. "Evolution is not a theory but a fact," the Thomist Percy asserts, against boring and futile fundamentalism.[55] The Catholic Percy praises "the Church's love and respect for the truth, including the truths of natural science," while being perfectly aware that the Church's respect for scientific truth has not really been unflagging.[56]

But the anti-Christian evolutionist is also characterized by angry self-denial, although the source of anger is less obvious. He asserts that Charles Darwin, along with Sigmund Freud and the other scientists, have shown that human beings are qualitatively no different from the rest of nature. Everything about every organism that exists, including human speech or language, can be explained by the requirements of environmental adaptation.

The antitheistic evolutionist contends that scientific curiosity should be directed toward the discovery of similarities or continuities in the various forms of biological development, and so toward the scientific abolition of perceptions of difference.[57] The right sort of research will show that the other species, such as the higher primates, also have the capacity for language, that languaged beings (computers) can be produced artificially that have all the human characteristics, and that intelligent life exists elsewhere in the cosmos.

The systematic or homogenizing efforts of science are on the way to dispelling the Christian or Western prejudice that causes human beings to be destructive of themselves and others and threaten the very existence of their environment. The hypothesis of science, soon to be completely verified, is that nature is simple, readily comprehensible, well ordered, and fundamentally good. Human beings are good by nature because they are not qualitatively different from the rest of nature.

The social and political thought of antitheistic evolutionists, popularized, Percy hilariously shows, by media experts such as Phil Donahue, tends to be an unsophisticated tale of progress. The history of human beings is the movement from repression, particularly religiously inspired repression, to scientific freedom or enlightenment. It is from murder, war, cruel inhibition and discipline, and belief in a supernatural being to peace, happiness, tolerance, affectionate promiscuity, and scientific atheism.[58] Because human existence, at its natural core, is unproblematically good, human beings, once freed from prejudice, can live in peace and contentment.

Percy never tires of showing the untruth or self-denial of the Donahue theory. The sexual life of our permissive times is anything but reasonable and peaceful. It is distorted more than ever by anger and anxiety, and so further from what is required to perpetuate the species, than ever before. Percy shows, in a very politically incorrect fashion, how naive Donahue and the other experts are about the meaning of our growing acceptance of and obsession with homosexuality.[59]

Most fundamentally, Percy observes that the antitheistic Darwinian or Freudian always exempts himself and his troubles from his observations. He does not even try to explain why human beings, alone in the cosmos, desire to know and to find joy in discovering the truth about all things. He is not curious about why only human scientists try so hard to prove that human beings are not unique and displaced in the cosmos. The irony is that Darwin and Freud, known for their theoretical radicalism, "were not radical enough. For neither can account for his own activity by his own theory."[60]

Percy gives the rather pathetic example of the excellent popularizing scientist Carl Sagan, who spent much of his theoretical life searching among the animals and throughout the universe for evidence that human beings are not alone. Sagan's evidence for extraterrestrial life is too weak to be science, although he is quite rigorous when describing reality that is not human. Percy concludes that Sagan did not want to admit that Sagan is lonely. What else does he really give but evidence of his ineradicable uniqueness? Sagan has not freed himself from the anxious disorder of being human, the experience Pascal says comes when human beings attempt and fail to discern their place in the whole.

Sagan's book *Cosmos* is a failed attempt at a self-help book, a failed attempt to cure himself of the human disorder that especially characterizes this century.[61] One reason the lonely Sagan longs for extraterrestrial intelligences is he believes he has reduced his fellow human beings to beings really incapable of giving or receiving love.[62] But Sagan does not understand or acknowledge his loneliness or much of anything else about human psychology. Percy writes of his "unmalicious, even innocent, scientism," the product of his unscientific abstraction from his own and others' distinctively human experiences.[63] And that naïveté explains his ridiculously unrealistic moral and political opinions. For Sagan, human aggressiveness, incredibly, "can be explained by our residual reptilian brains."[64] He cannot explain why our century has been either the most lonely or the most murderous yet.

The Thomist asks why Sagan, the Darwinians, and Freudians do not direct their curiosity to themselves, the most singular and remarkable phenomena in the cosmos. The truth is "humans are far more mysterious than any extraterrestrial . . . yet imagined."[65] A strictly empirical answer comes from the capacity for self-deception of languaged beings. The scientist wants to cure himself of his anxiety, described so well by Pascal. Self-denying or wholly impersonal science has its origin in a person who is worse than a fool.

Such a science is not an authentically comprehensive account of all that exists, but an impossible attempt to escape from the reality of personal disorder. For the impersonal scientist, the forms of inquiry into the traditional human questions about the soul, philosophy, poetry, novels, theology, and so forth, are diversions from the genuine or scientific pursuit of the truth.[66] For the Thomistic scientist, impersonal science is a diversion from a scientific search for the answers to the questions about human, particularly one's own, existence.

The criticism of impersonal science's materialism applies to all systematic attempts to explain all of reality, including Hegel's systematic idealism. The truth about human existence, the experiences of the self, will always remain a leftover to any system. What sent Percy thinking in the direction of his new science was Søren Kierkegaard's famous remark: "Hegel, said Kierkegaard, explained everything under the sun, except one small detail, what it means to be a man, or a woman, to be born in this world, to live, and to die."[67] The Hegelian cannot really explain the experience of individual as individual, the self-conscious mortal, and so he, as Alexandre Kojève explains, actually joins the materialist scientist in working to make impersonal science true. The self-denying systems of materialism and idealism are actually twin forms of Cartesianism.

CARTESIAN VERSUS THOMISTIC SCIENCE

The impersonal science that displaced Thomism Percy traces to Descartes. The Thomist calls that science incoherent. It is composed of two parts—mind and "stuff" or matter—which do not fit together. The human being is defined as a mind located in stuff, in a body, a ghost in a machine. The disembodied mind is, in principle, rational or well ordered and so objective or impersonal. So is the unconscious body, which obeys, with every other body, the impersonal laws of nature. But the Cartesian scientist cannot connect mind and body, and so he cannot explain how mind has access to the empirical world.[68]

The languaged being in whom mind and body intersect cannot be reduced to rational or impersonal order. That intersection, paradoxically, is both the true source of the human impetus to, and so the possibility of, science, and the source of ineradicable human perversity, which includes the scientist's self-denial. The Cartesian scientist tends to understand himself as a disembodied being, existing, in wisdom, above ordinary human existence, and to understand others, nonscientists, as bodies, as nothing more than organisms well or badly adjusted to their environment. He misses his own and others' human distinctiveness and what authentically connects him to them. The Cartesian scientist views himself, unrealistically, as alone by missing the social fact of science's origination in language. Consciousness, Percy remembers, means to "know with," and the isolated individual Descartes describes could not really be conscious.[69]

The Thomistic scientist accepts the fact of human distinctiveness or alienation and looks to science for evidence of the source of the gift of language to human beings. Evolutionary natural science, Percy shows, provides such evidence. Science means all that human beings can know and communicate to others, and it includes an investigation into what is singular about the human species and particular human individuals.[70] Percy's "scientific curiosity" points him in the direction of explaining man in "his perversity and uniqueness."[71]

Percy explains that the capacity of language was "a relatively recent, sudden, and explosive" development in the evolutionary process. Sometime between 75,000 and 35,000 years ago, the brain increased in weight about sixty percent in just a few thousand years. Much of the increase came "in the cortex, especially in those areas around the Sylvan fissure implicated in perception and production of speech." These speech perception and production structures are not found even in "the highest apes." These startling changes provided the natural equipment that made possible the "emergence of language, consciousness, self, art, religion, science."[72]

This sudden increase in brain size was "evolutionarily speaking" the almost instantaneous event that "[a]natomically speaking" was "the spectacular quantum jump that made man human." When placed on "the scale of evolutionary time"—millions and millions of years—the scientific evidence concerning how the human being came into existence does not contradict the biblical story of creation.[73] Why human beings suddenly and unexpectedly became human seems beyond the realm of evolutionary naturalism, but that they did is well supported by it.

There is more evidence still for man's mysterious natural distinctiveness. Percy notices that "the brain of the most 'primitive' man is not discernibly different from the brain of Beethoven and therefore cannot be accounted for by Darwin's theory of a gradual adaptation of a species to its environment."[74] The human brain came into existence almost at once and has remained virtually unchanged. Both facts are exceptions to Darwin's generally sound theory. We have already considered a third exceptional fact, the unique perversity of human behavior, much of which opposes itself to the species' preservation and adaptation.

From yet another perspective, the acquisition of language could not have been a gradual, evolutionary adaptation. Language is "an all or nothing" affair. Some birds fly well, others barely fly. But every normal human being, Percy explains, "has the capacity for uttering and understanding an infinite number of sentences in his language, no matter what the language is."[75] Strictly speaking, there is no such thing as a primitive human language, just as there is no such thing as a primitive human brain.

Percy never tires of mocking Rousseauean efforts—such as Herman Melville's and Margaret Mead's—to describe man in his primitive, well-ordered, natural simplicity. The existentialist novelist Fyodor Dostoyevsky, Percy laughs, would have made Billy Budd a "child molester" and so "a good deal more believable."[76] Percy also reminds us that Mead's Samoans, we now know, were not "an innocent, happy, Edenic people until they were corrupted by missionaries and technology." They "appear to have been at least as neurotic as New Yorkers."[77] Yet the return to natural simplicity on an enlightened basis is Phil Donahue's cure for the contemporary neuroses rooted in repression of his contemporary urban audience.

Percy shows that there is an empirical, natural foundation for the existentialist distinction between environment and world.[78] So Rousseau's portrayal of natural man as no different from the rest of nature is unscientific or romantic. There is scientific evidence for the experiences of human self-consciousness and alienation the existentialist describes. There is even some evidence to support the fundamentalist belief that man was especially created to be a self, or person, by a personal God. Even without Christian belief, Thomism makes human beings more at home with their homelessness than Cartesianism.

But Thomistic science does show that Christianity, or Judeo-Christianity, is the only religion compatible with the scientific evidence about human nature. Biblical revelation offers a plausible explanation for what the secular scientist cannot: man's extraordinary differences from the other creatures.[79] Human beings are sinful creatures uniquely born to trouble. But they also have infinite longing or love that points beyond all human experience. They are pilgrims or wayfarers in the cosmos, on their way to their true home elsewhere.

Percy himself concludes that "Life is a mystery, love is a delight," and neither can be reduced to impersonal, deterministic science of adaption and self-preservation. So he "refuse[s] to settle for anything less" than the true end of his human longing, "infinite mystery and the infinite delight, i.e. God."[80] He does not join Kierkegaard in believing faith to be an irrational leap toward absurdity, but Saint Thomas in holding that faith "is an assent which includes cognition. . . . [T]he Gospel is the knowledge that humanity truly longs for and needs to have."[81]

The Christian explanation for the natural fact of human distinctiveness, if believed, makes a human being "[a]mbiguously at home," or "at home with his homelessness." It allows one to both acknowledge and accept the limitations of one's "creatureliness," and so to really see and love other troubled, incarnated selves and to enjoy the natural pleasures of human life with less anxiety and diversion.[82]

For the Cartesian scientists, Buddhism, New Age Gaia, and other forms of pantheism are compatible with scientific truth. Those anti-Christian religions deny the reality of the experience of human individuality, of human beings' special place in the cosmos.[83] Percy agrees with Alexis de Tocqueville: Pantheism is the most seductive and untrue form of thought today.[84] It is an extreme form of self-denial, an inauthentic because incredible attempt to suppress the terrible misery of individuality. It is a theological expression of the Rousseauean lie that, because man is by nature one with his environment, his spiritual efforts should be directed toward restoring that unproblematic natural unity.

In a less polemical vein, Percy wrote in a letter to a philosophic friend that he viewed "Buddhism, and most of the great contemplative religions as 'scientific' in a broad sense, that is, as professing general truths which can be arrived at by anyone, anywhere and at any time." But this religious expression of philosophic truth about man and the cosmos in general does less than justice to the predicament of the particular human individual. Christianity and Judaism are "open to 'news,' of the singular (scandalous) event, the Jewish covenant, the Christian incarnation and news of same." Percy holds that man "by his very nature" as a dislocated, singular self is open to hearing the Bible's good news and not finding its truth absurd or impossible. Percy's theory of man stands not only in criticism of modern science, but to some extent in criticism of the moral teaching of philosophy and science in general.[85]

Percy affirms the philosophic view that "Both art and science are ways of knowing and as such are the greatest pleasures of which man is capable (Aristotle, Aquinas)." But a human problem is that those pleasures are "So great, in fact, that the ordinary pursuits of life are spoiled by contrast."[86] Those pleasures lead the philosopher, scientist, and artist to transcend the dreariness of ordinary life. The transcendence is real, Percy says, but it is not complete. Such pleasurable transcendence cannot constitute a whole human life. The understandable attempt at such total self-absorption is really impossible self-denial. The scientist, philosopher, and artist must periodically reenter the world of ordinary human selves, and most of their personal disorder comes from the fact that they do not have a science of reentry. They must go to "heroic lengths" to make the nontranscendent parts of their lives "tolerable."[87]

So Percy often criticizes Christians for their hostility to science or philosophy, for their denial of the truth and goodness of the experiences of the great natural pleasures. But he adds that "It is true that both St. Paul and God are on record as preferring simple folk to the overeducated, especially philosophers."[88] Simple folks know what philosophers and scientists characteristically deny. Human beings are not God, and they are all equally in need of a Creator. Philosophers, by confusing themselves with God through denial of the human goodness of ordinary life, deny what really connects them to other human beings.

The Cartesian scientist implicitly asserts his own divinity by virtue of his absolute transcendence of the reality he describes. That transcendence is his evidence that he is not an alienated creature. He replaces the biblical God with himself, because "There is no room in the Cosmos for an absolutely transcending objective mind and an absolutely transcending God."[89] The pleasure of scientific transcendence is so great and the experience of ordinary life so dreary in comparison that the scientist cannot bear to acknowledge that his existence is determined in any way by the latter. But the scientist cannot really explain why he, alone among human beings, is detached through thought from ordinary life. Nor does he really reflect on why his detachment is not complete.

SOCIAL AND POLITICAL SCIENCE

The contemporary American social and political world, according to Percy, is formed by the popularization of Cartesian theory. He agrees with that "remarkable fellow," Alexis de Tocqueville, by calling the Americans Carte-sians who have never actually read a word of Descartes. The pop Cartesianism of the Americans is really scientism, the "elevation" of a theory that does account scientifically for nonhuman nature into "an all-enveloping ideology."[90]

The ideology of scientism is always, in some way or another, a project for eradicating human nature in the name of science's truth. Its aim is to destroy the truth about the human perception of the truth in the name of the truth. The Americans' ideological deference to Cartesianism means that scientists, indirectly, have become sovereign. Laymen tend to surrender their personal sovereignty, their own judgments about their personal experiences, to the scientists' allegedly impersonal authority.[91] The constant, tyrannical danger of post-Christian, enlightened democracy is the elite claim to rule that denies the rights of others and the rule of law on behalf of scientific expertise.

The tendency for scientists to assume absolute rule cannot be blamed mainly on their pretensions. Ordinary human beings, confused and disoriented, turn to science for guidance. They hope that its great success in conquering and explaining the nonhuman world can find its culmination in the integration of human beings into that world.

A particularly perplexing contemporary paradox is that people feel more homeless than ever in the technological world Cartesian scientists have made with the intention of making them feel fully at home. They are anxious to hear that their homesickness is a misperception, that they ought to enjoy themselves in the unconstrained and prosperous environment that has been created to meet all their needs as consumers.[92] For "the ordinary denizen of modern technological society . . . nothing seems more natural . . . than [that] *they* [the scientific experts] know the answers."[93] And ordinary people think " 'They' not only know about the Cosmos, they know about me, my aches and pains, my brain functions, even my neuroses."[94] As Heidegger says, deference to the impersonal *they* is a way of surrendering the personal responsibility of living authentically in light of the truth.

The pop Cartesian experts—therapists, educators, Phil Donahue, Carl Sagan, and so forth—say that human beings should dismiss as a misery-producing illusion any experience that makes them anxious for no good reason in the midst of their good fortune. The experts' intention is therapeutic. As our pragmatist Richard Rorty explains, the aim is to correct through redescription the perception that produces the uncomfortable and unproductive mood. The experts tell people that everything has a scientific, materialistic explanation, or "can be reduced to the causes and effects of electron, neuron, and so forth."[95]

So anxiety, depression, and so forth are symptoms to be cured through a change in environmental stimuli or redressing a chemical imbalance with drugs.

But Percy observes that what Americans believe—or are told to believe by experts who they hope will provide answers for all the mysteries of human life—remains persistently contradicted by their personal experiences. They become pop Cartesians only through the denial of what they really know about themselves. But they become even more disoriented when they find complete self-denial impossible. They may consent to but they cannot really achieve self-surrender to experts.[96] The Americans, as the Pascalian Tocqueville first described, are restlessly dissatisfied in the midst of "affluence," experiencing "some sense of loss that he cannot understand."[97] Americans today cannot help but follow the Cartesian scientist's own example by exempting their own minds and actions from their understanding of science. The expert cannot really tell ordinary Americans why they remain or become more restless and anxious in fortunate material circumstances. The American may say he is but he often does not think or act as if he were simply a body in motion.

Part of what the American has lost is the language for articulating the true source of his restless dissatisfaction. He has been deprived of some way of explaining to himself and others why he experiences himself as more than a well-adjusted or badly adjusted organism. One consequence of the pop Cartesian impoverishment of language is "a radical impoverishment of human relations."[98] Human beings cannot say what connects one self to another, and so what makes one self lovable to another. The result is "that people are, by and large, probably lonelier than ever." Despite all the expert emphasis on human relations or getting along with others, loneliness remains "the twentieth-century disease."[99] The pop Cartesian is "a lonesome ghost in an abused machine."[100] So "despite an embarrassment of riches," he "is in fact impoverished and deprived, like Lazarus at the feast."[101]

Tocqueville actually explains with greater precision than Percy how the impersonal language of therapeutic expertise comes to dominate the thought of modern democracy. Tocqueville says that democratic social conditions—largely created by a dogmatic distrust of all authoritative belief, especially in personal claims to rule, as arbitrarily inegalitarian—make individuals feel too weak, too uncertain and disoriented, to find a standpoint by which to resist public opinion.

Domination by public opinion seems not to be undemocratic. It seems to be the rule of no one in particular. But democratic public opinion tends to be shaped by its growing tendency to be expressed in the language of impersonal or deterministic science. In democratic language, in Tocqueville's words, "metaphysics and theology . . . slowly lose ground." Democratic language tends to be formulated by pop Cartesian experts, who claim authority not on the basis of their personal judgments but of the impersonal or objective and abstract authority of science. The expert determination of public opinion also appears to be the rule of no one in particular.[102]

POLITICAL THOUGHT

The disorienting impoverishment of thought of contemporary Americans is present, in a more muted form, in American thought from the beginning. Percy seems particularly contemptuous of "The standard American-Jeffersonian high school-commencement Republican-and-Democratic platform self." This description of self is an untenable mixture of a small dose of Christianity with a large dose of Cartesianism, and it is lacking in the integrity of either of its parts. The Jeffersonian defines the self as "an individual entity created by God and endowed with certain inalienable rights and the freedom to pursue happiness and fulfill his potential." Thomas Jefferson defines man, officially, as a creature, but he holds that the creature was endowed with the purpose of pursuing this-worldly, rational, self-won happiness. So "It follows that in a free and affluent society the self should succeed more often than not in fulfilling itself. Happiness can be pursued and to a degree caught."[103] If this optimistic, pragmatic anthropology were true, most Americans today would be living sober, fulfilling, and reasonably happy lives. But that description is clearly not true, and the standard American self-understanding retains some force only because of the mixture of scientific expertise and patriotic prejudice.

Percy is capable of being even harder on this self-understanding. He calls it "the Western democratic-technological humanist view of man as a higher organism invested with certain traditional trappings of more or less nominal Judeo-Christianity." This definition is a "mishmash" anthropology that declares man to be free and sacred but leaves completely unclear what about him is free or sacred.[104] Its nominally Christian defense of the individual is undercut by its scientific view that man is a "higher" or particularly clever organism and no more.

So, for Percy, Jefferson's standard American self is not much different from Phil Donahue's. It is an early form of the soft utopianism characteristic of Cartesian progressivism. The American pursuit aims at creating a future "Where scientists know like angels, and laymen prosper in good environments, and ethical democracies progress through good education." Through the progress of science "the environment could be changed and man made to feel more and more at home." Scientific progress would inevitably be accompanied by moral progress "through education and the application of the ethical principles of Christianity."[105] That description captures nicely Jefferson's democratic faith in the beneficence of the right mixture of education, science, and Jesus. But it is also a description without authentic human beings, without a true account of the predicament of the self.

The modern world is replaced by the postmodern one for anyone who comes to see the naive untruth and massive failure of that progressivism. Our century has not been the coming of "universal peace and brotherhood," but a time of war, self-destruction, deranged, violent eroticism, and angry self-hatred. The world human beings have created for themselves is for angels and pigs—abstracted, unempirical beings that are absolutely transcendent or absolutely immanent. It is a world for those who can live wholly as scientists or wholly as consumers; it is not for human beings.[106]

Scientists such as behaviorists and structuralists say that the experience of self is a psychological or cultural illusion. Once it is recognized as such, it will disappear. The result should be a happy and reasonable life. From a political perspective, the consumer is described as a slave, a being without personal sovereignty or rights, not to be ruled politically but controlled like an animal.[107]

But Cartesian scientists also speak of the "autonomous self," or the ideological equivalent of the absolute self-mastery or transcendence claimed by the scientist. That self is liberated by technology and scientific education from the drudgery of material necessity and "the tyranny of the unconscious" for the pursuit of "its own destiny without God."[108] The theory of the autonomous self is actually responsible for most of the murder and gratuitous violence of our century. That self claims to have self-knowledge, but all it really has is freedom from belief for the impossible task of self-creation out of nothing. Because it believes in nothing, it readily "fall[s] prey to ideology," devoting itself, as it did to Adolf Hitler and Joseph Stalin, to misanthropic abstractions it mistakes for wisdom. Ideology so employed by allegedly autonomous selves is the cause of "abstract violence," of murder based on scientific self-denial. So the pretension of the autonomous self is the root of the contemporary phenomenon Hannah Arendt discovered, the banality of evil, or seemingly passionless and well-mannered terror.[109] As Pascal says, he who sees himself as an angel will act like a beast.[110]

The autonomous self cannot help but be proud. His pride, oriented in the direction of unprecedented political reform, surpasses that of any aristocrat.

This proud tyrant readily or ideologically comes to believe that he can remake the world as he pleases. He also comes to experience the existing world, without his redemption, as radically evil. In a perverse love of mankind, he compassionately takes upon himself the eradication of the misery of human disorder, which invariably becomes the murder of large numbers of particular human beings. The autonomous self is an extreme example of Percy's frequent observation that human beings are cruel because they are sentimental (and so Richard Rorty is wrong to say that cruelty is opposed most effectively by sentiment). The allegedly autonomous self lacks a tough or unsentimental, faithful and so serene acceptance of the limits of his worldly existence. Our century, Percy notes, has been both the most sentimental and the most murderous.[111]

But finally what leads the autonomous self to murder is less pride than a "suppressed fury" about the inexplicable contingency of its existence, about the fact that the self is not really autonomous but unsupported or accidental. Self-hatred lurks below the proud claims for self-knowledge and self-rule. That self-hatred produces hatred for other selves, and so resolute efforts at self-obliteration. What the autonomous self claims to do for itself human beings cannot really do, and that self is deranged by its ideological, destructive attempts to suppress that truth. The anger aroused by the false perception of autonomy, Percy even suggests, will be the cause of World War III,[112] and it was the cause of the first two world wars. Postmodernism, for Percy, begins with truthful reflection on the causes of ideology and world war.[113]

Most radically, modern science denies the reality of the experience of authenticity or truthful, undiverted self-consciousness that language makes possible and that is the foundation of the dignity of the human individual. That courageous experience, for Percy, is the true source of personal sovereignty and so of individual rights. The American Cartesians, beginning with Jefferson, cannot say what exactly about the individual is dignified or sacred. After Rousseau, Cartesians say with greater clarity and with sentimentality or compassion that the dignity of the individual depends on the surrender of his experience of being moved to anxiety and thought by his mortality. Compassion rooted in self-hatred leads to unprecented self-destruction.

PERCY'S SELF-HELP BOOK

Percy wrote *Lost in the Cosmos: The Last Self-Help Book* to replace the misanthropic and futile efforts by Cartesian experts to alleviate Americans' restless anxiety in the midst of prosperity. The longest piece of prose in that book is a theoretical "intermezzo of some forty pages,"[114] where Percy presents his Thomistic science, his theory of evolution and of man as a languaged being by nature. This theory, a combination of Peirce's semiotic empiricism and Heidegger's existentialism, can be called a realistic theory of human nature.[115] Percy said he "never will do anything as important" as writing this "semiotical account of the emergence of man."[116]

Percy knows this theoretical intermezzo may be the least persuasive part of his book. But, if understood and accepted, it is the "keystone" to his program of self-help.[117] Believers in pop Cartesianism, or secular humanists, will say, skeptically, that it is full of illegitimate theological baggage. Fundamentalists will think it quite superfluous. It is important, at least for Thomists, for those who hold that faith or revelation completes, but does not oppose, reason. It saves, for the believer, the truth of science and so the way of life of the scientist or philosopher. It is a scientific justification of what, by tradition, is called the poetic criticism of the self-denial or impersonality of science or philosophy. Science need not abstract from or deny the experience of the self. But it cannot end, in the name of reason, the mystery of human existence and so exclude the possibility that human beings were created. It shows that the self cannot be autonomous, but its origin is not necessarily accidental. For Percy the most profound and realistic of contemporary writers was the Thomistic artist Flannery O'Connor, who saw "both creation and art as the Chartres sculptor did, as both dense and mysterious, gratuitous, anagogic, and sacramental."[118] It may be for human beings to know that all of reality was created.

Percy's self-help is a scientific explanation for the apparent misery of Americans in the midst of prosperity, their dislocation, angry self-hatred, and derangement. He explains why "Mother Teresa of Calcutta" is right to say that "affluent Westerners" are more impoverished, in the crucial respect, than the poor of Calcutta.[119] Percy's theoretical intermezzo shows that "the impoverishments and enrichments of a *self* in a *world* are not necessarily the same as the impoverishments and enrichments of an *organism* in an *environment*." In truth, "the self in a world is rich or poor accordingly as it identifies its otherwise unspeakable self, e.g., mythically, by identifying itself with a world-sign, such as a totem; religiously, by identifying itself as a creature of God."[120] So we feel impoverished, or miserably alienated, because we believe we live in a "post-religious age." We believe we know we are not creatures (or totems, an identification that is completely incredible for us), but we really do not know what else we might be. So we engage unsuccessful strategies for self-denial, deferring to experts or making unrealistic claims for autonomy. As Pascal says, we tend to do what we can to divert ourselves from what we really know about ourselves.

Percy's postmodern observation is that, for Americans, "The pursuit of happiness becomes the pursuit of diversion," and that is why they are restlessly miserable in the midst of abundance.[121] They work not in pursuit of material comfort but to purchase diversions. The diverted self cannot be explained rationally or scientifically by the Cartesian expert. His life is unreasonable and unhappy. But the diverted self is closer to the truth than the Jeffersonian self. His frenzied self-avoidance is really a close encounter with the reality of self-ignorance. The diverted self becomes more clearly what it is as it frees itself from the Jeffersonian mishmash that once gave it self-confidence.

The pursuit of diversion becomes more insistent as it becomes more unsuccessful. The diverted self is gradually replaced by the bored self and the disappointed self.[122] The success of the Jeffersonian project, on one level, means the possibility of "increased leisure." But that leisure is accompanied by "an ever heightening self-consciousness." So leisure, perversely enough, comes to be experienced not as a human good but as a misery to be avoided.[123] The pursuits recommended by the Declaration's psychology are experienced as progressively less fulfilling.

Even sex, often suggested as the most successful of diversions, has become disappointing. Contemporary theorists are obsessed with genital sexuality, as seemingly the only way left for the transcendent ghost to reenter the real world of bodies. But the scientific or expert attempt to liberate the erotic from the Christian tradition of repression and familial responsibility has really produced the "trivialization" or "demotion" of eros "to another technique for need satisfaction of the organism."[124] The attempt to free sex from the distinctive longings of the self has not produced the mechanical contentment of animal rutting, but more disorienting dissatisfaction. Human beings still long to love other selves. Sexual relationships, properly understood, are part, perhaps the highest part, of communication between man and woman, two selves, in the social context of sharing a home, family, and life.[125]

Eventually, the result of the failure of diversions is the replacement of the bored self by the depressed self, the one anxious and melancholic enough to ponder self-destruction. But that self-destruction can take many forms. Suicide is one, but mental destruction or derangement is another. "The rational Jeffersonian pursuit of happiness" becomes "the flaky euphoria of the late twentieth century." For us, what passes for happiness is sometimes more inane than insane, a self-induced, superficial reverie. But Americans are sometimes too serious to take flaky reveries seriously. They experience themselves, often, as more free, which means more conscious of their homelessness, than ever before. That experience of freedom actually puts the self in a "curious and paradoxical bondage." It experiences itself as unfree to inhabit the world that it makes for itself and where it is told it longs to live.[126] The American, more commonly than ever, experiences the Pascalian truth that "to be born, to live, is to be dislocated."[127] He experiences the needs of the self or soul, the true source of homesickness in this world. But he lacks the language to account for them, much less pursue their satisfaction.

This scientific explanation of American impoverishment does not show that religion, meaning biblical religion, is true. But it does show that religion has not really been discredited by science and that human beings need it not to feel impoverished or deprived of something essential to their being. Knowing the true source of one's misery, even without belief in the personal Creator of the Bible, is some antidote for the misery. There is some pride and joy in knowing the truth about the mystery of the self, and the search for that truth is better than depression or diversion. If the search cannot eradicate the mystery of the self, it can at least make clear what makes one self lovable to another, the foundation for human community.

PERCY'S THOMISTIC POLITICAL PHILOSOPHY

Percy concludes his self-help book by going even further in defending the truth and goodness of Christian anthropology. He does not agree with the fundamentalists that Christian belief could ever give human beings stable self-certainty or free them from trouble. To be human is to be troubled, flawed, or sinful. Still, the possibility of Christianity's truth, the presence of the Church, can make this life better than bearable. It may even have that effect on non-Christians who know enough to know that they do not know enough not to believe, who are relatively free from scientific self-denial.

The second part of a fictional space odyssey is an account of the reasonableness of a non-Christian acknowledgment that the Church is a human good.[128] Percy introduces a man quite out of place, a strange sort of Stoic. Percy often explains that the pre–Civil War Southerners were Stoics, or self-confident, chivalric, militaristic, "magnanimous," honorable, secular, pre-Christian aristocrats. He also makes clear that this proud self-understanding, a certain kind of "natural perfection," has about disappeared from the world.[129] He does not present it as a contemporary self in his self-help book. The only stoic sort in the book until the last chapter is "Colonel John Pelham, Jeb Stuart's legendary artillerist," who appears mysteriously from the past on the Donahue show.[130] He finds the world of Donahue and his guests repulsive and incomprehensible.

The ship's captain for this odyssey is Marcus Aurelius Schuyler, a man from an old New York family with the same "dark" understanding of the human condition as the philosopher-emperor after whom he was named. He views human beings as more full of mischief and hatred than love. They love death more than life, war more than peace, and so they are almost surely destined for self-destruction. But, unlike the captain, they understand none of this. They are self-deceived, and their strongest motivations are unconscious.

The captain's view is darker than the Christian's, but they are alike in being free from the diversion of scientific optimism or progressivism. "He was like a Christian," Percy writes, "who has lost his faith in everything but the fall of man." His view was that of a pre-Christian philosopher. The captain is much more an idealization of features of Percy's intellectual "Uncle Will," the man who raised him, than a rebel soldier. Percy, remarking in an interview that "there is something to be said" for the "Stoic virtues," added that "My Uncle Will's hero was not this or that Christian saint but Marcus Aurelius."[131] Will's book *Lanterns on the Levee* expresses "a rather dark view" about the world and one's duty in the face of more or less inevitable defeat. Its pessimistic "paternalism" is that of the philosophy of "Greco-Roman Stoicism."[132]

But Marcus is also "sardonic," a suggestion that his dark view also has its pleasure. He enjoys being fully conscious of "playing the unflappable captain," and of taking on tasks that are "odd and necessary." He takes pleasure in living well with the strange contingency of his existence, in not losing his bearings by "sticking with his decisions," even as they probably lead to failure. He also takes pleasure in the fact that, after leaving behind all his worldly possessions, including his woman, he feels no compulsion to look back.

It would be too much to say that Marcus enjoys ruling. He is not, as Colonel Pelham was, a man of honor. He enjoys playing the role of ruling, but his pleasure is inward or self-conscious. His sardonic role playing is a form of pleasurable transcendence based on self-confident self-knowledge. It is evidence to himself that he can exempt himself from the consequences of the Fall.

The captain leads a mission in pursuit of intelligent life elsewhere in the cosmos. For the participants the mission will last eighteen years, but they will return to an earth four or five hundred years older. The men and women of the mission are organized according to the scientific principles of "programmed serial monogamy" and "open and free sexuality" to reproduce themselves, mostly because there are signs of the species' imminent destruction on earth. The abstract science breaks down and perverse and violent human behavior breaks out, but reproduction still occurs. The most unexpected breakdown is that the captain falls in love with and marries a particular intelligent and family-oriented woman, who becomes the mother of all the children born on the ship. One reason the captain fell in love with Dr. Jane Smith is that he could not fully comprehend or control her. She saw through his role playing and lied to him effectively. Marcus and Jane's love seemed to depend on the ironic recognition one had for the other's depth and flaws.

But that love also depends on Dr. Jane leading the captain to the human responsibilities of marriage and the family. By refusing to disconnect sex and even love from marriage, she shows the captain the truth about the social longings of the being with language. The eros of that being is not just of the rutting animal or the philosophic or scientific mind. Human life in a world is something other than transcendence or immanence. And so human beings are given joys and responsibilities not given to angels or pigs. To live well the human being must free himself from the scientific abstraction that causes him to believe that he is detached enough merely to be playing a role in this world.

The mission returns to an earth devastated by nuclear war. Landing in Utah they find Aristarchus Jones, an astronomer, three (two black and one Jewish) Benedictine monks, and about a dozen genetically malformed and misbegotten children. Aristarchus, who is as devoted to science as his Ionian namesake, and Abbot Liebowitz offer the captain two incompatible plans.[133]

Aristarchus says that civilization on earth is finished, but it might be reestablished on a firmly scientific foundation on a satellite of Jupiter. He sees the opportunity to actualize a radical version of the Enlightenment or Cartesian dream that reason might free human beings from their troubled condition. He is excited by the possibility of a "New Ionia," where people will live free from the "superstitions and repressions of religion," from the contentious mystifications of the Bible and Plato. They will live in peace, self-knowledge, and sexual freedom. The arts and sciences will flourish uninhibited. In the name of science, or the species' perfection, Aristarchus says the genetically malformed must be left behind. Nothing will be malformed in New Ionia.

Abbot Liebowitz sees the coming of the captain and the others, especially the children, as a miracle. He says they must all go to Lost Cove, Tennessee, where the effects of radiation may be minimal and life may well be sustainable. They must go, to state the obvious, to repopulate the cave. The abbot takes the side of Plato and the Church against Ionian or apolitical science. But this cave is "lost." It is for the lost, for beings who, as the Church says, will never feel completely home in this world. They cannot help but experience their self-consciousness or transcendent freedom.

The abbot suggests this journey because his task is to perpetuate the Church, and the children are potential priests. He gives an elegant, theological version of Percy's science, including evolution and anthropology, speaking of "ensoulment" rather than the emergence of the self. He criticizes the Church, as a Catholic Jew, for not loving science and art more. His hope is to repopulate the University of Notre Dame with Jewish scientists. He realistically tells the captain and his party that they will not escape the predicament of soul or self merely by leaving planet earth. Without his help, they will be "lost in the cosmos" without hope or love. The Church, not science, the earth, or some new planet, points to the home they are seeking.

Percy does not have the captain make one choice or the other. He does suggest that if he chooses Lost Cove it will be because of the influence of the woman he loves (who sees how religion protects marriage, the family, human community, and the mystery that is the foundation of the love of one human being for another). The choice is left for the reader. As a thought experiment, Percy imagines for us the consequences of each choice for the captain.

New Ionia is based on the principles of freedom without God and self-knowledge through absolute honesty. Honesty is secured through "group self-criticism," which aims to abolish secrecy and lying. More generally, New Ionia is based on "the principles of Skinner's Walden II, modified by Jungian self-analysis, with suitable rewards for friendly social behavior and punishment, even exile, for aggressive, jealous, solitary, mystical, or other antisocial behavior." In the name of self-knowledge, manifestations of human experiences of self are to be eradicated. In the name of honesty, antisocial or personal experiences are punished. But, in truth, only the being ironic enough to lie and keep secrets can tell the truth to himself about himself or really be honest. And there are no real experiences of the goodness of human life in New Ionia. The substitute supplied to make life bearable is the "euphoria" caused by a drug. So much for self-knowledge.

The captain remains "somewhat ironical" about the group exercises, viewing them as a new sort of AA meeting. He finds no pleasure in his irony, which has become a reaction against human beings who have been almost free from the consequences of the Fall through behavior modification and drugs, or almost without selves. His only pleasures are sex with any well-formed body or bodies (and so not with his old wife, who sulks, showing that she still has a self) and Shakespeare and Mozart, who remind him of the world's human or troubled past.

It is impossible to see how the sciences and arts could flourish in New Ionia. There are no restless selves who long for the truth and seek absolute transcendence from the dreariness of ordinary life. There are just two miserable, superfluous selves. New Ionia has solved every human problem, it seems, but that of the captain's self. His irony reminds us of that of Alexandre Kojève, the resigned Hegelian, at the end of history. That irony is directed toward a world composed of beings without irony and so incapable of loving or being loved. Percy contends that "Skinner's *Walden II* is probably the most depressing book written in this century."[134]

In Lost Cove, we find the captain "watch[ing] ironically yet not without affection" two black priests saying Mass in the cave. The community is flourishing with all sorts of human beings, including the most malformed and misbegotten. Marcus sits "above the cave" with a community of "good friends," a variety of dissidents and unbelievers. The love and hatred of political life ("of us against them") are returning, along with racism, feminism, war, and religious fanaticism. Wherever there is love of particular troubled selves for others, there is hatred too. The captain's thought is "Jesus Christ, here we go again," and he laughs.

His new view of the consequences of the Fall is somewhat ironic and somewhat affectionate. It is not at all sardonic, and he has lost interest in playing the role of ruling. The human condition seems just as inevitably flawed but much less dark to him. It is more comic and genuinely mysterious. The mistakes and sins of the past are being repeated. The Church, strangely, actually seems to make them possible. The compensation, Percy explains, for all the "nuttiness" of Lost Cove is the "joy there. And there ain't no joy in New Ionia or Walden II."[135]

Marcus enjoys his friends and family, the love and affection of others. He's happy with his wife, satisfied with being monogamous.[136] He also likes liquor and pork and just being alive. He still does not believe, and he remains somewhat detached. But ordinary life is now more than bearable. He knows why he has affection for the priests and their Church. He knows, as he did not before, the limits of his independence. His freedom depends on the cave; his skepticism depends upon belief, and his pleasurable experiences of the goodness of life depend upon his love of others. He knows he is more alike than different from other human beings. He lives well with all sorts of misbegotten selves, because he knows that he himself is far from free from trouble or disorder.

Percy seems, at first, to be repeating the view of classical political philosophy that science and philosophy depend upon politics and religion. The disappearance of the cave would also be the end of the philosopher. The eradication of the distinction between man and God would be at the expense of all that is distinctly human. But Marcus actually has an enlarged or Thomistic view of his dependence. The scientist or philosopher is not free from experiences of the self. He should not even pretend to transcend absolutely ordinary life, or the cave, nor should he deny the truth about other selves' partial but real transcendence. As a self or ensouled, he depends—and not primarily in a utilitarian fashion—on other selves for his perception of the goodness of human life.

Philosophers have something to learn from priests (and Catholic writers who are also philosophic) about how to enjoy life. At home with their homelessness, they are free to be "at home in the worldly sense of being at home," to enjoy the good things of the world "in recognition of their creatureliness and limitations."[137] The second space odyssey ends or almost ends as Percy's novels do, with the experience of a human being who gets a glimpse of the real or natural evidence for "the goodness and gratuitousness of created being."[138]

The self-help offered by *Lost in the Cosmos* is that Peirce/Percy or Thomistic science, the latest scientific development, shows that there is no substitute for Socratic or dialectical inquiry into the truth about the human self or soul. Such a search into the mystery of the dislocation of the self or soul can help people live better lives and provide the foundation for our otherwise empty talk about human dignity and human rights. This inquiry only points to evidence to the possible truth of biblical revelation, but it can be good for human beings even though they do not believe. It will emphatically not produce absolute certainty, perfect happiness, or an untroubled world. Even Socratics (such as Marcus), Catholic or otherwise, remain flawed mortals, born to trouble, but they have no illusions that they can fundamentally transform their condition through their own efforts. It goes without saying that we should not defer to the authority of priests, although we should listen to what they have to say. But neither should we defer to Cartesian experts who incoherently deny the very existence of the soul or self. The only way to judge the truth of the help Percy offers is to begin by trusting one's own judgment about one's own personal experiences.

THE WRITER AT THE END
OF THE (MODERN, AMERICAN) WORLD

Percy understands himself as a writer or artist, part Thomistic or anti-Cartesian philosopher and part novelist. He says that artist-writers in America today do not really believe they have much influence. They have a "secret envy" for the dissident writer Aleksandr Solzhenitsyn, who brought the state to its knees by opposing it with the truth. Percy even observes that for the writer "there are things worse than the Gulag," such as having one's telling of the truth have no influence on the world.[139] So he joins Solzhenitsyn in his perception that America, in one important respect, more effectively opposes the truth than did the Soviet Union. Percy remarks ironically that "the novelist . . . despite his well-advertised penchant for violence, his fetish for freedom, his sexual adventurism, pronounces anathemas upon the most permissive of societies, which in fact permits him everything."[140] Such a society permits him everything but to be taken seriously, to communicate with his community. No matter how bizarre or deranged either his writing or personal behavior become, he is barely noticed.[141] He has the freedom to predict the catastrophe that must come from anxious and angry self-denial. But his prediction joins thousands of others, most of which are really loony, and most people seem sensible enough not to take any of them seriously. Percy, the Catholic Socratic, joins Allan Bloom, the atheistic Socratic, in complaining most of all about the polite indifference with which their thoughts are received.

The artist-writer yearns for recognition, for social and political evidence that his perception of derangement is real and so really influential. He is not absolutely certain that his perception of madness is not itself madness.[142] The Socratic and the novelist both know that it is absolutely impossible to experience as good the truth alone. The Thomist and novelist know that all human beings have selves and so must share some of their joys and miseries. The Thomist and novelist view themselves as part of "the world of men" and not just part of a small community of artists or scientists.[143] Percy wrote novels and not just theoretical essays because he had reason to hope that a wide audience can share his personal perception of the way things really are for human beings today.

The artist wishes not to be socially displaced, but to be understood, or to be part of a community based on a shared understanding of human displacement. He longs, in part, to be located in a "lost cove." He would prefer as a human being, in some ways, to celebrate the ordered self-understanding of the community in which he lives, to build a literary Chartres.[144] But the artist-scientist, the Socratic philosopher, also has reason to appreciate his deranged time, when civilization is in an advanced state of decay, at the end of the world. There "man is exposed in his nakedness," and it is possible to get "a view of man abstracted from this or that culture."[145] It is easier to experience and share the truth about human existence freed from the shared illusions of culture. Love in the ruins is between two particularly needy, undeluded selves who know, far better than human beings usually do, that love is not an illusion.[146]

So one reason Percy's thought is postmodern is that he can say that, despite or because of its derangement, "the present age is better than Christendom." At one time, "everyone was a Christian and hardly anyone thought twice about it. But in the present age the survivor of theory and consumption becomes a wayfarer in the desert like St. Anthony, which is to say, open to signs." It is both easier and harder but, in the best case, better to be a Christian or Jew today. It is a good time to experience one's openness to the truth about being, including one's own being.[147]

PERCY AND AMERICAN POLITICS TODAY

The contemporary Thomist or Tocquevillian Percy was a strange sort of liberal. He separated himself from other liberals with his view of the genuinely natural foundation of human liberty, and so on the authentically human foundation of personal sovereignty and rights. He sought to make clear, against the mishmash Jeffersonians and their Cartesian/Rousseauean successors, what view of the human self or soul was required to protect effectively the human pursuits of life, liberty, happiness, love, and God. Contrary to secular liberals such as Rorty, he denied that democratic ideals provide a sufficient reason or motivation not to be cruel. Principled opposition to cruelty really depends on a Thomistic anthropology, which shows that the great cruelty is the attempt to eradicate cruelty altogether. Percy's political judgments depended, finally, on his perception that Christianity is distinguished from Cartesian science and the world's other religions by its emphasis on "human creatureliness, the self in its vagary, individuality, and folly." Hinduism and Buddhism both deny the reality of the individual, the self, and so they deny the human perception of reality itself.[148]

America was founded on an incipiently utopian, misanthropic Cartesianism, and so the history of America has not mainly been progress toward a more free and rational life. Percy compares the sophistication and nobility of *The Federalist,* campaign documents aiming to elevate already intelligent voters, with contemporary politicians, who flatter the paltry and venal "little man."[149] He does not follow Tocqueville by looking to political life to reduce American restlessness and derangement. The ennobling effects that life may have had, which Percy appreciates in his understanding of both the South's aristocracy and Calvinism, have no chance of being widely felt today. The space odyssey does not point to the return of America, but to the birth of a civilization being built on the ruins of America and the West. Percy's faith is in human nature and God, and not in America as such. He claimed he did not see our century "in such dark terms" as his uncle, but he might not have disagreed with him on America's decline and fall.[150]

Percy says that Americans today, particularly young persons, find politics, like other diversions, disappointing. He says at one point that it is not political life as it is actually practiced that disappoints. Instead, it is the shallow way it is portrayed in the media. But that is the way most Americans experience political life. The great technological achievement that is the media is what makes Tocqueville's political teaching obsolete.[151]

The fact that our political life is disappointing did not make Percy, for all practical purposes, a political radical. He rejected, as a Christian and as a Thomistic scientist, the legitimacy of political action based on aristocratic contempt for democracy. He was a principled and occasionally politically active antiracist, and he was attached to the Kennedy-Johnson Democratic Party for its promotion of civil rights. He saw no real alternative to the West's self-destruction but the "glimmer of hope" he saw in America's liberal democracy.[152] He was a strong anti-Nazi and anticommunist, and he was especially irritated by Catholic idealists who would criticize Ronald Reagan's social policies but not the atrocities of the Sandinistas.[153] Percy separated himself from many alleged existentialists by not blaming capitalism or economic injustice much for human misery. "However serious the situation of the mass man of the West, it seems hopeful in comparison with that of the Soviet consumer."[154]

Percy often mocked the redneck chauvinism, oligarchic narrowness, and WASPishness of the Republicans. But he voted once for Reagan despite being repulsed by his perception of the president's forgetful personality and much of Reaganism. He was, reluctantly, in alliance with the cultural conservatives, opposing the moral permissiveness of the anxious secular humanism of the liberals. That humanism is really pop Cartesianism or scientism, and so fundamentally antihumanistic. It produced the unproblematic acceptance of abortion, euthanasia, and so forth, allegedly to improve the quality of life, but really in opposition to the flawed mystery of human existence. Percy said quite bluntly that "legalized abortion . . . is yet another banal atrocity in a century where atrocities have become commonplace."[155] Political projects based on the scientific inability to recognize human uniqueness tend toward misanthropy or nihilism.

So Percy was not really at home anywhere in America's moral and political life. He even planned "a short religious-political work damning the Right and Left in U.S. life," and that anger was a large source of his novel *Love in the Ruins*. He searched for the center that "did not hold" between "the goddamn silly radical student-professor Left and the country-club Christian Right."[156]

The novelist as novelist "is more apt to feel at home with the hardheads, the unbelievers, rakes, drunks, skeptics, Darwinians, than with the Moral Majority."[157] He finds his place with the philosophers outside the cave. So Percy said often that there is nothing more obnoxious than a self-certain, politically confident fundamentalist. But he adds that "just because the Moral Majority comes out for morality doesn't mean that one should be immoral." Percy's alienation, as a Thomistic Christian, is partly from politics simply. He wrote that political theory joins scientific theory in not being able to account for the self.[158]

Percy, given his view of human freedom, was no political determinist, technological or otherwise. He believed that it is possible that human beings might use their great power wisely, and he wrote of "man's increased *responsibility* in the technical age."[159] But his general view seems to have been that people are now too anxious, angry, and otherwise deranged to recognize their predicament and accept the help they need to act well. He did not think his self-help book would lead to social or political reform, although he hoped that it would help some lonely individuals undertake the search that would lead them to each other and to God.

Percy did not say what Allan Bloom or Leo Strauss did. He did not think that the future of philosophy depends on the resolute efforts to defend America or the West. He was much less of a historicist. Human nature in all its manifestations—including philosophy or science—will surely emerge from the ruins. His faith in human nature was partly scientific. But he also believed Christ's promise that the Church will last until the end of time, which means the memory of the West and its great books will never be completely extinguished. Percy emphatically did not believe in the transience of all things human. He thought that Bloom, a tricky nihilist, did.[160] The spiritual longings of human beings really are somehow satisfied, but they will never cure the disorder of the self through their own efforts. The self will remain elusive, an ineradicable leftover from the Cartesian efforts at comprehension and control.

Percy may have agreed with the classical political philosophers even more than Bloom by affirming a sort of cyclical view of human history. The possible or likely self-destruction of the West gives us plenty of room for reasonable hope. We can expect that human beings will make the same mistakes, get in the same sort of trouble, love and hate, lie and tell the truth the next time around. Contrary to the hopes and fears of thinkers from B. F. Skinner to Friedrich Nietzsche, they will remain human and so sinful beings. One reason the self-destruction of the West gives us hope is that it is evidence that we have, by nature, inextinguishable longings that make the Christian description of our situation as a wayfarer in this world no more preposterous than its scientific rivals. Love in the ruins may be the human alterative to the end of history.

PERCY'S POSTMODERNISM

Here I am taking the liberty of describing what, in my view, postmodernism rightly understood is, using Percy's thought as an example. Postmodern thought is a reaction against modern rationalism or science, and to some extent rationalism simply, for their futile attempt to eradicate the mystery of being, particularly human being. It is a reaction against the systematic pretensions of both Hegelianism and behaviorism and other forms of scientism. The postmodernist opposes the view that human misery is rooted most fundamentally in either material deprivation or imaginary illusion. Human beings have religious longings that cannot be satisfied by social or political reform. The longings cannot even be focused wholly on this world.

Percy shows that postmodernism is to some extent both post-Christian and postpolitical. It is reflection based on a world where religious faith is no longer strong, no longer really at the foundation of culture, where human beings characteristically live according to an enlightened secularism, deferring to impersonal expertise. It is reflection on a world where human beings are no longer strongly engaged in political life, where they do not have much of the spirited self-confidence that comes with participation in rule. It is reflection on a world where individuals are isolated and lonely, anxious and confused about longings they cannot understand or even articulate. But it is also a reflection on the continued existence of both human loneliness and the possibility of the love of one lonely self for another.

The postmodern thinker notices the failure of modern or pragmatic efforts to eradicate the mysterious and elusive experiences of the self. So he restores to thought the discredited hypothesis that those experiences might have a foundation in human nature, that human nature is not an oxymoron. He is in one respect more rational than the modern rationalist, because he refuses to rest content with the inexplicable, unempirical incoherence of Cartesian dualism, or with the unempirical hypothesis that history or human distinctiveness has or could come to an end through human effort. The truth is that existence is not made up of detached minds and instinctually determined bodies, two well-ordered but disconnected systems. There is plenty of evidence for the real or natural existence of the disordered, perverse being with language. But the postmodernist's rationalism is limited by his perception that the cosmos is not really a cosmos, because alienated beings with selves are really there. There is no homogeneous or wholly consistent account of being, because of the mystery of human being. Reason, or what we really can know, points beyond itself to the possibility that being is created, that human persons are created in the image and likeness of a personal God.

The postmodern philosopher or scientist does not exempt his own thought, experiences, and action from his science. He considers how and why he longs for and can really know much of the truth. He is a contemporary Tocquevillian, noting with wonder and thinking about the fact that human beings are particularly restless and anxious in fortunate material circumstances. He is, finally, grateful for indomitable human resistance to expert determination. Human beings will never experience themselves mainly as clever animals adjusting well or badly to their environments.

NOTES

1. Lewis A. Lawson and Victor A. Kramer, eds., *Conversations with Walker Percy* (Jackson: University Press of Mississippi, 1985), 4.

2. Walker Percy, letter to Shelby Foote (23 June 1972), in *The Correspondence of Walker Percy and Shelby Foote,* ed. J. Tolson (New York: Norton, 1997), 165.

3. Percy, letter to Foote (25 July 1970), *Correspondence,* 146.

4. Percy, letter to Foote (17 September 1971), *Correspondence,* 156.

5. Percy, letter to Foote (10 September 1980), *Correspondence,* 169.

6. Walker Percy, *Signposts in a Strange Land* (New York: Farrar, Straus, and Giroux, 1991), 257.

7. Ibid., 117.

8. Walker Percy, *The Message in the Bottle* (New York: Farrar, Straus, and Giroux, 1975), 45.

9. Percy, *Signposts,* 282.

10. Ibid., 278.

11. Walker Percy, letter to Ken Ketner (27 February 1989), in *A Thief of Peirce: The Letters of Kenneth Laine Ketner and Walker Percy,* ed. Patrick Samway (Jackson: University Press of Mississippi, 1995), 130–131.

12. Percy, letter to Ketner (19 August 1989), *A Thief,* 158.

13. John F. Desmond, *At the Crossroads: Ethical and Religious Themes in the Writings of Walker Percy* (Troy, N.Y.: Whitson, 1997), 135–145.

14. Percy, letter to Foote (3 February 1971), *Correspondence,* 156.

15. Percy, "Science, Religion, and the Tertium Quid," in *A Thief,* 98–99.

16. Percy, *Signposts,* 134; Percy, *Message,* 11–12.

17 Walker Percy, *Lost in the Cosmos: The Last Self-Help Book* (New York: Farrar, Straus, and Giroux, 1983), 163.

18. Walker Percy, letter to Ketner (11 April 1987), *A Thief,* 13.

19. Percy, *Lost,* 105.

20. Ibid., 143.

21. Lawson and Kramer, *Conversations,* 217.

22. Percy, *Signposts,* 128.

23. Ibid., 126–127.

24. Ibid., 110.

25. Percy, *Lost,* 178.

26. Ibid., 55.

27. Ibid., 178.

28. Percy, *Signposts,* 136–137.

29. Ibid., 288.

30. See Desmond, *At the Crossroads,* 118–125.

31. Percy, *Lost,* 55; Percy, *Message,* 45.

32. Percy, *Signposts,* 256–257.

33. Ibid., 257.

34. Ibid., 135.

35. Percy, "Science, Religion, and the Tertium Quid," 113–114.

36. Percy, *Signposts,* 135, 151, 257.

37. Percy, *Message,* 63.

38. Percy, *Signposts,* 258.

39. Ibid.

40. Percy, *Message,* 19.

41. Percy *Signposts,* 238.

42. Lawson and Kramer, *Conversations,* 28–29.

43. Percy, *Signposts,* 134–135.

44. Percy, *Message,* 24.

45. Lewis A. Lawson and Victor A. Kramer, eds., in *More Conversations with Walker Percy* (Jackson: University Press of Mississippi, 1993), 155.

46. Percy, *Signposts,* 260.

47. Percy, *Message,* 5, 286.

48. Lawson and Kramer, *Conversations,* 43–44.

49. Ibid., 63.

50. Percy, *Lost,* 113n.

51. Percy, *Message,* 277.

52. Ibid., 18.

53. Lawson and Kramer, *More Conversations,* 145.

54. Percy, *Signposts,* 113–114.

55. Percy, *Lost,* 161.

56. Percy, *Signposts,* 301.

57. Percy, *Lost,* 163. The summary of antitheistic evolutionism here is put together from various places in *Lost in the Cosmos.*

58. Ibid., 66, 232.

59. Ibid., 40, 44, 186.

60. Percy, *Signposts,* 277.

61. Percy, *Lost,* 172–173, 192–193n.

62. Ibid., 178.

63. Ibid., 192–193n.

64. Ibid., 217.

65. Lawson and Kramer, *Conversations,* 298.

66. Percy, *Signposts,* 213.

67. Lawson and Kramer, *Conversations,* 73.

68. For Percy's last and maybe best statement on the incoherence of Cartesianism, see *Signposts,* 272–294. Also, Lawson and Kramer, *Conversations,* 60.

69. See Percy, *Lost,* 87n, 102n.

70. Percy, *Signposts,* 207.

71. Ibid., 114.

72. Ibid., 118–119; Percy, *Lost,* 160–163.

73. Percy, *Signposts,* 119.

74. Percy, *Lost,* 160.

75. Percy, *Signposts,* 119.

76. Ibid., 203.

77. Lawson and Kramer, *More Conversations,* 155.

78. Percy, *Signposts,* 126.

79. Lawson and Kramer, *Conversations,* 205.

80. Percy, *Signposts,* 417.

81. Ralph C. Wood, *The Comedy of Redemption: Christian Faith and Comic Vision in Four American Novelists* (Notre Dame, Ind.: University of Notre Dame Press, 1988), 149.

82. Percy, *Lost,* 139.

83. *Lost,* 11; Percy, *Signposts,* 283.

84. *Democracy in America,* volume 2, part 1, chapter 7.

85. Percy, letter to Ketner (27 February 1989), *A Thief,* 130–131.

86. Percy, *Lost,* 143.

87. Ibid., 142, 147.

88. Ibid., 156–157.

89. Ibid., 167.

90. Percy, *Signposts,* 194, 272; Lawson and Kramer, *More Conversations,* 232–233.

91. Ibid., 297.

92. Percy, *Message,* 143; Percy, *Signposts,* 210–211, 252.

93. Percy, *Signposts,* 297–298.

94. Percy, *Lost,* 119.

95. Lawson and Kramer, *More Conversations,* 232.

96. Percy, *Lost,* 74.

97. Lawson and Kramer, *More Conversations,* 82, with Tocqueville, *Democracy in America,* volume 2, part 2, chapter 13.

98. Percy, *Signposts,* 210.

99. Percy, *Conversations,* 308.

100. Percy, *Message,* 44.

101. Percy, *Lost,* 74.

102. Tocqueville, *Democracy in America,* volume 2, part 1, chapter 15 in the context of volume 2, part 1, as a whole.

103. Percy, *Lost,* 12.

104. Percy, *Signposts,* 228–229.

105. Percy, *Message,* 25.

106. Ibid., 3–7.

107. Percy, *Lost,* 13.

108. Ibid.

109. Ibid., 157, 189–190.

110. Lawson and Kramer, *Conversations,* 140.

111. Percy, *Lost,* 211, 214.

112. Ibid., 192.

113. See Percy's novel *The Thanatos Syndrome,* which is discussed in the next chapter.

114. Percy, *Lost,* 83.

115. See ibid., 85–87n.

116. Lawson and Kramer, *Conversations,* 285.

117. Lawson and Kramer, *More Conversations,* 145.

118. Percy, *Lost,* 157.

119. Ibid., 80.

120. Ibid., 122.

121. Ibid., 186.

122. Ibid., 185.

123. Ibid., 70.

124. Ibid., 192.

125. Ibid., 9.

126. Ibid., 13.

127. Lawson and Kramer, *More Conversations,* 163.

128. Percy, *Lost,* 225–263. Otherwise unattributed quotes in this section are from these pages, those of the second space odyssey.

129. Percy, *Signposts*, 46, 83–88.

130. Percy, *Lost*, 50.

131. Lawson and Kramer, *More Conversations*, 126.

132. Lawson and Kramer, *Conversations*, 58.

133. "Liebowitz" is probably a typo in *Lost*. See Percy's appreciation of the Catholic science fiction novelist Walter M. Miller's *A Canticle for Leibowitz* in *Signposts*, 227–33. Liebowitz provides the Catholic answer to Aristarchus, the Ionian founder of science in Sagan's *Cosmos*.

134. Ibid., 287.

135. Ibid., 288.

136. Ibid., 287.

137. Percy, *Lost*, 135.

138. Percy, *Signposts*, 221.

139. Percy, *Lost*, 158.

140. Percy, *Message*, 110.

141. Percy, *Lost*, 153, 158.

142. Percy, *Signposts*, 157.

143. Percy, *Lost*, 119.

144. Ibid., 145.

145. Percy, *Signposts*, 218.

146. Lawson and Kramer, *More Conversations*, 74–75.

147. Percy, *Signposts*, 314.

148. Percy, *Lost*, 11–13, 40.

149. Percy, *Signposts*, 267.

150. Lawson and Kramer, *More Conversations*, 126.

151. Percy, *Lost*, 185.

152. Ibid., 13, 55. See Lawson and Kramer, *Conversations*, 58.

153. For the details of Percy's life, including his political opinions and very occasional and limited political activity, see the hugely informative biography by Patrick H. Samway, S.J., *Walker Percy: A Life* (New York: Farrar, Straus, and Giroux, 1997).

154. Percy, *Signposts*, 258.

155. Ibid., 340.

156. Percy, letter to Shelby Foote (25 July 1970), *Correspondence*, 146–147.

157. Percy, *Signposts*, 159–160.

158. Ibid., 160, 312.

159. Ibid., 258.

160. Lawson and Kramer, *More Conversations*, 231.

4

SEX, DRUGS, POLITICS, LOVE, AND DEATH

W alker Percy's novel *The Thanatos Syndrome* presents and criticizes the pragmatic project he finds at the core of modern science and scientists.[1] Their aim is to eradicate human self-consciousness, including self-conscious mortality. In uncovering this aim, Percy partly agrees with the Hegelian Alexandre Kojève, who says that history has come to an end, the human project has been completed, because human beings are no longer animated by what distinguishes them: their awareness of their mortality. Percy also partly agrees with Allan Bloom, Kojève's most penetrating student, who wrote a best-seller saying that contemporary America, the product of philosophic or scientific thought, is in the process of putting death to death. Richard Rorty, *the* contemporary American defender of pragmatism, cheerfully accepts and writes to perfect the America Bloom calls antiphilosophic or inhuman. We do well, Rorty says, to regard the experience of self-conscious mortality as not useful and so not true.[2] Percy disagrees with Kojève, Bloom, and Rorty by having reason to believe that this scientific, pragmatic project cannot succeed completely.

Dr. Thomas More, the old-fashioned or dialectical practitioner of "psycheiatry" who is the political hero of *The Thanatos Syndrome,* explains that what terrifies people most is not sex, crime, or poverty. They have trouble "knowing who they are or what to do with themselves." Their perplexity increases when they are not doing what "*They,* the experts" say they should be doing. *They* cannot explain why wealthy, intelligent, and attractive people should be miserably unproductive "for no apparent reason" (67, 74–76, 88). The experts, More suggests, are the *they* philosopher Martin Heidegger describes, those who "*do not permit us anxiety in the face of death.*"[3] Their expertise means to keep the individual from being touched by the awareness of his own mortality. Their judgment is that such experience is not good for human beings. They aim not to permit the individual the experience that opens one, courageously, to the truth about oneself.

115

For the experts, anxiety "is a symptom to be gotten rid of." For Heidegger, "it may be a summons to human existence, to be heeded at any cost." For Percy, "it is a matter of some importance to know which it is."[4] But Percy's view of Heidegger's "summons" may not be Heidegger's own. As Lewis Lawson has shown, *the* book that shaped *The Thanatos Syndrome* is the philosopher-theologian-priest Romano Guardini's *The End of the Modern World.* According to Guardini, anxiety in the face of the "great crises" of human life, "conception, birth, sickness, death . . . reveal[s] truths which cannot be mastered by modern techniques," those truths that constitute the mysterious misery and goodness of human existence. The ultimately futile but life-destructive project of modern science, especially "medical science," is "the rational conquest of sickness and death," or the obliteration of that mystery, including the mysterious human perception of the truth.[5]

PSYCHOTHERAPY

The Thanatos Syndrome's "only message," Percy says, is that it is "better to be a dislocated human than a happy chimp."[6] Beginning perhaps with René Descartes and certainly with Jean-Jacques Rousseau, modern thinkers have tended to choose the chimp.[7] Their political project became reducing "a stressful human existence to a peaceable animal existence" (180). The effort to eradicate stress completely, to purge human existence of consciousness of death, Percy explains, has produced a century of death, an unprecedented amount of ideologically motivated killing. He connects the apparently benign and compassionate projects of scientists today to reduce suffering and improve the quality of life with those of the Weimar scientists who eventually assisted in the killing of the Jews.

Pop Cartesian, pro-chimp therapy has failed so far. Rorty's pragmatic, linguistic therapy denies the truth that human experiences of self and so human language have a natural foundation. They cannot really be described out of existence. But according to Percy, the dominant tendency in psychotherapy today is actually the use of drugs and chemicals to suppress the moods of anxiety and depression.[8] This method, by altering one's natural functioning, seems to succeed where Rorty fails.

The chemotherapeutic scientist agrees with the pop Cartesian philosopher that anxiety and depression are treatable symptoms of a disease to be cured in the name of an orderly, stress-free, nice, reasonable life. Why should human beings be unnecessarily miserable, especially when that misery is the source of so much socially undesirable behavior? The old-fashioned answer is that such experiences of self or soul point one in the direction of the truth and are integral to human nature or the human condition. But the scientist's reasonable response is that when the experience is eradicated, by whatever means, the alleged reality to which it points—the soul or self—also disappears.

The disease of which anxiety and depression are symptoms is self-conscious mortality. Human health, both mental and physical, is greatly improved, not by futilely denying, but by actually destroying what separates human beings from the other animals. As Rousseau first explained, unselfconscious man, whom he too simply called natural man, is a model of mental and physical health.

The Thanatos Syndrome presents an ambitious, illegal experiment, a pilot project with national potential, of government-funded physicians and scientists to treat the water supply of a large section of Louisiana with a self-suppressing chemical, heavy sodium. The scientific hypothesis of these chemotherapists "is that at least a segment of the human neocortex and of consciousness itself is not only an aberration of evolution but is also the scourge and curse of life on earth, the source of wars, insanities, and perversions—in short, those very pathologies which are peculiar to *Homo sapiens*." Translated into nonscientific language by the novelist Kurt Vonnegut, the hypothesis is that "the only trouble with *Homo sapiens* is that parts of our brains are too fucking big" (195). It is Rousseau's hypothesis, with one difference. Rousseau distinguished between animal nature and human history. Natural man, considered precisely, is an oxymoron. The chemotherapists observe that human beings are actually naturally different from the other animals. That natural difference is the source of all the pathologies peculiar to human history. Human distinctiveness is a natural aberration, to be corrected on behalf of evolution's general intention.

Human beings function better when the functioning of the part of the brain that produces self-consciousness is suppressed. They actually become what Rorty describes them to be, extremely clever animals and no more. Contrary to Rousseau's view that unselfconscious human beings must be stupid, chemical treatment actually makes them much more clever. Their brains, no longer impeded by self-deceptive moodiness, calculate and remember far better. Their language, no longer bloated by the poetic, dialogical articulations of the self, moves toward the powerful binary language of the computer (68–69, 192–196).

Human sexual desire becomes healthy or completely uninflamed and unperverted by the longings of the self. Sex becomes merely mechanical rutting for the purposes of procreation and the satisfaction of bodily desire and no more. So it becomes open and casual, undistorted by vain self-deception, lies, and guilt. It is no longer perverted by the longing of one self for another. It is simply the presentation of one's body, or one's sexual parts, to another. Human sex becomes like chimp sex, no longer face-to-face. Human beings no longer act perversely to negate their instincts for self-preservation and enjoyment when freed from consciousness of self (20–21, 68–69).

Human beings also become more energetic and self-confident. The chemical treatment also has the effect of increasing the body's production of endorphins, a "natural high." So there are no more "hang-ups" or inhibitions. People are "always psyched up but never psyched out." Without the disorders not found among the other animals, human possibilities, because of the species' singular cleverness, become unlimited (192–196).

The scientist-physicians add that chemical treatment has become a social imperative today. We live in a time of extreme social disorder, because we live in a time of very disordered selves. Society is infected with a new form of the "plague," this time a more moral or psychological than physiological one. Surely society "has the right to defend itself" against the consequences of the family's decline, the underclass's demoralization, drug abuse, and so forth (218). It appears, as Rousseau said, that the effects of the aberration of evolution grow over time.

But social decay can be replaced with progress with the self's eradication. Human beings really can flourish in contentment in the midst of abundance. The chemotherapists assert, against Rousseau, that human health or perfection is compatible with high civilization. Civilization and technology originally may have come into existence and depended upon experiences of self, but their future can be secured by clever animals with computer-brains.

The eradication of the self, perhaps most fundamentally, is required for human beings not to become progressively more dissatisfied with modern science's apparent failure, which is perhaps the primary cause of the disorder of our time. "The trouble is," as Percy explains, "the sciences for the last 200 years have been spectacularly successful in dealing with subhuman reality . . . with extraordinary progress in learning about the cosmos, but also extraordinary lack of success in dealing with humanity as humanity."[9] So the progress of science has actually made human beings more aware of the elusiveness of what distinguishes them: their selves. They feel more dislocated than ever, because there is more evidence than ever that the self is some sort of leftover in the cosmos. "Western man's sense of homelessness and loss of community is in part due to the fact that he feels himself a stranger to the method and data of his sciences."[10]

Scientists stubbornly and expertly deny the reality of the self or soul, and so they deny the reality of the feeling of dislocation. The cosmos, they say, really is a cosmos. There cannot be any leftovers. But the genuine failure of modern science can become success if science really eradicates, not just futilely denies, what it cannot explain. So chemical treatment "zaps" what scientists otherwise might have to acknowledge to be inexplicable deviancy or error. It serves the truth, paradoxically, by depriving human beings of the experience of the wondrous search for the truth about oneself. In the name of the truth, they are deprived of knowledge of the truth about their own contingency and mortality.

Chemotherapy promises to *make* modern science wholly true. That science, when examining human beings, becomes progressively less empirical over time. It abstracts from the truth about the self or soul. By so doing, it becomes less a scientific description and more an ideal for human transformation. The ideal is to perfect human beings by freeing them from their flaws, their malformation. That ideal cannot be realized through linguistic therapy or propaganda, as Rorty believes, or through political revolution, as the Marxists believed. In both cases, the natural foundation of the self resists merely ideological efforts at destruction. But because the self does have a natural foundation—it is not the arbitrary political or poetic creation of human beings—perhaps it cannot resist chemicals that alter its natural functioning. Why cannot science change human nature?

PSYCHE-IATRY

Dr. More dissents from the dominant therapeutic method, the treatment of symptoms with chemicals. That dissent seems, at first glance, to be the foundation of his dissent from the scientists' political project. His resolute action thwarts their experiment, defending effectively the rule of law and the protection of rights. But as a man of science, a physician dedicated to the alleviation of human misery, he could not help but be attracted to the project's proclaimed scientific, compassionate purpose and initial success. He had to learn what was wrong with the experiment through his experience with its results (328).

More calls himself "a psyche-iatrist, an old-fashioned physician of the soul" (16). He practices "one-on-one therapy with depressed and terrified people" (366). His method is dialectical; we might say Socratic. He talks with but mainly listens to his patients, as they "plumb the depths of their depression." He encourages them "to believe that their anxiety and depression might be telling them something of value" (67).

More believes his method is empirical. It is distinguished by its attentiveness to the details of the way human speech articulates human experience. The truth is that human beings are anxious because they experience themselves as dislocated. Coming to terms with such strange, terrible experiences, and wondering about them, is what makes life "more tolerable" (6). In More's view, wondering about the terror of the self's dislocation is an inescapable part of the human condition.

The "best thing" the "shrink" can do is help each patient "render the unspeakable speakable." The unspeakable, the source of human speech, is the self. The deepest cause of "free floating anxiety" is the "unnamed longing" somehow at the core of the self. But human beings are also mysteriously given the capacity to live well enough with the self's consciousness of its dislocation and finitude, of time and death. More's amazing, finally inexplicable, experience is that human beings can feel better without chemicals by talking about what eludes their complete comprehension and control. His "psychiatric faith" in the ability of the self to come to terms with what it really knows through dialectical investigation comes from what he has seen for himself (6, 13–18, 67).

What the patient needs to know to begin to live well is that the Cartesian experts who deny the reality of the self do not speak the truth, or the whole truth. He needs to know that it is perfectly reasonable for a self-conscious mortal to be restless and miserable in fortunate material circumstances. He needs to articulate what he really experiences about the mystery of his own being. He needs to know that failure, far more than success, is characteristic of the human condition, and how "even [to] take pleasure in the general fecklessness of life." Nothing opposes the pragmatic core of modern science more than the truth that one can be a happy failure (77). Happiness, in truth, comes most readily when one does not pursue it, when one does not imagine that it is a state of being somehow within one's control (89).

More's psyche-iatric method, getting at "the root of the trouble, the soul's own secret, by venturing into the heart of darkness," takes months or years of talking and listening (13). His view is that each soul or self is particularly worthy of thought. It presents haunting questions that make one miserable, can occupy one's whole life, and may never adequately be answered. The success More's method achieves is through illuminating what the questions are and why one is haunted by them. It cannot turn anxiety into pleasure. But there is a compensatory pleasure in self-understanding, in the amazed wonder that comes with seeing how strange human beings, beginning with oneself, really are.

For Percy, More "is a closet Jew or Christian whether he likes it or not," because his psyche-iatric view of the individual's life as "find[ing] himself in a predicament which is a profound mystery to which he devotes his whole life to unraveling" is based on Christian anthropology.[11] But Percy also knows that this Christian view of the self's mysterious dislocation could be true even if a Christian God does not exist, as the existentialists thought. It is a view that one can discover to be true through one's own observation of others and self-exploration, even if one does not believe in God. Joseph Cropsey has recently discovered that experience of "human loneliness in the cosmos, which pervades our being," may first have been articulated, if rather covertly, by Plato.[12]

Cropsey's Plato is quite the atheist, even a dogmatic atheist. But, as Christopher Bruell complains, if existence or "the whole" is fundamentally mysterious, how do we know that God does not exist, that, as Percy puts it, the fundamental news is so bad?[13] Psyche-iatry, properly understood, is also Christian in the sense that its anthropology has to acknowledge the possibility that the news is good, that we are created by a provident God. Percy calls that "exploration" of the human being's "openness" to that possibility "a different story" from the genuinely scientific articulation of anthropology or what we can really know about the human self and its situation.[14] It is one he does not tell in his philosophical or scientific writing and only calls attention to in his novels.

More had been a Cartesian scientist. He believed he had discovered the technique with which to diagnose and treat the world's madness. He was as "grandiose, even Faustian" as the chemotherapists. Concluding that he, far more than the world, had gone mad, he prescribed prison for himself (67, 103). The treatment worked fairly well in moderating his selfish disorder, and it made him a better psychiatrist. He says it cured him of his "vanity," or "the secret sardonic derisiveness of doctors in general." He thought prison "restored my humanity." So he learned to speak with his patients "as fellow flawed humans." He came to acknowledge that he was not free from their selfish disorder and suffering by virtue of his scientific knowledge. He believed that he no longer viewed their merely human flaws and troubles with contempt (81).

Prison helped More become a physician of the soul, a genuine empiricist (43). He started to see with amazement how strange—both troubled and brave—people really are. He became curious about them. He distinguished himself from his fellow scientist-physicians by giving particular human beings "considerable thought" (81). He worried no longer about "modern man" or "the human condition" or God, grandiose abstractions, but about particular individuals. His horizon became more empirical as it became more modest or small scale (67).

Scientific detachment is ordinarily really from the dreariness of ordinary human life, including the ordinariness of one's own life when one is not engaged in scientific inquiry. More's detachment is from the characteristic and false pretension of science, that ordinary life is not worthy of thought. The scientist, through his inquiry, characteristically to some extent diverts himself from his own experiences of self, from what he shares with all other self-conscious mortals.

More's attention to the way human speech reveals human reality, the depth of the self, makes him a dialectical, not a Cartesian, scientist. He agrees with the physician-novelist Percy that the " 'sentences' of art, poetry, and the novel ought to be taken very seriously indeed since these are cognitive, scientific, if you will, statements that we have about what it is to be human."[15] But even More's involvement in the troubled self-exploration of others is, to some extent, a diversion from his personal disorder. He is slow to connect what he learns from sharing in the self-exploration of his patients to himself, his family, political life, and his longing for God. It is not until near the novel's end that More really completely stops thinking of himself as a scientific "genius," as somehow exempted from ordinary human troubles and longings.[16] Only then does he fully become what he believed himself to be as a psyche-iatrist, "a flawed human being caring for another through language."[17] He finally learns how radically he must distinguish himself from the Cartesian chemotherapists.

More makes claims for the scientific superiority and human worthiness of his psyche-iatry. But he is unpretentious enough to suspect that his preference for the old-fashioned method might be pretentious. His approach might be scientific in the sense of being based on an accurate description of human self-consciousness. But as a way of alleviating human misery, it is inefficient, uncertain, and at best partially successful. Its time-consuming focus on the individual seems to make it irrelevant in the struggle against social disorder. More acknowledges that the chemotherapists might deserve to have carried the day because they get results: "If one can prescribe a chemical and overnight turn a haunted soul into a bustling little body, why take on such a quixotic quest as pursuing the secret of one's very self " (13)?

Would not science progress rapidly, discovering certain answers to fundamental questions, if the soul, with its mysterious disorder, were simply eradicated? Then Cartesian or materialistic science would really become science, a complete account of all bodies and so all that exists. The quest for self-knowledge becomes more than "quixotic" only when the self disappears altogether. But who would undertake the quest if there were no selves? Who would desire and so come to know the answers to the fundamental questions?

THE ILLEGAL EXPERIMENT WITH CHEMICALS

More, the physician, is devoted to human well-being. He identifies well-being with health and freedom from suffering, mental and physical. But he also identifies it with what is integral to the human condition, personal or dialectical responses to the anxious experience of dislocation. His individual approach to psyche-iatry makes him a defender of personal sovereignty against scientific expertise.

More's two views of human well-being are in tension. As long as one has experiences of self, one will be somewhat more miserable and less healthy than one might otherwise be. The surrender of personal sovereignty seems to be what is required to produce a well-ordered life, freed from cruel suffering. The exercise of personal sovereignty or liberty brings into existence a world with love and wonder but also one with anxiety, anger, fear, hatred, perversion, exploitation, and war. More's experience with the consequences of the scientists' experiments forces him to reflect on the choice between stressful, troubled, and sometimes cruel human existence and peaceful, well-ordered, and content animal existence.

When More begins to notice that his patients, for a reason not yet discovered, have lost their experiences of self, he cannot decide whether they are better or worse off. They are more physically healthy, and in every way less disordered. They are free from terror, rage, and guilt (21). They are, from the physician's or psychiatrist's perspective, seemingly cured. They neither desire nor seem in need of treatment. But More adds that they are somehow "diminished" (86), and he calls their psychological and physiological changes in the direction of contentment "regression." They have lost their sovereignty, liberty, distinctiveness, or greatness.

The scientific argument for social responsibility initially attracts More, and he accepts the "impressive evidence of social betterment." In one sense, "society is like an organism," and the eradication of the personal cause of social disorder can be justified in terms of society's self-preservation (234–235).

More tends to agree that a plague-like crisis can justify the temporary suspension of rights. After all, what is good for society's self-preservation as an "organism" is also good for the individual's preservation as an organism. All that is lost is the self, that which seems to oppose itself perversely to the organism's self-preservation, both individual and social.

We can say that this argument for self-preservation seems Hobbesian. But the individually oriented psyche-iatrist puts forward, although tentatively, two related Hobbesian rejoinders. More wonders about the experiment's illegality, about its usurpation of the authority of democratic political sovereignty. When he is encouraged to be the "devil's advocate," or speak from his "own expertise" or not in his own name, More also ironically calls attention to "the technicality of civil rights." The experimenters are "assaulting the cortex of the individual without the knowledge and consent of the assaultees" (209). For Thomas Hobbes, the foundation of the sovereign's power, and so the rule of law, is the individual's reasonable consent. One's natural, personal sovereignty is the source of political authority. More cannot help but wonder whether the doctors can be trusted with the unaccountable power over individuals they have assumed. They are treating their very large number of patients not as beings with rights but as animals to be controlled.

More, alone among the scientist and physicians, is capable of raising the question of rights. His political dissent comes from his knowledge of the self. He knows that human beings are capable of living well with their personal sovereignty. They have, as even Hobbes says, the capacity to tell the truth to themselves about themselves. They do not need to—and in fact cannot consistently without chemical treatment—defer to expert control of their experiences for their own good.

More differs from Hobbes concerning the foundation of rights. In so doing, he shows that Hobbes's foundation is inadequate, that by beginning with fearful avoidance of death one ends up with the rule of experts. For Hobbes, human beings by nature are both miserably afraid of death and free to do what they can to preserve themselves, to act methodically in response to their fear. Their goal is safety or peace. But they never really achieve their goal, because their best efforts cannot free them from the fear that comes with self-conscious mortality. Perhaps the more safe they really are, the more afraid they feel, which is why Hobbes says human beings become particularly troublesome in times of peace, prosperity, and good government. Freed somewhat from their struggle against necessity, they cannot avoid reflection on their inevitable failure.

If the human goal really is safety or peace, then the chemotherapists might really deserve our consent. They claim to have secured for human beings what they could not secure reliably for themselves. They have freed them from fear and anxiety about death. As a result of the treatment, people actually feel safe and secure. For More, personal sovereignty does not come from one's freedom to attempt to defeat death. It comes with one's capability to live well with one's own fear and anxiety, by coming to terms with the inevitability of death, with genuinely self-conscious mortality. For More, the person Hobbes describes, working incessantly to avoid the inevitable, is self-deceptive. The person Hobbes describes does not really tell the truth to himself about himself at all.

More's ambivalence about and initial reluctance to push the issue of the defense of rights comes in part from his awareness that perhaps most or all human beings would consent to the chemical suppression of their self-consciousness if they actually could experience a before and after comparison. His immobilizing thought is that Hobbes or, better, Rousseau might be in a deep sense right. More has the chemotherapist Dr. John Van Dorn take an extremely potent dose of heavy sodium as part of his plan to foil the experiment. More actually wins Van Dorn's consent by telling him honestly that the chemicals will produce no effects in him that he would not want (344).

More's decisive action against the experiment is not based primarily on his judgment about the treatment's evil effects on individuals. It has to do with the requirements of their self-defense against other selves. The trouble with the experiment is the scientists' vain, tyrannical decision to exempt themselves from its consequences. In Hobbes's terms, they aim, as all tyrants do, to bring the natural equality of human beings to an end by turning themselves into masters and others into slaves. That desire for mastery, Hobbes says, is natural. Percy agrees, adding the explanation that its source is the naturalness of the anxious self.

That desire for mastery exists in us all to some extent, although most of us aim mainly at self-mastery or self-defense. Those aiming to master others must prevent that desire from manifesting itself effectively in others. Hobbes recommends the use of fear, calling attention to its reliability. But the chemotherapists say, quite rightly, that fear is not nearly reliable enough, and it is unnecessarily cruel. They claim to replace fear with compassion, with a project to eliminate all cruelty and so the need for lawful or political order from the world.

ANGER

In addition to the sexual and linguistic regression, More notices the absence of anger and partisanship in his patients. He detects "a certain curious disinterest. . . . No arguments, no fright, no rage, no cursing the Communists, no blaming the networks, no interests," no clash of ideologies (85). He was less inclined, in one sense, to view the absence of this quality as regression.

While in prison, surrounded by angry, ideological, passionate men, More wondered about the source of such "rage." He lost interest in the actual content of arguments, and he became extremely reluctant to engage in argument himself. He concluded that those who argue are really afraid of the "abyss." They take pleasant refuge in argument from what they really know. Passionate liberals and passionate conservatives, More notices, need each other like lovers do. Anything, even "violent disagreement, even war," is better than nothing (35, 87).

More's view of the world combines a perception that responsible, credible political and religious conviction is impossible in our time with his faith based on experience in the ability of individuals to live well in light of death. This incoherence explains why he is much more attentive to individual cases than to political life or God, and perhaps why he too easily accepts the inadequate view that society is like an organism. The cause of this incoherence seems to be More's own unacknowledged, anguished or angry atheism. He says one reason he has focused his curiosity on particular individuals is he does not "know what to make of God." He claims not to give "Him, Her, It, a second thought" (67), but he really diverts himself from what he thinks he knows. Not having acknowledged or come to terms with his anger, More is unable to live as well without God as some of his patients. He cannot really undertake his own "interior quest" as long as he denies his interest in and longing for God.[18]

More sometimes muses that ours has been an angry, ideological, murderous century because it has been an atheistic one. Human beings kill for empty abstractions in response to their miserable disorientation in the absence of God (87, 330). Chemical treatment, of course, quickly removes one's perception of the abyss. Overnight, it seems at first, it has changed our century's character by removing the cause of gratuitous killing and war.

More distinguishes between the talking and listening of his dialectical method and polemical argument. The former, genuinely Socratic, aims at truth or self-knowledge. The latter, although it may actually be more often called Socratic, angrily and anxiously covers over the truth by opposing itself to listening (34). The "passionate arguer," in fact, has no interest in individuals and individuality. The racially enlightened liberal, for instance, has "no use for individual blacks." The less angry or displaced Southerner who has little use for ideology and is sometimes unjust actually knows and likes particular black individuals (35). Argument opposes itself to self-understanding in all its forms.

More makes this distinction between dialectic and polemic too radically or apolitically. He is far too reluctant to argue even on behalf of personal sovereignty or individual rights. A chemotherapeutic physician says after the experiment failed that More actually had no argument against its "ultimate goals." It is clear that by then More knows there is such an argument, but he still does not make it in his own name (346–347).

But More also becomes somewhat aware that his detachment from argument is a form of self-denial. He is told, correctly, that while he is personally involved with his patients, he is detached from his own family and his own concerns. He admits that his "parenting skills" are poor (205), and he refuses to acknowledge his anger even when he discovers that his wife had a sexual relationship with Dr. Van Dorn. His political action is, in large measure, a result of that unacknowledged anger, a passionate defense of his own wife and children from those who would abuse them. "There is a great difference," More says in reflecting upon one of his patient's troubles, "between being angry and knowing that you are angry," and one result of psyche-iatry is discovering that one is angry (13).

Anger, More shows us, does not just cover up the abyss. It is a defense of what one loves, a natural consequence of the experience of the goodness of human life. The chemotherapists, by eradicating anger, also eradicate the spirit of resistance to their illegal, tyrannical project. They destroy what leads oneself to resist destruction by another. Anger, a manifestation of self, leads human beings to perform acts of gratuitous cruelty and even to commit suicide. For other human beings the angry protection of self is required to protect one's body from the disorder of other selves. Only in a world without selves at all could human beings defend themselves adequately without anger. So More does not do well to say that society is like an organism, because its components—human individuals—are not simply organisms.

More, in another sense, connects the absence of anger with regression. Disinterest, or the absence of partisanship, also manifests itself in More's patients as a lack of curiosity. Curiosity begins with interest in oneself (79), and without such self-interest, everything interesting strange or diverse about human beings disappears. What remains is a "sameness . . . a flatness of affect"

(85). Individuals lose their context as "encultured creatures," because culture originates in self-exploration and self-expression (69). They also lose their capacity to tell jokes, which is really a way of venting anger (76). Not only do they stop lying, but there is no longer any space for their ironic detachment (82).

SEXUAL LIBERATION AS SEXUAL REGRESSION

The chemical treatment produces among Louisianians what Allan Bloom claimed to find among America's students: flatness of soul. Human beings are no longer touched or moved by death. Without thanatos, as Freud says, there is no eros. Without love, or passionate longing and attachment to one's own, there is no anger or hatred.

More soon discovers that the mode of liberated human relations praised by pop Cartesian experts has actually come into existence. Freed from the twinship of love and death, human beings finally really enjoy sexual liberation, the unencumbered openness of the "encounter group." Before chemical treatment, those who preached easygoing openness and relativistic permissiveness were actually "quarrelsome and ideological" themselves. Their propaganda did nothing to ease their own troubled souls, or have the effect they intended on those they attempted to influence. After chemotherapy, More really does discover an "open community" with "creative relationships across stereotypical bonding," casual promiscuity. Human beings live more contentedly in what is "less like a couple's retreat than a chimp colony" (84–85). Only in a colony of selfless chimps could one find the simple, honest openness that is the alleged goal of the "sexual revolution."

The goal of the centuries-long pop Cartesian moral revolution has always been liberation from the repressive, guilt-ridden effects of Platonism and Christianity, the moralism that has distorted Western civilization. Cartesianism has always pointed toward a return to "the old nature religion, a nonsexist, pre-Judeo-Christian belief, nothing less than becoming one with nature and with yourself" (81). Radically modern religion, as Alexis de Tocqueville for one noticed, is pantheism, a radical rejection of the anxious, disorienting experience of individuality.[19] It is the religion compatible with the modern, Cartesian view of the cosmos.

Pantheistic oneness, in Percy's view, is really the spiritual form of Cartesian self-denial, a denial of the experiences that separate the self from the rest of nature or the cosmos. Compared with Christianity, it is obviously a regression in the direction of illusion. But neither the sexual revolution nor nature religion can prevail in the Christian or post-Christian world through linguistic therapy or political reform; human beings cannot help but experience their claims as untrue. They can only become true as the result of chemotherapy. Before seeing the effects of the treatment, More reacted derisively when he heard obviously untrue pop Cartesian propaganda. After seeing their effects he had to acknowledge that perhaps the distinction between human and chimp reality had actually disappeared. He had to consider the possibility that science could make pantheism true.

THE SCIENTISTS

More's initial judgment concerning the scientists' experiment was ambivalent because he did not appreciate the role of the scientists themselves in the experiment. In their absence, he saw both good and bad in the effects he observed and in the experiment's proclaimed goals. With the scientists' presence, the effects of the experiment turned out to be different and more complex than More had originally thought. Finally, he did not decisively oppose science but the scientists, those who irresponsibly exempted themselves from the treatment they prescribed for others. The experiment was foiled and destined for failure anyway, because it was less a product of detached scientific objectivity than a projection of the scientists' own unexamined troubled selves. The scientists, not science, were responsible for the key decisions that constitute the experiment (326).

The physicians and scientists came close to imagining that by brutalizing others, they would divinize or angelize themselves. Their imaginations, in Percy's terms, tended to be Cartesian. Their science can account for the well-ordered existences of angels and animals but not for the human self. By freeing others from their disorder, they imagined it would also free themselves. The scientists imagined themselves operating outside political life or the law, creating a world in which its restraints would be obsolete. They viewed themselves, by virtue of their scientific knowledge, as having no need for legal or conscientious restraint, and those they treated would act in an orderly fashion without conscience or the law. Law and conscience are unreliable means of restraining troubled, flawed mortal selves. The chemotherapy would leave nothing imperfect or malformed in the world.

The physicians and scientists did not *quite* mean to divinize themselves or brutalize others. They imagined themselves as retaining some, but not all, human qualities. They meant not to control thoughtless automatons but to rule, if tyrannically, human beings. They, quite romantically, believed that through the experiment's success they would be freed from their own personal misery while remaining human.

For Percy, a romantic imagination is one freed from the rigor of empirical, including self-, investigation. Its source is the scientists' Cartesian premise that the self or soul does not exist, which really means they have put their personal experiences outside the scope of science. The "scientifically minded person become[s] a romantic because he is a left-over from his own science."[20] By not engaging in dialectical psyche-iatry, scientists divert themselves from the fact that all distinctively human qualities flow from self-consciousness, and one cannot experience curiosity, wonder, or love without experiencing anxiety and dislocation in view of one's contingency and mortality.

The scientists quite unscientifically imagined that a perfectly well-ordered world could be a human one. Because they are neither perfectly wise nor really detached from the troubled concerns of flawed mortals, their imaginations were distorted. They repeated the error of Karl Marx, who said, quite incoherently, that human beings could somehow remain human at history's end.

The designers of the chemical experiment did not intend to produce superchimps. Both the physician Dr. Bob Comeaux and the scientist Dr. John Van Dorn thought in terms of a beautiful human perfection. Comeaux aimed at perfect human innocence, whereas Van Dorn sought an unprecedented, unencumbered human excellence. Comeaux's thought was distorted by his reactionary, racist anger, Van Dorn's by his sexual perversion.

Comeaux began by imagining for himself the identity and life of a cultivated Louisiana aristocrat. He was actually "Bob Como of Long Island City." As a white, urban ethnic, his fearful anger was directed against the young black "punks" who roam unsocialized and outside the law (198–199). He wanted those criminals to behave (347). But Como was not simply a fearful racist. He was, quite understandably, repulsed by the "monuments of bare ugliness" that characterize modern, urban, democratic life generally (198). He moved south, where he had heard and read that life was once beautiful and blacks were a docile part of that life.

Comeaux aimed to "restore the best of the Southern way of life" (213), believing that living that life would free him from personal disorder, his fear and anger, and for the pure perception of ordered beauty. His admittedly "corny" or abstract view of that life did not come from experience. More muses to himself: "If there is such a thing as a Southern way of life, part of it has to do with not speaking of it" (60). The beautiful South of Comeaux's imagination comes in large part from the Hollywood version of *Gone with the Wind*. He aims to restore a world that never existed anywhere but in a romance.

In Comeaux's world, blacks are docile, but without the cruelty of the master and his overseer, and without the degraded, feigned slavishness of "Uncle Tom." Like any Northerner, he knows the way the masters treated their "niggers" was cruelly unjust. He replaced the relationship that did actually once exist between master and slave with that of "Uncle Tom Jefferson and his yeoman farmers and yeoman craftsmen," a relationship formed largely by Jefferson's imagination (198). Comeaux's ideal is a combination of Hollywood and Jeffersonian romanticism. He imagines himself the new and perfected Uncle Tom Jefferson, paternalistically and benevolently caring for well-behaved, industrious, and genuinely contented blacks.

This South, to emphasize the obvious, is no restoration. It could only become possible through the chemical "zapping" of black selves, the source of their resistance to and discontent with white benevolence. With the treatment, the world in Comeaux's part of Louisiana does come to correspond largely to his ideal. Young punks are transformed into intelligent, industrious apprentices. The "darkies" are once again singing in the field, and without the legal reinstitution of slavery (266, 327). The black farmers and laborers have lost their desire for freedom. They have been freed from the distinctively human cruelty of longing for what one does not have.

Percy clearly means to criticize Jefferson's own romantic tendencies, which characterized Southern agrarianism from his time onward. Jefferson obscured even from himself his ideal's dependence on the rights-denying injustice of slavery. Both Jefferson and Comeaux were scientists and masters. The pride of the master who exempts himself from his science, as the rights-protecting Jefferson certainly understood in principle, distorts his political vision.

Comeaux refuses to acknowledge that the newly docile blacks are, despite their intelligence, really subhuman. Their art and music he accepts—on the authority of an anthropologist—as evidence of the return to primitive—but still human—innocence (198–199). For More (and Percy), anthropology is an incoherent, unempirical science, infused at its core with Rousseau's romanticism. Those such as Margaret Mead who claim to have uncovered *human* innocence are obvious frauds. Anthropology, Percy explains, is part of the Cartesian-Rousseauean dogma of contemporary science that human beings are in no way flawed or troubled by nature: "Thou shalt not suggest that there is a unique and fatal flaw in Homo sapiens or indeed any perverse trait that cannot be laid to the influence of Western civilization."[21]

Comeaux is attracted to anthropology because he accepts, although with a crucial alteration, its Rousseauean imperative. Human beings, according to Rousseau, have made themselves miserably restless. Once they know their misery is self-created, perhaps they can uncreate it. Comeaux knows that restless human misery is natural, and so he really knows he is not quite restoring primitive innocence. He believes that human beings can—with scientific knowledge in the service of romantic idealism—alter nature to create human innocence. But his correction to Rousseau is only sound in part. Rousseau was right to say that an innocent, untroubled, docile being could not be a human one.

Comeaux aims to create the well-ordered soul and society imagined by aristocrats, but without their sometimes cruel and unjust use of legal coercion. But in his pursuit of his angry, political goal, he could not avoid depriving those whom he desired to control of their freedom. His anger is really directed against the very existence of the self or soul, of what disturbs the beautiful order or harmony of nature, but what is also the source of all distinctively human beauty.

Comeaux's angry opposition to human freedom is clear in his praise of the benefits of physiological regression in women. The chemical treatment has replaced the menstrual cycle with estrus. Women used to be in heat most of the time, and so they could not help but be trouble for men and themselves. After the treatment, they are rarely interested in or capable of doing what leads to reproduction. The result is no more "useless" sex, no more promiscuity, and "natural population control." The troublesome and ineffectual techniques of birth control and abortion are no longer needed (196). There is no more sexual deviancy because there is no more sexual freedom. Comeaux, the moralist, creates a world, not of sexual liberation, but of liberation from sex.

There is, more exactly, no more human eros. Without experiences of self, human sexual response contracts, because it is no longer inflamed by distinctively human longings. Sexual or erotic freedom, understood as the product of that mixture, is at the core of human freedom. It really would have to disappear for the world to become well ordered. The moralistic use of science creates a world without the need for personal restraint or morality.

Comeaux does have some anxiety about his project. He often attempts to engage the skeptical More with "Socratic questions" or "dialoging" about it (34, 190, 194, 201, 346–347). Reminding us of Rorty's pragmatism, he asserts that his scientific inquiry has left the great controversies and intellectual quarrels of human history behind. They have not been dialectically resolved, but rendered irrelevant (196). He mocks More's prudish recitation of the facts about sexual regression and abuse by saying that More is accusing him, in effect, of "corrupting the youth of Athens" (329). He wants More to acknowledge the force of the evidence that he has eradicated human suffering and improved the quality of life (190) and that More's opposition to Comeaux's project is simply a matter of "style" or snobbery (347). But More says Comeaux reminds him of prisoners, who use anger to hide emptiness (34). One problem with Comeaux's identification of himself with Socrates is that he actually works to suppress the natural corruption or perversity of the young that might lead the youth to Socrates.

At the core of Comeaux's project is the perception that human life as it actually exists is no good. He sees no beauty in and so has no love for its flawed, mortal freedom. His is the experience of an extremely disordered, desperate, unscientific, death-denying self, and his experiment based on his romanticism is really incompletely successful self-deception. Comeaux ends up admitting his efforts at re-creation have failed; he still does not know "how to act" (347). Because he does not know how to die, a true Socratic would say, he does not know how to live.

SEXUAL LIBERATION AND HUMAN EXCELLENCE

Dr. John Van Dorn, the other director of the chemical experiment, knows all too well that human flourishing depends upon sexual freedom (218). He is contemptuous of the "castrating" moralism of the "ham-fisted social engineer[ing]" of Comeaux and his kind. Van Dorn's own, more finely tuned, goal is to zap only some of the self. His goal is to liberate the creative energy of eros from being impeded by repressive moralism or guilt. The social engineer has only the "short-term" goal of controlling misbehavior. Because he has "no ultimate goals," he does not see that the patient must remain "human enough" to achieve them. "Excellence," of course, is the end of being human, meaning artistic and scientific excellence (219).

Van Dorn believes he can alter human nature slightly to combine different forms of excellence—"the high sexuality of the Don [Giovanni] and Einstein without the frivolity of the Don or the repressed Jewish sexuality of Einstein"—in single human beings (220). Chemotherapy is the means to achieve such an unprecedented combination, to actualize, we might say, the ideal represented by Socrates. The new genius, once created, will have no need for chemicals. His brain and eros will combine for self-sufficient, untroubled, philosophical liberation.

Van Dorn, "the Renaissance Man" (200) dedicated to excellence in all its forms, is the founder of a private school for young children, dedicated to "Greek ideals of virtue" (252). The Greeks defined virtue as excellence, and that definition has, in Van Dorn's eyes, nothing to do with moderation or self-restraint. He has, as did the Greeks, a "theory of the nature of man," which is that the "highest achievements . . . derive from sexual energy" (219).

Excellence has been thwarted by the tradition of moral repression that has held the West back "since St. Paul" (200). Because the chemical treatment does not free human beings from tradition or convention for a life according to nature but actually alters their natures, it would appear the excellence really has been thwarted more by the self than by the West. But Van Dorn is clear that the antierotic or moralistic, including Comeaux's, view of virtue is Christian, not Greek. Van Dorn believes he has stated in modern or more scientific terms the Greek connection between erotic longing and intellectual excellence. He is part of the intellectual movement that rejects Christianity and Christian Platonism by recovering the true spirit of the Greeks at the origin of high civilization and scientific liberation.

Van Dorn, "Dr. Ruth of the bayous" (200), believes that Sigmund Freud stated scientifically what the Greeks understood imperfectly. All forms of human energy or eros are actually derived from sexual eros. The soul or self is really a reflection of the body and its needs. This theory, for More and Percy, is really a form of Cartesian self-denial. It is also a denial of the qualitative distinctions that separate the various forms of human excellence.

Van Dorn's Greek-Freudian (Nietzschean?) theory is really a particularly incoherent form of Cartesianism. He acknowledges that human beings must be sexually free — or have intense, complex, and perverse sexual drives — in order to pursue human excellence. So he concedes implicitly that human eros is qualitatively different from that of chimps. But he does not reflect on what that difference is. He seems too self-satisfied, too vain, to engage in self-reflection. His evidence for the relationship between the chemical treatment and unprecedented excellence is the increase in SAT scores of the treated students (219). But he seems not to have noticed or acknowledged that they have lost the curiosity, beginning with self-curiosity or self-consciousness, that actually impels one to pursue intellectual or artistic greatness.

But More also knows that Van Dorn's use of Freud is based on a misinterpretation of at least his mature thought. His incorrect view is that one's anxiety is caused by a lack of sexual satisfaction. Those like Van Dorn with particularly strong sexual drives can easily become extremely anxious, so anxious they can't cope with daily life (73–74). Anxious frustration impedes human flourishing. A strong sexual drive is evidence that one is destined for greatness, if only that energy can be liberated or discharged. (According to Percy, the mature Freud was actually more incoherent. He did not attempt to reduce his own curiosity and scientific knowledge to his sexuality; he simply "exempt[ed] himself and his truth-telling from the sexual dynamics of other human psyches."[22])

Van Dorn's misinterpretation of Freud is really a misunderstanding of his own anxiety and sexual desire. He deceives himself about his attraction to the young. His academy prides itself in the development of minds with "the tough old European Gymnasium-Hochschule treatment." Van Dorn immediately rephrases: "We work their little asses" (219). He and his staff claim, to themselves and others, to be interested in both the children's bodies and minds, and they explain to themselves that what they do to their bodies will contribute to their mental development.

The law says that Van Dorn wants to abuse children, and that his strong, perverse sexual desire is a threat to others unless restrained. Van Dorn claims that his natural excellence, his scientific knowledge and sexual drive, places him above the law, which originated in moralistic hostility to excellence. He acts well in using whatever means necessary to liberate bodies and minds from the tradition of repression the law embodies. But the law, of course, is especially necessary to protect others from extremely disordered and clever selves, those who use their minds to find arguments and techniques to impose themselves on others. More's political intention becomes to employ the law to hold Van Dorn and his staff humanly responsible. He does not hesitate to mislead the law enforcers to achieve the law's intention (338).

Percy's view is that Van Dorn's vain, anxious self has distorted his eros in a way that distances it from its proper or lawful purpose. Van Dorn's project is the effectual truth of all projects for sexual liberation. They are conceived by the perverse to free perversion and exploitation from legal restraint. Contrary to the propaganda of the perverse and clever, human sexual activity ends up further away than before from ready, honest satisfaction. Van Dorn's genuine, self-suppressed theory of life is "the jaybird wisdom" of the behaviorist B. F. Skinner: Once one denies the existence of the self, the honest conclusion is "The object of life is to gratify yourself without being arrested." The best way to become a successful jaybird, Van Dorn discovered, is to turn everyone else into a chicken (90).

Van Dorn was troubled enough to seem more in need of chemical treatment than his students. The huge dose More finally induced him to take, in fact, is what freed him from his unlawful and irresponsible inclinations. As a human being, he was especially in need of and vainly uninterested in old-fashioned psyche-iatry. So he aimed to cure others, not himself. His science and idealism were rooted not primarily in care for others or passion for the truth but in anxious self-deception and an unlawful desire to molest children.

Contrary to his intention, Van Dorn's experiment, like Comeaux's, ends up depriving those treated of their sexual freedom. The dose given to the children in the academy was large enough to deprive them of all experiences of self, of anything that would cause them to resist the staff's sexual advances. More has to admit that the selfless children exhibit no psychological signs of suffering or abuse. Their acquiescence in various forms of molestation seems quite uncoerced or unfearful (330). But abuse still occurs because the molesters intend to molest, depriving those they abuse of their freedom and dignity in order to do so.

Van Dorn, when pressed by More, drops excellence as the experiment's justification. He turns instead to love and "caring," which become possible with the removal of "the mental roadblocks" from "human relationships." He claims to have created a world without cruelty or hate (303). The Greek ideal of virtue reduces itself to the easygoing promiscuity of the chimp colony. Van Dorn really has removed the children's mental roadblocks, but not his own. The children have become too simple, and he is too perverse, for there to be a genuinely human relationship between them. Van Dorn is not their teacher, and they are not his students. There is nothing open or honest or loving about his approach to them.

The source of Van Dorn's desire to molest children is his desire to escape from the disorder of the human self. He longs to free sexual satisfaction from the mystery of human love, from the mixture of flesh and spirit that is the relationship between a mature, individuated, and flawed man and woman. He longs to reduce human sex to a mechanical act, to achieve full satisfaction by controlling and so really knowing his sexual object. Even in the most intimate human communion, one self eludes another to some extent. Free human selves can neither wholly know nor wholly control each other.[23]

Van Dorn does come close, at least, to reducing the children to the bestial innocence of Rousseau's state of nature. But he has not purged the sexual act of its perversions by the self. He himself is not innocent. His desire to dominate — to lord it over those he controls—and his identification of eros with conquest are peculiarly human and theoretically Cartesian.

Van Dorn is not only a molester but a pornographer. His photos and films portray "demure, even prissy" children engaged in every act imaginable with each other, his staff, and himself. More reports that "what sticks in the mind about the photos is not the impropriety but the propriety" (291). The selfless or almost selfless children experience themselves as doing nothing wrong. Van Dorn seems to enjoy gazing upon what appear to be well-ordered natures.

This pornography comes from the mixing of science with romanticism or sentimentality. Flannery O'Connor, doubtlessly Percy's source for this thought, explains that "Pornography . . . is essentially sentimental, for it leaves out the connection of sex with its hard purposes, and so far disconnects it from its meaning in life as to make it simply an experience for its own sake." The theory of pornography is that sexual satisfaction can be separated from the joys and miseries of self-conscious mortality, from the responsibilities of human life.

According to O'Connor, "sentimentality is an excess . . . in the direction of an overemphasis on innocence. . . . We lose our innocence in the Fall, and our return to it is through the Redemption. . . . Sentimentality is a skipping of this process in concrete reality and an early arrival at a mock state of innocence." Sentimentality, finally, is the thought that human beings can redeem themselves from themselves. It is the Rousseauean thought that their disorder can be overcome through human effort. The mock innocence of sentimentality, O'Connor goes on, "strongly suggests its opposite," tyranny and violence.[24] The one who longs for innocence, the problem is, is not innocent at all, and he must work to destroy human nature, the truth about human deformity or Fallenness, to achieve his objective. He must employ any means necessary to achieve the impossible, tyrannical, escapist goal of bringing human history to an end. He works to do what only God can do, to return human beings to innocence by freeing them from the consequences of sin.

This longing for innocence Percy presents as an inescapable part of human nature. In a general sense, it is rightly called a longing for the Garden of Eden, for man's original, unsinful existence. But it is also a longing for one's own preconscious existence, for each person's original unity with his mother. As Lewis Lawson notices, all of Percy's protagonists have a "personal yearning for a restoration to the lost mother figure."[25] All human beings experience themselves somehow as alienated from this original unity, suffering from the inescapable loss that is the birth of self-consciousness through the acquisition of language. The child's awareness of his separation from his mother is the result of the mother's gift of language to the child, a gift that makes possible both love and awareness of time and death.[26]

Dr. More's attempt to escape from self-consciousness, and so from time and human responsibility, was his confused, drunken period with the mothering Lucy Lipscomb at the plantation Pantherburn. There he experienced disjointed "memories" or solitary reveries and regressions into a romanticized childhood and the plantation's mythic past that dissociated him from the real world of time. He also succumbed briefly to the surrender of his sovereignty to a woman who seemed to combine sexual and motherly love for him (104, 161–166). More had to escape from Lucy's influence to act responsibly and to experience the ordinary joys of this world without melancholy or paranoia (348), the latter the result of the ultimate futility of all escapist diversions.[27] Drinking, especially, "frees one from the necessities of time," but not completely or permanently. The permanent solution to the despair of regression is suicide (173, 348).

The longing for regression is misanthropic, for the destruction of all distinctively human experience. It is a longing for the impossible that usually produces romantic impotence. But when joined with science it produces projects for human destruction.

Comeaux's partly conscious goal is the sexual regression of the whole species—a reverse of the process of evolution that brought the languaged being into existence. Van Dorn's unacknowledged goal is personal sexual regression—a reversal of the process of separation through the personal acquisition of language that made him a human individual. They both aim at a world without distinctively human eros, the mixture of the experiences of self or soul with bodily desire.

Comeaux rightly sees Van Dorn's pornography and pedophilia as perversion. Van Dorn rightly sees the threat Comeaux's castrating moralism poses to human excellence. But what Comeaux does to the "darkies" Van Dorn does to his "students." The desire for regression, mixed with science, becomes the desire for control. The scientists aim at knowledge through power, to eradicate human alienation through domination. But their desire to scientifically eradicate the mystery from human existence is as impossibly romantic as the desire to return to the womb.

For More and Percy, one antidote for regressive longing is love for other alienated selves, a mysterious, joyful compensation for human misery. But that longing, which has two parts, the "genital need for penetration" and the "psychic need for merger,"[28] is never perfectly satisfied. The longing for unity or wholeness remains because the self is elusive. Percy agrees with Blaise Pascal that the longing for wholeness or to be free from the consequences of sinful separation can only be completely satisfied for conscious selves by union with God.

The other antidote for regressive longing is the natural pleasure that comes when the child begins to name and so know the world. This "beginning of consciousness of language and speech" is also a social experience of communication with other alienated selves. Anxious experiences are painful in themselves, but even that pain can be accompanied by pleasure when one attempts to speak or write about them for others. Percy himself takes pleasure in "naming" human alienation as "the Judeo-Christian view of man in trouble," and as "the way man is" by nature. The psyche-iatrist assists his patient in experiencing the pleasure of such naming.[29]

MODERN UTOPIANISM

The differences between the moralistic, antierotic Comeaux and the libertarian Van Dorn turn out not to be very great. They both aimed to bring into existence a world where they could control others without resistance and where the ideas of the rule of law and personal rights or sovereignty would be obsolete. They thought their combination of scientific knowledge and idealistic imagination put them above the law and conscience, in the realm of the angels (180). They both drew upon their personal disorders to construct imaginary, romantically incoherent projects for human perfection. Instead of achieving human perfection, they both ended up depriving those they treated of their distinctively human qualities. They deprived them of both eros and thanatos, of the capacity to be moved either by death or love.

The rule of law is needed to protect flawed, self-conscious mortals from each other. Law is for responsible beings capable of choosing irresponsibly in response to selfish experiences of hate, anger, vanity, love, and sexual perversity. The rule of law aims to protect beings with rights or the capacity to exercise personal sovereignty, those who know or ought to know better than to trust one another too much. The simple political message of the novel is a defense of constitutional democracy against the tyrannical aspirations of experts.

Hardheaded scientists become incurable romantics when considering the world's political future. Their science abstracts from the truth about the self or soul. Modern utopianism is irrational, because it begins by putting the self and its experiences—which are even the source of science—beyond the scope of science. The scientists too readily imagine a scientific escape from the constraints of ordinary human experience, the law, and personal anxiety (64).

Because of their origination in the desire to escape merely human constraints, projects to transform the world in the name of alleviating human misery or perfecting the quality of life are especially to be distrusted. They are actually rebellions against human existence as such. The scientists, finally, are in rebellion against the anxiety and terror that come with the experience of the truth about one's own death. By avoiding a close encounter with their own deaths, they do not see what is real about their own and others' existence.

The other, more ineffectual antagonist of the chemotherapists in the novel, Father Rinaldo Smith, finds the scientists' romantic refusal to face and live well with one's own death contemptible. He calls the chemotherapists "the Louisiana Weimar psychiatrists" (232). He does not mean to call them Nazis or proto-Nazis, although Nazism is perhaps some mixture of angry racism and an incoherent effort to find a material foundation for human excellence. Their death- or self-denying use of science in the service of romantic imaginings is readily exploited by Nazis. Father Smith actually admired the SS members, who, unlike the Weimar doctors, lived resolutely in the face of death. They realized that devotion to an ideal required the risk or sacrifice of life, and so they lived more admirably, or closer to the truth, than the science and scientists they led to serve their ends.

The genuine devotion of science, as expressed by the Hippocratic Oath (127), is to the goodness of the life of the individual, which is really the goodness of the self or soul living in search of the truth about oneself. That devotion to the truth about the uniqueness and worth of human individuality stands in criticism of Cartesian science, which tries to lose the self in some materialistic account of the world. The Nazi SS tried and failed to lose the self in some "organic" conception of the nation, race, or people. But once the truthful devotion of science was abandoned, the open affirmation of death seems preferable to and easily prevailed over romantic self-avoidance (241–256).

The novel's lesson is partly about the contemptible moral weakness of the scientists and so of their projects, so easily foiled by More, and the strength of projects that might follow in the wake of that weakness. Percy's thought about the moral weakness of science and scientists seems to be Pascal's: Modern science is a diversion from the truth. It cannot really free human beings from the greatness and misery of their true experience of their anxious, contingent dislocation.

EUTHANASIA

More also had to learn the connection between the scientists' and physicians' ambitious, illegal project and the judgments they made within the law. They are "Qualitarians." They aim to use science to improve the quality of life by alleviating human suffering, curing all human infirmities, and promoting human dignity. They operate "Qualitarian Centers," which are not only legal but generously supported by government funding. These centers engage in "pedeuthanasia" and "gereuthanasia." More, the nonexpert, notes those terms are euphemisms for "disposing of infants and old people" (199).

These practices had the support of a "consensus of child psychiatrists," the American Psychological Association, and the Supreme Court. All the experts agreed. The Supreme Court had promulgated a "Right to Death." That right encompasses both "the right of the unwanted child not to have to suffer a life of suffering and abuse [and] the right of the unwanted aged to a life with dignity and death with dignity" (199). The right to death corresponds with the right not to be unwanted. They seem to replace the right to life, which is ineffectual without the right to be wanted.

The "unwanted child" is actually not a child at all. It had been redefined as a "neonate" by the psychologists. They judge it "does not attain its individuality until the acquisition of language." The Supreme Court in *Doe v. Dade,* drawing upon scientific expertise, decided that the child "does not acquire its legal rights until the age of eighteen months—an arbitrary age to be sure, but one which . . . is a good ballpark figure" (199–200). The child's right to death really is a euphemism for the denial of the right to life.

Ridiculous arguments about the right not to be unwanted are smoke-screens. The scientists make judgments about the quality of life. They say that those whose physical deformities or mental limitations place them below a level of "acceptable quality" are to be killed. These judgments have little or nothing to do with the child's perspective, which is admittedly unknown. That the family and the state have the right to be freed from excessive struggle and expense and the right to protect the quality of society or the species from the malformed makes sense only if the child has no rights. The Nazis readily appropriated this Qualitarian argument for their pursuit of racist, nationalistic purity, and they honestly abandoned euphemisms about rights and compassion.

This sort of reasoning, which abolishes the distinction between abortion and infanticide, is not at all far-fetched. It is a small extension of the logic of actual Supreme Court decisions and much of the scientific establishment in

America today. Justice Blackmun's opinion for the Court in *Roe v. Wade* defers explicitly to the expertise of the medical community, and it barely hides its arbitrariness with its elegant and seemingly scientific division of the pregnancy into three trimesters for the purpose of constitutional measurement. Blackmun's opinion is actually a clever argument for all or almost all prenatal abortion. The Court was most arbitrary in distinguishing between prenatal and postnatal life. There is no reason recognized by scientists for saying that human life begins at birth.

Percy's own view is that *Roe v. Wade* was part of an effort to "suppress an embarrassing scientific fact." It is another example of experts attempting to deny one's personal sovereignty, or the capacity to acknowledge and act upon what one really knows. The Court, in effect, tells "the high-school biology teacher" that his view "that the fertilized human ovum is an individual human life" is merely "his personal opinion" and he has no right to teach it as true. The teacher "Like Galileo . . . caves in, submits, but in turning away is heard to murmur, *"But it's still alive!"*[30] Percy is emphatic that what he knows about "the onset of individual life is not a dogma of the Church but a fact of science."[31]

Yet the Court in *Doe v. Dade* actually seems to share More's view about what distinguishes human beings and the source of human liberty. More says that self-consciousness and so personal sovereignty or rights depend upon the human capacity for language, which really does not develop until around the eighteenth month. So one could say that until that point children have no rights. More's argument against abortion and pedeuthanasia, to the extent it remains uninformed by religion, depends upon his reasonable distrust of scientific judgments about the rights of others. That secular argument, we can say, is good enough for opposing those who would make Qualitarian or compassionate exceptions to the right to life. In Percy's words, "once the principle gains acceptance—juridically, medically, socially—[that] innocent human life can be destroyed for any reason—then it does not take a prophet to predict what will happen next."[32] The Court in *Doe v. Dade* (and *Roe v. Wade*) stands accused primarily of naïveté. The Court thought it was permitting the woman's choice of abortion in certain circumstances, but the scientist-physicians interpreted its decision as giving them a right to kill (334).

Pedeuthanasia does quite effectively free a child from suffering a low quality of life. But all children suffer and are otherwise flawed or to some extent malformed. So a consistent, nonarbitrary application of the right to die rather than suffer would kill them all. But no one with a view of the human future would make that choice. Scientific judgments about life and death, More had to learn, reflect the doctors' distorted views about the species' order and excellence. They want to free us all from all that is malformed and misbegotten. But as Rousseau explains, human beings were well ordered according to nature only before they learned about the inevitability of one's own death. What Rousseau says about the state of nature, Percy, if not More, would say about the Garden of Eden.

The connection between abortion and pedeuthanasia and gereuthanasia is clear in recent Courts of Appeals' decisions, which have used the Supreme Court's arguments in favor of abortion to abolish the distinction between withdrawing medical treatment from those who are undoubtedly near death and physician-assisted suicide, which is really killing by doctors. For now, the courts say a doctor needs the consent of the patient before he can kill. But, as Leon Kass observes, there is nothing to prevent a doctor from using various techniques to induce incurable people to "experience a right to choose death *as their duty* to do so."

Kass goes on to say that we can expect that right to a humane death with dignity to be extended to the mentally incompetent, the retarded, deformed infants, Alzheimer's victims, and so forth. What will soon disappear is "the distinction between the right to choose one's own death and the right to request someone else's." With the eradication of the Hippocratic "taboo" against physicians killing for any reason, "medicine ceases to be a trustworthy and ethical profession," and "It should surprise no one if physicians, once they are exempted from the [legal] ban on the private use of lethal force, wind up killing without restraint."

As Percy shows, physicians, just like the rest of us, cannot be trusted to operate outside the law, which exists primarily to protect human lives from selfish exploitation by others. The court once again stands accused of naïveté in justifying exceptions to the right to life in the name of compassion and quality of life. This humanly destructive development in thought and action is the result of our inability "to act humanly in the presence of finitude," and the only antidote for it is to learn how to accept and love the dying, who most of all "need our presence and encouragement."[33]

But the Qualitarian physicians, particularly Comeaux, did think about those they killed, and he really did want to reduce the amount of suffering in the world (346–347). The chemotherapeutic approach to curing the disease of human self-consciousness began in the Qualitarian Centers. The neonates were peacefully put to sleep, Comeaux says with no awareness of irony, "like the babies they are." The adults were given a "state of the art" mixture of secobarbital and THC, "the active constituent of marijuana." The result, Comeaux reports, is euthanasia in the precise sense, a serene and joyous acceptance of death without suffering (351). The right mixture of drugs eradicates human misery, which is not primarily physical suffering. Death can come without fear, anxiety, and angry resistance. Human beings are no longer touched by it. So they have the serenity that the philosophers, and the joy the theologians, praised but perhaps never fully experienced themselves.

Comeaux's last, "simpleminded" thought is that "good is better than bad, serenity is better than suffering" (351). That way of evaluation is strangely simple for a scientist because it abstracts from or denies the goodness of the human capacity to desire and know the truth. But a simple thought might be true, and the truth might be self-destructive or misanthropic. Perhaps all we can say for certain is the self-surrender required for the abolition of suffering is impossible. So Percy once said that *The Thanatos Syndrome*'s "idea" is "that no technology, however designed, however advanced, can aid one in the search that I find is integral to the human condition."[34]

THE HOSPICE AND PSYCHE-IATRY

More, having foiled the Qualitarians' illegal project, insists that their government-funded center be closed and all the patients be turned over to Father Smith in a reactivated hospice. (The priest's hospice had been defunded and depopulated by the government.) The doctors reluctantly surrender what they regard as their legal right to kill to avoid More's exposure of their illegal activities.

More has no idea whether the bizarre and seemingly ineffectual priest can handle this responsibility. He could not, in fact, do so for long. More certainly has not abandoned science in favor of religion, but he now regards the priest as his ally. Whatever his practical shortcomings, he is much more trustworthy than the doctors. The hospice approach is an alternative to chemically induced euthanasia. It allows the dying to retain their personal sovereignty. Its premise is that self-consciousness and euthanasia are not incompatible. Human beings, as More discovered, have the capacity to live well, really better, with the fact of their impending death.

The priest knows that judgments about the quality of life do not depend upon the presence or absence of suffering. Dying human beings have selves or souls, something of value, which allows them to discover and accept human compensations for suffering. The priest finds himself at home only among those who know they are dying, and he has no desire to redeem them from themselves. He speaks with them about religion only at their initiative. For the psyche-iatrist, Father Smith's approach to death is more scientific than that of the doctors, more in accord with and open to the truth about human beings.

The priest says the dying are "his kind," because they do not lie. He adds: "Everyone else lies. Everyone else is dying too and spending their entire lives lying to themselves." The dying are happy, "happy to tell the truth after a lifetime of lying," and no one else is (244). Most people actually make themselves miserable in their self-deception, in their futile attempt to avoid human misery. They erroneously believe that genuine self-examination would make them more miserable. Not only is euthanasia possible without drugs, only the dying live well in light of the truth. Comeaux and Van Dorn live badly finally because they refuse to count themselves among the dying. The hospice provides a truly human education, learning how to die.

Father Smith's connections among death, truth, and human happiness are More's and Percy's. The happiness available to human beings depends upon telling the truth to oneself about oneself. But most human beings avoid that truth, what they really know, by refusing to live in the present. For the most part, to be human, to have a self, is largely to perceive and to be unable to live well with time. To begin to take human life seriously, Percy holds, is to begin to "think about the nature of time," or to stop diverting oneself from such thought.[35]

More notices that patients in a doctor's waiting room are bored, full of "page-flipping anxiety, the frowning sense of time building up." Only after their selves are zapped can patients lounge in the present, "out of time, as relaxed as the lions on the Serengetti Plain" (310). More also notices the strange fact that most people, including himself most of the time, both love and "can't stand" their children. They are rarely with them "in love" in the present. Instead, they regret the ways they have failed them in the past and worry and plan for their futures (46–47). So only beings without selves, lions and chimps, and the dying, who tell the truth, can live without boredom and anxiety in the present. Only the dying can really enjoy life, and only they, as Percy says, "become aware of what is real."[36]

Father Smith also observes that the dying know that the nearness of their death has made them repulsive to their loved ones. So they usually grow to hate them. But he adds, almost in spite of himself, that "The best thing I ever did for the living was, in a few cases, to make it possible for them to speak with truth and love to their dying mother and father—which of course no one ever does"

(244). His own experience contradicts his extreme conclusion that only those who are about to die tell the truth. Others can do so by finding the dying, self-conscious mortals, lovable. They do what human beings rarely do. They become conscious of what makes a particular human being lovable.

Father Smith's general view was that his "fellow man, with a few exceptions" are "either victims or assholes" (243). If it were not for his experience at the hospice, he would come close to agreeing with the chemotherapists. Human life is miserable and contemptible, of lower quality than unconscious life. The priest is perfectly aware of how un-Christian and misanthropic this perception was. It caused him to prefer members of the SS, because they were so clearly "ready to die," to ordinary, romantic, self-deceptive, feckless, bourgeois individuals, including his own parents. He finally became a priest to choose life over death, but that choice did not clearly alter his opinion about most human lives (241–246, 257).

More's psyche-iatric view is that Father Smith's observations are too extreme, and the Christian view is actually more true than he thinks. Ordinary human life is flawed and feckless, but it is not wholly irresponsible, uncourageous, and self-deceptive. People are stranger and more courageous than the priest says, and they are worthy of more than our pity and contempt. More is more attentive and thoughtful about the lives of particular human beings, and less angry about human mediocrity, than the priest. The psyche-iatric view is that most human beings experience terror and anxiety, or failures of self-deception. They have the capacity to live fairly well with those experiences and to find some human compensations through dialectical self-exploration for their misery. The priest to some extent shared the chemotherapists' unempirical misanthropy because he too was too detached from his fellow, flawed mortals. For him, the choice of life over death was too extreme.

TENDERNESS AND THE GAS CHAMBER

My purpose here is to give Percy's argument for the goodness and ineradicability of the human self or soul. So I will not dwell on the perplexing speeches, action, and inaction of Father Smith, or the interplay between him and More. They clearly learn from each other. The priest's perspective is superior to More's both in his unwavering opposition to the chemotherapeutic project and in his immediate understanding, based on his German experience, of the broader political consequences of making any exceptions to the right to life.

More is too attentive to the lives of particular human beings, and so too slow to make theoretical and political connections. He aims to divert himself from the political life, the senseless, ideological killing, that has dominated our century, as well as from God or His absence. His incoherent, unacknowledged anger prevents his personal observations from becoming the foundation of political philosophy or theology.

Father Smith presents a theological explanation that makes sense of our century's killing and he finds hope that it may soon be over. We have been deprived of faith and left to our own resources, but he may have found a sign that faith may soon return (365–366). But More's discovery is actually that individuals are not as deprived as the priest thinks they are, although he does not consider the political relevance of that discovery, which is the inevitable failure of the various ideological projects, the monstrous mixtures of science and romantic idealism. He might also have better evidence than the priest that Christianity might actually be true.

We cannot ignore Father Smith's most astounding political statement. He tells More that "tenderness always leads . . . [t]o the gas chamber." He seems to do so in response to a remark More made concerning the tenderheartedness of Charles Kuralt. The doctor does not take the connection seriously. He knows that television journalists are not murderers in disguise (128).

But Father Smith goes on to give his "final word," which is more precise and plausible. The disguised murderers are the tenderhearted who combine love of and theorizing about "Mankind." Lovers of Mankind "in the abstract" like Walt Whitman are harmless, pleasure-giving poets. Jean-Jacques Rousseau and B. F. Skinner, theorists of mankind, are also harmless and actually present instructive, if incomplete or reductionistic, accounts of human behavior. But those who combine abstract love with reductionistic theorizing, "Robespierre or Stalin or Hitler," are humanly destructive. They terrorize and murder millions of particular human beings "for the good of Mankind" (129). They kill, as an act of love, to make abstract theory or poetry—scientific idealism—true. What separates those theorist-lovers from the Louisiana Weimar psychiatrists is their personal strength, their readiness to acknowledge and act upon the necessity to kill. Their idealistic visions may differ in scale or grandiosity, but perhaps not fundamentally in form.

By acting out of tenderness or compassion for mankind, those theorist-lovers seem to imitate Christ. They use their knowledge and imaginations actually to bring into existence the world without suffering He promised. But Christ is no theorist; He has no need or desire to think abstractly or love abstractions. He loves particular human individuals, and He does not destroy persons in response to His personal disorder or weakness. Mankind in the abstract is what is left without the individuality or diversity that flows from the self. But without the self there would be no theory and no love. No amount of killing or terror can eradicate that contradiction, and so there is no limit to what theoretical lovers of mankind might attempt to do.

More views Father Smith's explanation as another example of grandiose theoretical madness. To be fair, the priest does not present much detail. But More still might have connected what he learned from his small-scale psychiatric practice to the priest's large-scale account of political manifestations of expert hostility to the truth about the self.

It is almost too easy for us to take Father Smith's astounding words seriously. One reason is that they are obviously meant to express Percy's intellectual debt to a brief, pointed essay on death, politics, and Christianity by Flannery O'Connor, the contemporary writer for whom Percy has the highest praise. Percy has quite unconvincingly denied that he had O'Connor's essay in mind when he wrote *The Thanatos Syndrome*. He admits novelists have reason to deceive, and his books are full of nods to O'Connor.[37]

O'Connor's essay is her introduction to *A Memoir for Mary Ann*. This remembrance, written by the Sisters who ran the Our Lady of Perpetual Help Cancer Home, concerns a three-year-old girl who came to the home with death seemingly imminent. She confounded the doctors by living well with the Sisters until her death at age twelve. Mary Ann, to use Percy's terms, looked extremely misbegotten and malformed, with a huge, disfiguring tumor on one side of her face and one of her eyes removed. From a Qualitarian perspective, her life was unacceptable. She had no productive future, and she endured much physical suffering. The Sisters wanted to convey the goodness of Mary Ann's life, lived "full of promise" with the presence of death always near.

O'Connor, despite her obvious embarrassment about the memoir's many literary flaws, pronounced that it had achieved its purpose. It got her thinking about "the mystery of Mary Ann." She "was an extraordinarily rich little girl," because she was taught by the Sisters and mysteriously found the personal capacity to do more than merely endure her condition, "but to build upon it." Her unobtrusive and enjoyable "education for death" was by "women . . . who love life so much that they spend their own lives making comfortable those who have been pronounced incurable."[38] The Sisters, of course, remind us of Father Smith, and Mary Ann of the dying in the hospice who live well enough to have no need of a cure. But the priest, a rather theoretical man, denies that his love of the dying has anything to do with the love of God, and he says that only the dying live well. It would not occur to the good Sisters, who love life so much, to say anything so extreme.

O'Connor goes on to become a bit theoretical herself. She reminds us that "Death is the theme of much modern literature," and we know that Percy made one of the clearest contributions to that literature. The failure of the scientific effort to conquer death, and the atheism that effort implies, have made us intensely aware of how inevitably death determines our lives.

The bishop who preached at Mary Ann's funeral, O'Connor reports, "said the world would ask why Mary Ann should die." She corrects him, saying that the question "everywhere" in our age is "why should she be born in the first place." And that "popular pity" is everywhere in literature, "discredit[ing] the goodness of God" with "the suffering of children."[39] In light of the experience of the cruelty of human suffering, we cannot say why it is good for any human being to be born. Human existence is a miserable accident, and if there is a God we have to blame Him for his capricious cruelty.

To discredit God's goodness in this way is really to affirm His death. If God is not good, He does not exist or He does us no good. If that is so, then it would appear that human suffering, all awareness of death more than death itself, is pitifully pointless. The central tendency of our age is, in the name of pity, to destroy the good that is human life. As O'Connor explains, "If other ages felt less, they saw more, even though they saw with the blind, prophetic, unsentimental eye of acceptance, which is to say, of faith. In the absence of this faith now, we govern by tenderness. It is a tenderness which, long since cut off from the person of Christ, is wrapped in theory. When tenderness is detached from the source of tenderness, its logical outcome is terror. It ends in forced-labor camps and in the fumes of the gas chamber."[40]

People in ages of faith accept as given the realities of human suffering and death, believing that they are beyond human control. They have the reasonable faith that human life is nonetheless good, and they unsentimentally accept the responsibility, given by God, to live well. By feeling less, they see more. Even if we say there is no Christ, we have to say that they live more in light of the truth than those governed by tenderness wrapped in theory. The pity the person Christ has for us does not point to the extinction of our personal existences but mysteriously, prophetically to our genuine perfection. Faith or hope in the pity of Christ is not self-pity or the sentimental wish to be free from the experiences of self.

Tenderness wrapped in theory is really a claim to "govern," to dominate politically, to eradicate the experiences of suffering and death. The theorist can find no theoretical reason why we were born to die, and so in the name of love he struggles to perfect his theory. That theory's "logical outcome" is the terrible efforts of the Communists and the Nazis to eradicate human individuality, the diverse mixtures of the good and the grotesque that constitute "human imperfection."[41] Such terror aims to make the world perfectly comprehensible to and so completely governed by pitying, in truth self-pitying, theorists. The terrorist wages war against the mystery at the core of human existence. O'Connor says that "the basic experience of everyone is the experience of human limitation."[42] Like Percy and the psyche-iatrist, she notices that "The mystery of existence is always showing through the texture of . . . ordinary lives, and . . . this makes them irresistible to the novelist."[43]

Father Smith's emphasis is more single-minded than O'Connor. He says that the chemotherapeutic project will end up with the killing of Jews. The eradication of the Jews is at the core of the Cartesian project to do away with human distinctiveness or disorder. Dr. More never does figure out exactly why the priest is obsessed with Jews. But we can easily, with the help of Percy's other writing.

The priest is looking for some sign that God has not abandoned the world, and so that all the signs that point to His existence have not disappeared or been deprived of meaning. At one point he says all he can find is the Jews. They, he says, cannot be "subsumed" or "assimilated" into some general, impersonal theory (123–124). Actually all he can find are the Jews and the dying. Most human beings, he believes, have been deprived of faith, sin, and guilt, the signs of the self born to trouble. He presents himself, when not with the dying, as a solitary lunatic (359). He fears that all the scientists have to do is kill the Jews and deprive the dying of their self-consciousness, and nothing distinctively human, no sign of God in the world, will remain.

Dr. More sees nothing singular about the Jews, but he sees signs of the self in the ordinary human experience of his patients. The psyche-iatrist, as psyche-iatrist, would not know to look for the Jews. Percy agrees with both psyche-iatrist and the priest, seeing further than either, and so he allows them to learn from each other. He says that the Jew and the self "are the only two signs in the post-modern age which cannot be encompassed by theory."

The self is "the portion of the person which cannot be encompassed by theory," the part "conspicuously without a place in the modern world." It is the part that experiences itself as an anxious leftover unexplained by the experts, the part that originates the dialectical search aided by the psyche-iatrist.

The Jews, Percy contends, also "cannot be subsumed under any social or political theory," which "is why they are hated by theorists like Hitler and Stalin." The Jews offend because they claim "that God entered into a covenant with a single tribe, and no other." But "Christianity is doubly offensive because it claims not only this but also that God became one man, He and no other." Percy explains that "by 'the Jews' I mean not only Israel, the exclusive people of God, but the worldwide *ecclesia* instituted by one of them, God-become-man, a Jew."[44] The claims of Judeo-Christianity about the personal God and human particularity, and so about the truthful foundation of the experience of the self, are most offensive to modern scientists and theorists. The theoretical war against the Jews, the program for their extermination, is really against the truth about God and the self. Killing the Jews is an act of tenderness, an effort to free human beings from the human experience they signify.

Percy and O'Connor, contrary to our tenderhearted, pragmatic theorist Richard Rorty, say the mixture of theory and excessive sentimentality of secularized Christianity culminates in the unprecedented cruelty of our age. Too much feeling, one result of the absence of faith, causes one not to experience what is good about human life. That experience depends upon the acceptance of suffering, especially the acceptance of the awareness of death. When the person of Christ, Who recognizes all human beings as persons or beings with souls or selves, is replaced by impersonal or abstract theory, we can no longer recognize the good in the face of a particular, brave, strange, deformed, dying girl. The pity the tenderhearted feel for her, to emphasize again the obvious, they really feel for themselves, despite their good health, personal prosperity, physical beauty, and scientific knowledge—their high quality of life.

O'Connor agrees with Percy (and Father Smith and Dr. More) that our mysterious capability for acceptance is made comprehensible and so easier by faith in Christ, but she may disagree with them by insisting that the unsentimentality of acceptance depends on that faith. More's and even the priest's faith in the self, in the dying, is stronger than their faith in the actual existence of the personal God. It seems to me that Percy, a sort of Catholic Socratic, someone who sees what both the Jews and the self signify, did not think that acceptance—although its foundation is undoubtedly mysterious—depends necessarily on O'Connor's faith, a faith that he shared. The dying, who include some affected by psyche-iatry, can be happy enough in light of the truth without faith.

The patients at Father Smith's hospice and Mary Ann at the Sisters' cancer home were educated for death. They unflinchingly recognized the truth about the limitation of human life, and so both the sinful, self-deceptive perversity and the free, courageous, truthful acceptance that characterize that life. The patients at the Qualitarian Center were denied the truth about death, and so about good and evil. Even if acceptance is possible without faith, it is also faith's "necessary precondition." Unless one is really conscious that this life must end, one cannot really hope for another.[45]

Perhaps we can say that Percy and O'Connor agree that psyche-iatry, the Socratic way, cannot moderate effectively the extreme derangement or dislocation of our post-Christian, postmodern age. The treatment is too personal and uncertain. Large-scale acceptance, and so a political life devoted to the capacity for personal sovereignty, may depend on the truth of Father Smith's prediction of a return of faith. The return of genuine, dialogic self-examination among our theorists, the process required to toughen their hearts and quell their romantic idealism, may require the replacement of the equation of Cartesian self-denial with intellectual enlightenment with the return of the intellectual credibility of something like Thomism, the view that revelation or faith completes and is not incompatible with what we know by reason or science.

The novel's affirmation of the truth of Thomistic natural law is Dr. More's coming to see something of the identity between the Catholic and the genuinely scientific or psyche-iatric understandings of the world. He acknowledges the possible value of that "connection," distinguishing between Catholic and Protestant or Cartesian-influenced Christianity. The Catholic sacrament is the real "mixing up of body and spirit" in the person of Christ. That reality of "the Eucharist" is what "horrified" More's Presbyterian wife (402, 384). The sacrament is a sign of the truth about the self, of a being in the world that is neither pure body nor pure spirit. It is also a sign about the truth about human eros or love, and so of the falsity and futility of the Cartesian effort to eradicate all malformation from the world. More came back to the celebration of Eucharist although he did not yet actually have faith in the God Who became man (395).

There is surely a connection between More's complete reentry into ordinary life, enjoying simple human pleasures (such as recreational vehicles and Disney World) with his wife, children, and other feckless, troubled selves, and his concluding openness to the anthropology of the Catholic Church as signified by the sacraments. Percy explains that "the sacraments, especially the Eucharist . . . confer the higher significance to the ordinary things of the world, bread, wine, water, touch, breath, words, talking, listening."[46] More's psyche-iatry, by itself, allowed only his entry into the remarkable lives of his ordinary patients. It did not affect sufficiently his own life, because he partially exempted himself and his own from his theory. His theory remained distorted by a Cartesian residue, which his resolute action combined with the words of the priest removed.

The novel ends hopefully, if not quite prophetically. More has again become Father Smith's friend, and he listens to him more. He occasionally serves Mass for him, although he tells the priest honestly that he is too uncertain to be religious. Father Smith, formerly suspicious, now approves of More's psycheiatry, and More even makes an ironic remark to his wife that suggests that he has begun to admit that he thinks about God (370–371). The doctor has certainly become less self-deceptive and more accepting. He is more able to enjoy the present in love with his wife and children, and his parenting skills have improved considerably. He has less need to drink to escape from the burden of time, largely because he is more able to talk to the woman he loves. But a psyche-iatrist still needs patients, "the lonely hearts, the solitary, aching consciousness," those More calls "my kind of people" (367). Because the chemical treatment was so slow to wear off completely, More became uncertain concerning whether this sort of person would ever return for his help.

Finally, one of his patients, Mickey La Faye, a woman who was before her chemical treatment and is now again strangely terrified by a dream about some stranger, returns to Dr. More for help. She says, "I think the stranger is part of myself," and when More asks her who the stranger might be, she replies, "the deepest part of me." The last two lines of the novel are "She opens her mouth to speak. Well well well" (372). More has become certain that human well-being is talking about the strange depths of the self. The thanatos syndrome properly understood is integral to the human condition, and it is one not to be cured by human effort. From one view, as Percy says, the " 'human condition' . . . is essentially a terminal illness."[47] The efforts for its cure, even through the killing of millions, are based on a mistaken view of the quality of human life. The novel ends with a certainty about the strangeness and goodness of human dislocation, and only the possibility of faith in the person of Christ.

We may learn from More, or at least from his self-deception or unacknowledged anger, that whether or not there is a God, part of the strangeness and goodness of man is what Percy calls his "incurable God-directedness."[48] But if man is to find God, he must begin by "communicating" what he really knows about himself to others. Both self-knowledge, or reflection on the direction of his incurable longing, and the "human connection" are good in themselves, whatever the ultimate results of the search.[49]

As John Wauck nicely sums things up, Percy says men need both God and women. The love of a woman, another embodied, mortal, strange, wonderful self, is the self's unique, mysterious, and perhaps more than ample compensation for its unique misery, even if one cannot believe in God.[50] Still, the "movement . . . toward God" is helpful even for loving women and all the other joys of this world. Through that movement, Percy says, his characters "become themselves, not abstracted like scientists but fully incarnate beings in the world."[51] The good that is one self's love for another is perfected in the experience of oneself fully transparent before God.[52]

NOTES

1. Walker Percy, *The Thanatos Syndrome* (New York: Farrar, Straus, and Giroux, 1987). All page references in the text are to this book.

2. See chapter 2.

3. Martin Heidegger, *Being and Time,* trans. J. Macquarrie and E. Robinson (New York: Harper and Row, 1962), 297–298.

4. Walker Percy, *Signposts in a Strange Land* (New York: Farrar, Straus, and Giroux, 1991), 259.

5. Romano Guardini, quoted by Lewis Lawson, "Tom More: Walker Percy's Alienated Genius," *South Central Review* 10 (Winter 1993), 50.

6. Lewis A. Lawson and Victor A. Kramer, eds., *More Conversations with Walker Percy* (Jackson: University Press of Mississippi, 1993), 202.

7. On Percy's early and enduring opposition to Rousseau, see the letter he received from Shelby Foote (19 November 1949), *The Correspondence of Shelby Foote and Walker Percy,* ed. J. Tolson (W.W. Norton, 1997), 20–21. The Rousseau discussed throughout this chapter is that of *The Discourse on Inequality.*

8. Lawson and Kramer, *More Conversations,* 187.

9. Ibid., 237.

10. Percy, *Signposts,* 252.

11. Ibid., 178.

12. Joseph Cropsey, *Plato's World: Man's Place in the Cosmos* (Chicago: University of Chicago Press, 1995), 121.

13. Christopher Bruell, review of Cropsey, *American Political Science Review* 90 (March 1996), 170.

14. Percy, *Signposts,* 278.

15. Ibid., 288.

16. See Lawson, "Tom More," passim.

17. Ibid., 50.

18. Lawson and Kramer, *More Conversations,* 79.

19. Alexis de Tocqueville, *Democracy,* volume 2, part 1, chapter 7.

20. Walker Percy, *The Moviegoer* (New York: Knopf, 1961).

21. Percy, *Signposts,* 395.

22. Ibid., 277.

23. John F. Desmond, *At the Crossroads: Ethical and Religious Themes in the Writings of Walker Percy* (Troy, N.Y.: Whitson, 1997), 66–71.

24. Flannery O'Connor, *Mystery and Manners* (New York: Farrar, Straus, and Giroux, 1959), 157–158. See Desmond, 90–91.

25. Lewis A. Lawson, *Still Following Percy* (Jackson: University Press of Mississippi, 1996), 11.

26. Ibid., 159, 227.

27. See Desmond, 114–115.

28. Lawson, *Still Following*, 148.

29. Lewis A. Lawson and Victor A. Kramer, eds., *Conversations with Walker Percy* (Jackson: University Press of Mississippi, 1985), 217–218.

30. Percy, *Signposts*, 342.

31. Ibid., 341.

32. Ibid., 350–351.

33. Leon Kass, "Dehumanization Triumphant," *First Things*, no. 65 (August/September 1996), 15–16.

34. Lawson and Kramer, *More Conversations*, 307.

35. Ibid., 73.

36. Lawson and Kramer, *Conversations*, 41.

37. See Lawson and Kramer, *More Conversations*, 194, 229.

38. O'Connor, *Mystery*, 223–224.

39. Ibid., 226–227.

40. Ibid., 227.

41. Ibid., 228.

42. Ibid., 131.

43. Ibid., 133.

44. Percy, *Signposts*, 312–314.

45. John Edward Hardy, *The Fiction of Walker Percy* (Urbana: University of Illinois Press, 1987), 253.

46. Percy, *Signposts*, 369.

47. Lawson and Kramer, *More Conversations*, 59.

48. Percy, *Signposts*, 261.

49. Lawson and Kramer, *More Conversations*, 75. The best secondary literature on this novel emphasizes more than I do its theological dimension. See in particular Lewis Lawson, "Tom More: Walker Percy's Alienated Genius." This article contains many wonderful insights, and I recommend it be read as a necessary supplement to mine.

50. John Wauck, "Fables of Alienation," *The Human Life Review* (Spring 1991), 73–94. Wauck's witty account of Percy's message also should be read with mine. Consider especially his summary of Percy's refutation of every form of abstract or self-denying devotion to beauty (the diversions of theorists and artists): "a particular man can very well do without the Ninth Symphony—the life of the individual, the life every person actually leads, will go on without it. . . . One man's need for another person is utterly unlike mankind's need for Beethoven, and love is the expression of this unique need" (93).

51. Percy, *Signposts*, 388.

52. Søren Kierkegaard, *Fear and Trembling* and *Sickness unto Death* (Garden City, N.Y.: Doubleday/Anchor Books, 1954), 163, with Lawson and Kramer, *Conversations*, 49. See Desmond, *At the Crossroads*, and Lewis Lawson, *Following Percy* (Troy, N.Y.: Whitston, 1988) for all sorts of insights into Percy's indebtedness to Kierkegaard. But Percy's reading of Lawson's analysis of his debts caused him to recommend that the critic look less for Kierkegaard and more for Thomas and Thomism in his novels (Patrick Samway, *Walker Percy: A Life* [New York: Farrar, Straus, and Giroux, 1997], 250–251).

5

MORAL REALISM VERSUS THERAPEUTIC ELITISM: CHRISTOPHER LASCH'S POPULIST DEFENSE OF AMERICAN CHARACTER

C hristopher Lasch, professor of history and the provocative, best-selling author of ten books, including *The Culture of Narcissism,* called himself a social critic, which means he was much more than a historian.[1] Such a critic, Lasch said, "holds a mirror to society, revealing patterns that might otherwise go undetected," and then he "passes judgment."[2] Lasch's judgments were in defense of the fact that human beings experience the truth about themselves and nature. They know, when they are not deluding themselves, that they are limited in many ways by their natures as embodied beings. They are self-conscious mortals, haunted always to some extent by death. So the need for character or virtue to live well with what we really know is ineradicable. The modern attempts to dispense with virtue by re-creating human identity are degrading illusions. They are also misguided, because human joy and love depend upon death. A genuinely truthful and morally responsible human being is grateful for the invigorating challenges his distinctive existence gives him.

Lasch's realism has two parts. He is a philosophical realist, convinced that human beings have knowledge of a natural and personal reality that exists independently of their making. He is also a "moral realist," opposing the fantastic efforts of modern utopians who aim to create a world where morality would be superfluous. There the distinction between good and evil would simply be replaced by the distinction between healthy and sick.

Lasch's realism makes him in one respect a Tocquevillian. He shared *Democracy in America*'s perception that the Americans tend, in principle, to be Cartesian.[3] They are superficial rationalists who understand reality in terms of two rational systems, minds and bodies. So they divide human experiences into those of pure mind and pure body. Lasch agrees with the best Tocquevillian of our time, the novelist and philosopher Walker Percy, who called American theory a kind of therapeutic pop Cartesianism.[4] The elite or expert class incoherently both describes human beings as nothing but animals well adjusted or poorly adjusted to their environments and aims to reduce them to that subhuman condition.

The antidote to such Cartesianism, really an ignoble and fantastic diversion from the truth about fundamental experiences of the self-conscious mortal, is realism. Lasch, who never wrote as a believing Christian, approached Percy's twentieth-century Thomism almost in spite of himself. Like Percy, his study of the original or Socratic intention of psychoanalysis is the basis of both his criticism of the truth-denying intention of today's knowledge class and his turn to Christian psychology as a source expressing the ineradicable truth of human alienation.

Lasch's distinctive and profound contribution to contemporary thought is his connection of class analysis to psychoanalysis, reminding us of Alexis de Tocqueville's connection between Jean-Jacques Rousseau's history and Blaise Pascal's psychology.[5] My intention here is to bring to light this philosophical dimension of Lasch's populism, his defense of what remains of the character of Americans.

CLASS ANALYSIS

Lasch saw the Cartesian reduction of human reality to minds and bodies reflected in the development of the American class structure. His main concern was class analysis of American life. His analysis was not detached or nonpartisan. He thought one class is more admirable and lived more in light of the truth, and he encouraged that class to fight the "culture war" against those who would reduce its members to less than free and responsible beings.[6] But Lasch was careful to present populism rightly understood. (He admitted, for example, that racism has been part of American populism, and he praises its ebbing as one of a very few positive recent social developments.[7])

The true goal of populism is "universal competence," or "a whole world of heroes." This "strenuous and morally demanding definition" of the good life is threatened by elites who aim to produce "a society of supremely contented consumers," people who live unmoved by the truth about their existence.[8] The populist aims to universalize the practice of virtue, to make every human being an aristocrat of character. The elite aims to make virtue unnecessary or obsolete, by eradicating the difference between most people and thoughtless and readily controllable animals or machines.

Universal competence is the thoughtful, responsible, effective exercise of personal sovereignty by each human being. Lasch saw it as the devotion of the American Founders and Abraham Lincoln. Lincoln embraced it through his description of the American goal of "universal education." He said "that [each] particular head . . . should direct and control that particular pair of hands." All "citizens of a free country" are "expected to work with their heads as well as their hands." So a free country is not divided into two classes, one that thinks for the other.[9] The division of society into mental and physical laborers, Karl Marx was right to say, is the end of democracy. "The American revolution had made subjects into citizens," and the elite establishment of such a class system returns most citizens to subjection.[10]

In Lasch's view, the history of America has been away from democracy properly understood to a rather extreme separation of mental and physical laborers. It has been toward the welfare or therapeutic state. The mental laborers have compassion for those who have become dependent on their thought. They claim to work to alleviate the suffering of the others, but they cannot plausibly claim to have respect for those for whom they claim to think. Genuine respect only comes through "admirable achievements, admirably formed characters, natural gifts put to good use."[11] A society that does not expect everyone to be an admirable citizen is not a democracy.

Double standards masquerading as compassion create the paternalistic and degrading distinction between first- and second-class citizenship.[12] They make life too easy for everyone. There is nothing admirable in being a pitied victim. It is easier and otherwise self-serving for the elite to pity fellow citizens "than to hold them up to impersonal standards" that if met really would entitle them to equal respect. The self-indulgence of compassion allows both classes to shy away from the hard work really required to raise the competence of everyone. Compassion-based toleration is really a form of apathetic indifference for the characters or souls of our fellow citizens.[13]

The virtue the pitying or "caring class" means to deny others is that exhibited by "those who refuse to exploit their suffering for the purposes of pity."[14] Members of that class fraudulently attempt to reduce virtue to words they know to be merely flattering, the rhetoric of indiscriminate self-esteem. But those words do not make people feel good, only cynical.[15] They cannot really mask the harsh reality of the absence of achievement. The absurd idea, for example "that a respect for cultural diversity forbids us to impose the standards of privileged groups on the victims of oppression" is "a recipe for . . . incompetence."[16]

A particularly absurd form of this dismissal of standards is Carol Gilligan's difference feminism. For women "to pit themselves against a demanding standard of perfection" is to "masculinize" themselves or engage in self-denial. Women, Gilligan contends, are too caring, cooperative, and compassionate, too concerned about relationships to really regard such standards as "impersonal" or gender-neutral.

Lasch responds that any argument for the equality of citizens concerns not the difference, but the similarity, in admirable human characteristics. Women, in truth, not only can be kind but have the same capacity for cruelty as men. So they are capable of being integrated into a world "where quality of ideas or workmanship counts for more than 'relationships.'" And they are capable of criticizing an excessive concern with the quality of relationships as petty and confining. If women can be equal citizens, it is because they can earn the respect of men, and not just their concern or support.[17]

For the caring class, "Compassion has become the human face of contempt," which is why a genuine democrat or populist is "unambiguously committed" to the principle of respect justly accorded admirable deeds.[18] Lasch calls Martin Luther King Jr. "a populist in his insistence that black people had to take responsibility for their lives and in his praise of petty bourgeois virtues: hard work, sobriety, and improvement."[19] Lasch opposes Marx on bourgeois virtue: It is what *keeps* an individual from functioning merely as a cog in a machine under capitalism. That virtue is what really protects the people from elite manipulation.

The utopia the compassionate or therapeutic elite claims to pursue is one with an abundance of agreeable jobs and a "life easy for everyone." But technological innovations and information revolutions have, in truth, mainly "widened the gap between the knowledge class and the rest of the population." Despite the unprecedented availability of information, "the public knows less about public affairs than it used to know."[20] People do not know because there is no reason for them to know. There is no national debate on public issues. There is almost no American political life.

The knowledge class does not believe it is possible to educate most people to be citizens. They deny the truth of the premises on which democratic citizenship is based. For Frederick Douglass, Lasch observes, "The power of speech—given through the equivalent of a classical education—gave him access to the inner world of his own thoughts and to the public world in which the fate of his people would be decided for better or worse." True and meaningful speech about his personal identity could ennoble his people. But our educators today seem no longer "to believe in the reality of either the inner world or the public world, either in a stable core of personal identity or in a politics that rises above the level of platitudes and propaganda."[21] The knowledge class, ironically, no longer believes in the personal or political efficacy of the pursuit of knowledge, particularly self-knowledge. There is no self to know.

The knowledge class now holds that "personal identity" is an arbitrary and unstable personal construction and that political speech is empty of any meaning but the pursuit of power. The truth about truth, freedom, and dignity is that they do not really exist. There is no point of view, no self, from which one can either know or defend one's own liberty or dignity. This therapeutic theory about personal emptiness both reflects and is the source of "a new kind of dependence, the dependence of the consumer on the market and the provider of expert services, not only for the satisfaction of their needs but for the definition of their needs."[22]

Lasch emphasizes that both corporate capitalism and the bureaucratic state engage in need creation. Their shared therapeutic theory is a sort of self-fulfilling prophecy. It both describes and creates beings whose seemingly materialistic or bodily needs really come from the manipulative minds of experts. The welfare or therapeutic state and corporate capitalism both work to have the knowledge class give content to the dependent class.[23]

So the elitist aim of the members of the expert class is to bring political life to an end. They describe and create beings incapable of being spirited and thoughtful citizens. Here Lasch seems to echo Tocqueville. The easy control of dependents solves the problem of "social discipline." But it also "makes it more and more difficult for political leaders to mobilize public support for their policies." The welfare or therapeutic state is, at heart, more weak than strong, because it excels at preventing, not doing. Interest in and sacrifice for the common good depends upon some participation in making public policy.[24]

Lasch, again like Tocqueville, sees that the restoration of the public spirit of citizens requires considerable decentralization and voluntary involvement in political life. It also involves the freeing of personal experiences and intimate relationships from the reductionistic discipline of expert manipulation.[25] But the expert class is too full of easygoing contempt and aversion to risk really to care for, much less act on behalf of, the souls of their fellow citizens.[26] So "to break the existing pattern of dependence and put an end to an erosion of competence, citizens will have to take the solution of their own problems in their own hands."[27]

PSYCHOANALYSIS

For Lasch, the movement of the history of psychoanalysis from Socratic introspection to therapeutic "coping" mirrors the degradation of the knowledge class.[28] Originally, psychoanalysis was "linked to a long degree of speculation in which self-knowledge is seen as the beginning of wisdom." So its subject matter, the pursuit of the truth about the human soul or self, "drew it irresistibly toward the existential questions that have always defined religious discourse."[29] The original, Freudian psychoanalysts pursued a Socratic alternative to religious answers to those questions. They aimed to understand, not transform, human experiences. They "held out no cure for injustice or unhappiness," but they attempted to explain them as features of the normal human experience of alienation.[30] Psychoanalysis at its best is the discovery of a "moral realism that makes it possible for human beings to come to terms with the existential constraints to their power and freedom."[31]

The human experience of shame, the original psychoanalysts discovered, is in response to one's knowledge of "the contingency and finitude of the human condition, nothing less." That is why the suffering of shame "is so closely associated with the body," which necessarily escapes our effort at control and "reminds us, vividly and painfully, of our inescapable limitations, the inescapability of death above everything." What makes a human being ashamed, finally, is his knowledge of his "bondage to nature."[32] The experience is that of a self-conscious mortal. So the original psychoanalysts saw a close connection between shame and curiosity.[33] To eradicate one would be to eradicate the other. The being who seeks knowledge or science is, among other things, ashamed. A world without shame would be one without scientists and philosophers.

But shame "refers, above all, to the irreducible element of mystery in human affairs."[34] Human beings do not know why they, alone among the animals, are alienated mortals. The truth about their own being necessarily eludes their complete comprehension and control. So shame is also "a kind of outrage in the face of whatever is mysterious."[35] It is a rebellion against the limits of philosophy or science, and so shame can lead to futile attempts to overcome those limits through science.

Human beings cannot help but long for a world without shame and without mystery. But the original psychologists knew that such an existence is both impossible and undesirable for human beings. The longing is really "to be free from longing." It is "a backward quest for absolute peace." The longing is for freedom from all that characterizes human existence, from the alienation or "malaise" that distinguishes the human condition as such.[36] Lasch's affirmation of "Nietzsche's connection between shame and mystery" is his affirmation of the greatness and misery of human existence against Rousseauean romanticism.[37]

The history of "the psychiatric profession" is its movement away from this affirmation. Its aim has become "behavior modification" and "management of symptoms," often with the help of drugs. It achieves "fast relief," not "deeper understanding." This change in approach, at first glance, seems both democratic and scientific. Introspective psychoanalysis "cost too much, last[ed] too long and demand[ed] too much intellectual sophistication from the patient." It also "often ended in failure, even after years of extensive self-exploration."[38] It culminated, at best, in the discovery of mystery and only the alleviation of anxious unhappiness. But symptoms can be managed with physiological certainty and without raising the unanswerable existential questions that occupy the soul.

If drugs can free us from the pain of shame and mystery, then is it unscientific or dogmatic to hold that mystery or the experience of ineradicable limits is intrinsic to human nature or the human condition? If it is, then shame can now be dismissed "as the vestigial remnant of an outmoded prudery."[39] Psychotherapists now say that shame is an unnecessary experience that gets in the way of a healthy and happy human existence.

The psychotherapeutic view is that what gets in the way of science and health is the human capacity to be moved by the truth about one's own death. So the new "technology of the self," which brought into existence "an elaborate network of therapeutic professions," is based on the "now-familiar insistence" that there is no depth or stability to human identity. So through technological transformation human beings can "achieve a state of mind beyond freedom and dignity,"[40] beyond shame and curiosity.

The original fear was that modern technology would enslave human beings to machines. The new "hope is that man will become something like a machine in his own right."[41] B. F. Skinner "scandalizes" twentieth-century liberal, therapeutic humanists by showing that the therapeutic goal is neither liberal nor humanistic. He simply thought through the implications of their assumptions and prejudices. The denial of moral responsibility in favor of the compassionate eradication of misery leads to the expert destruction of human liberty. So therapeutic democracy is actually "an oligarchy of experts, who claim no powers or privileges beyond the impersonal authority of science."[42] The technological experts on the self simply aim to eradicate all personal experiences, to make impersonal science wholly true. The conquest of nature is really the conquest of human nature, the reintegration of human beings into subhuman or unconscious nature.

Lasch connects the original psychoanalytic with the religious and existential objections to therapeutic pragmatism. The old psychoanalysis, by showing the intractability of human mystery and misery, leads human beings, against its scientific intention, to religion. Socratic philosophy, Lasch suggests, does the same.[43] The new psychotherapy, by treating human experiences as symptoms to be cured, more coherently attempts to replace religion by science. It aims to eradicate scientifically the experiences that brought religion into being.

The problem remains that psychotherapy would eradicate the shameful, curious being who is the source of science. The new psychotherapy can neither account for nor affirm the experience of the scientist. The old psychoanalysis, unrealistically, pointed to the universalization of the introspective, scientific experience of Socrates. So one reason it failed is that it could not "satisfy the growing demand, in a world without religion, for meaning, faith, and emotional security."[44] Psychotherapy aims to make emotional security easy by eradicating the needs for meaning and faith.

The therapeutic cure destroys "the very sense of moral responsibility." Human weakness and willfulness, manifestations of human individuality or "sin," become "sickness." No one is truly culpable or responsible. The being freed from responsibility is reduced from a citizen or sovereign individual to a "patient unfit to manage his own life." Therapeutic antimorality "delivers" the diseased "into the hands of a specialist for cure." So the populist Lasch notices the "close connection . . . between the erosion of moral responsibility and the erosion of the capacity for self-help."[45] The sick are not blamed but pitied; they cannot cure themselves.

ELITE SELF-PITY

The new psychotherapy seems to achieve the goal of science through its technological reduction of selves to readily manipulable machines or animals. Because human needs become nothing but a therapeutic creation, the therapist achieves human wisdom by knowing what he makes. The members of the dependent class become dependent on the knowledge class for their very identities. The aim is to reduce the dependent class to nothing but consumers of expertise. But the new psychotherapy is not, most radically, a tyranny of experts. It is a reflection of the moral weakness or self-denial of the knowledge class. The cure that class proposes for society as a whole it really imposes on itself. The pity its members claim to feel for others they really feel for themselves.

The foundation of this self-pity is today's extreme separation of mental and physical labor: "The thinking classes are fatally removed from the physical side of life." They only consume the results of but never do "productive labor." They are dependent on the manual labor of others. So their world is abstracted from "the palpable, immediate, physical reality inhabited by men and women." They too easily forget they are natural beings, or beings with bodies. But they also "have no experience of making anything substantial and enduring."[46] They have no experience of what beings with minds can really accomplish with their hands. Their Cartesian abstraction does not comprehend the limits, joys, and deserved pride in accomplishment of real men and women.

The knowledge class's largely successful creation of an artificial, controlled environment for itself is the source of its "central dogma" that all reality is socially constructed. All that exists is a willful, mental construction. This dogma is a denial of both the existence and the goodness of a reality that exists independently of human will. It comes from a class obsessed with control: "In their drive to insulate themselves against risk and contingency — against the unpredictable hazards that afflict human life — the thinking classes have seceded not just from the common world around them but from reality itself."[47]

The members of the thinking class actually aim to replace the harsh reality of conscious, embodied existence with their self-creation. Their separation of themselves from the working class is really a separation from their own embodiment. Their distinctive, "enlightened" values are really opposed to moral realism. Their therapeutic antimorality is really a way of attempting to escape the human necessity to come to terms with the existential limits to their power and freedom.

What usually passes for postmodernism really is "hypermodernism," the tendency toward unlimited exaggeration of the least admirable and most seductive features of modern society. The attempt to dominate nature or reality becomes its artificial simulation. In "hyperreality" or virtual reality, human control is freed from "the intractable resistance of physical materials." Intelligence becomes "hyperintelligence," the purpose of which is not to understand "the real world" but "the world simulated by computers." Man himself becomes, Lasch emphasizes, "hyperman." This "pitifully shrunken, driven creature" is "subservient to the machines who demand his frantic attention." His artificial world never really comes under his control. There is nothing more contemptible than hyperman's futile, petty, fearful, anxious, antirealistic "hyperactivity."[48]

Hyperman denies the possibility of real perception of the world that human beings might share. So he denies the possibility of persuasion through rational public debate. On the basis of this dogma, he no longer tries to persuade the moral majority of the truth of his values. The intellectual secession of the thinking class from reality is also from the moral and physical world occupied by most human beings. It is, as Richard Rorty says, secession for the creation of a private or class-based fantasy, which is the foundation for its "alternative" institutions, its gated communities.[49]

Therapy, in this light, becomes a way of protecting that fantasy from the reality of human beings who do not share it. Moral privatization or permissiveness means exempting not only the dependent class but the knowledge class from common moral standards. Lasch on occasion admits that this extreme division of labor tends to make both classes too one-sided or unrealistic to live genuinely admirable and truthful lives. Both classes lose contact with the sense of continuity and permanence in human affairs that makes human excellence and civic life possible.[50]

Lasch dismisses communitarianism as it is usually understood as basically an elite construction, an implausible mixture of moral permissiveness and public trust and philosophy. The rejection of moral realism implied by moral privatization is destructive of all community. Communitarians are usually "more interested in the responsibility of the community as a whole than individual responsibility." But communal trust really depends upon the respect of one responsible individual for another.[51]

THE MODERN PROJECT'S FUTILITY

The postmodern or hypermodern doctrine is incoherent. Rorty, for example, puts forward his version of the social construction of reality as a recognition of human contingency. Nothing human is stable; all human experiences are described into and may be described out of existence. But this assertion of radical contingency is meant to be the prelude to rational control of human identity through description and redescription. A genuine acknowledgment of contingency would be of what is beyond expert comprehension and control: God, nature, death, and so forth.

The hypermodern assertion of control actually produces a deeper perception of genuine contingency, "a feeling of inauthenticity and inner emptiness," the absence of "a strong, stable sense of selfhood" that is the foundation of personal resistance to manipulation. One unacknowledged postmodern perception of the knowledge class is the emptiness of human, and especially of one's own, existence. The human self is a meaningless accident that is worthy of pity.[52]

The deepest perception of contingency is of the futility of self-denial. Hypermodern man remains haunted by death, by what really cannot be conquered by talk or drugs. Hyperman cannot completely forget that he is not really hyperman at all. Human beings have not really mastered their environment until they have really comprehended and brought under their control "life's secret." So "the utopian possibilities of modern technology in its purest sense" depend on "a revolution in genetics" that could prolong life indefinitely.[53] But there is, in truth, no imaginable way of postponing death forever, without bringing the whole universe under human control.

Accidental death will always remain a possibility, and eventual death will always remain a certainty. Turning death from an ennobling, challenging necessity into an unfortunate possibility makes human existence more accidental, or at least more determined by accidents, than ever before. Human beings surely become more risk-averse, or more ignobly defined by fear of death. The knowledge class is more progressive or pitiful than the working class, because it is less likely to accept the necessarily limited and tragic character of human existence. It will always be the case that "the shadow of death hangs over our pleasures and triumphs, calling them into question."[54]

Technological control, undertaken in the name of compassion, makes human beings more pitiful than ever before. They are more dependent than ever on forces beyond their control. Lasch applauds the ecological movement insofar as it makes clear the inescapability of our dependence on nature.[55] But the knowledge class is particularly badly equipped to live well with that knowledge. It remains in rebellion against "the ancient religious insight that the only way to achieve happiness is to accept limitations in a spirit of gratitude and contrition." So it vacillates between the unrealistic, emotionally immature extremes "of attempting to annul those limitations and bitterly resenting them." The knowledge class childishly refuses to acknowledge the connection between human happiness and suffering.[56] So it is in rebellion against "the central paradox of religious faith: that the secret to happiness lies in renouncing the right to be happy."[57]

THE RETURN TO SUPERSTITION

The technological war against death is unwinnable. Its great but limited success makes us more aware of and more unwilling to come to terms with human limitations. Lasch observes that today it is "increasingly difficult to accept the reality of sorrow, loss, aging, and death." People, particularly members of the knowledge class, are more anxious than ever, and such experiences "have intensified the mechanisms of denial."[58]

So high technology is actually the cause of "the revival of ancient superstitions," particularly pantheism in the form of New Age spirituality. Pantheism is the illusion that opposes itself most radically to the truth about human alienation or individuality. It attempts "to restore the illusion of symbiosis, a feeling of absolute oneness with the world." That superstitious illusion grows as the technological form of the fantasy of absolute mastery fades.[59]

Pantheism is the effort at "a complete surrender of the will" that comes with the failure of human willfulness.[60] Lasch agrees with Tocqueville that it is the most seductive modern doctrine because it denies most radically the truth about human individuality.[61] He also agrees with Percy that the self-denial of New Age/Eastern religion is most compatible with the impersonal claim for comprehensive truth of modern science.[62] Prideless individuals who attempt to lose themselves in pantheistic reveries deserve both our pity and our contempt.

Lasch explains that pantheism is the theological expression of the narcissistic solution to fear of death. The narcissist "does not acknowledge the separate existence of the self," and so "he lacks any conception of the difference between himself and his surroundings." He is unaware of his own death and so lacks any "determination to stay alive." His particular existence has no significance; it is indistinguishable from the rest of existence.[63]

The narcissist or pantheist rebels against "the pain of separation" that constitutes individuality or selfhood by denying the truth of its existence.[64] Radical individualism, the modern assertion of unconstrained freedom, actually makes life so miserably contingent that it culminates "in the radical repudiation of individualism." Everyone and everything, the narcissist or pantheist says, is identical to everything else.[65] The radical repudiation of difference is really a repudiation of *the* human difference. Pantheism is the most rational of religions insofar as it describes a whole without incoherence or alienation. It describes a world without mystery, including the mysterious being who can really long for and know some of the truth about his own existence. Pantheism is the most unrealistic or untrue of religions for human or alienated beings.

So science, contrary to its intention and expectation, has not really replaced religious superstition. Sophisticated twentieth-century life is a mixture of "hyper rationalism and a widespread revolt against rationality." The failure of rationalism really to produce hyperman, to purge the mystery of self-conscious mortality from human existence, has produced intensified "feelings of homelessness and deprivation." These feelings are largely in reaction to the contradiction between the promise of the modern project to bring nature under human control and the reality that the mysterious limitations of human existence persist.[66] Human beings have been deprived by the therapeutic language that describes only hyperactivity of the words for articulating and coming to terms with what they really know about their existence.

The modern or postmodern knowledge class romantically aims to "recreate natural harmony in history." But the foundation of human or historical freedom, in truth, "is precisely the inescapable awareness of man's contradictory place in the natural order of things." So "The distinguishing characteristic of selfhood . . . is not rationality but a critical awareness of man's divided nature." Selfhood necessarily includes "the painful awareness of the gulf between human aspirations and human limitations." Citing the Augustinian Reinhold Niebuhr, Lasch says that man is neither wholly rational hyperman nor wholly harmonious Rousseauean natural man, but an incoherent mixture of the two.[67] As the Pascalian Tocqueville said, man is the beast with the angel in him.[68]

Lasch never claimed to be a Christian, and he opposed using religion merely to achieve some social or cultural goal. The realist's concern is religion's truth. But the Augustinian psychology of Christian realism is always true: "The modern world has no monopoly on fear of death or the alienation from God. Alienation is the normal condition of human existence." What distinguishes "the modern temper" is the intensity and pervasiveness of the rebellion against this truth.[69]

POPULISM: THE WORKING CLASS AND THE CULTURE WAR

Lasch's populism is rooted in his Socratic and religious moral realism. He opposes the modern elite's futile rebellion against nature and God, and he holds that human excellence is living well in gratitude with one's limitations. He observes that the therapeutic effort to reduce most human beings to thoughtless dependents has not succeeded completely. Lasch agrees with his fellow antitherapeutic thinker Philip Rieff that "the persistence of old-fashioned moralities among the 'less educated'" is a reason for hope for the future of guilt, moral responsibility, and religion.[70]

In our time, the people have a more truthful and morally demanding view of the good life than the elite. Although Lasch's class analysis owes much to

Marx, he is not a Marxist because he sides with the "petit bourgeois" class's "deep reservations about the progressive scheme of history." Lasch accepts that class's populist critique of indefinite progress, therapeutic enlightenment and entitlement, and "unlimited ambition."[71] Generally, socialism was an elitist or intellectual movement, much more opposed to the morality of the herd or "bourgeois philistinism" than to capitalist elitism. Its attack on bourgeois or the ordinary person's culture was far more effective than its attack on capitalism.

Bourgeois virtues, in truth, are populist virtues, the qualities required of "active, self-respecting citizens."[72] Their ennobling practice is undermined by socialism's characteristically modern, therapeutic promise to dispense with virtue or self-restraint altogether. Socialist and capitalist elitism have had the same morally corrosive effects.[73] Both the capitalist market and the therapeutic state weaken "the character forming discipline of the family, neighborhood, school, and church." Both tend to transform all of human life in a standardized and degrading direction if not resisted. Lasch agrees with the Marxists about the market, and with the conservatives about the welfare state.[74]

The knowledge class has identified working class's antiprogressive culture—its religion and morality—as "authoritarian prejudices." A preference for working over talking, the recognition of the limits of science, and the affirmation of honor are parts of the pathology called the authoritarian personality. Any choice for authority over unconstrained freedom is not primarily unenlightened but unhealthy. So moralistic or realistic positions need not be opposed by argument. They are symptoms of a disease that might be cured.[75]

The disease is a pathologically childish desire for security. The progressive theory of history shared by all versions of the modern knowledge class is a movement from childhood to maturity, a story of "emotional and intellectual growth." So all forms of "cultural conservatism" and "any respect for tradition" are dismissed as forms of clinging to childhood. The nonauthoritarian individual is the one who accepts without flinching "the burden of maturity."[76] His pride is in his disillusionment, his ability to live well without faith.[77] But in Lasch's own view, nothing is more childish than the modern effort to free human existence from all dependence, and premodern culture and tradition, whatever their shortcomings, tended to embody a largely lost moral maturity. "In an age that fancies itself as disillusioned," Lasch observes, "one illusion—the illusion of mastery—remains as tenacious as ever."[78]

Psychologizing social science is one weapon among many, and one that Lasch himself uses, in the moral or cultural war between the classes. Perhaps the key issue in this war today is abortion. The "working-class ethics of limits" affirms the dignity of motherhood and "a biological view of human nature" that includes fixed and desirable differences between men and women. The knowledge class's "enlightened ethic" opposes "biological constraints of any kind" with the "insistence that women ought to assume 'control over their own bodies.'" The separation of sex from reproduction makes it possible to bring both under human control, to liberate them both from illusion or mystery.[79]

The right-to-life movement opposes the elitist drive for reproductive autonomy with the perception that not only sex and love but being human itself are good, and are mysteries beyond our comprehension and control. The denial of the mystery of selfhood or personhood implicit in the pro-choice position leads logically to genetic engineering and other willful judgments about "the 'quality of life.'" The result could easily be the consignment of "whole categories of defective and superfluous individuals to the status of nonpersons." The elitism of the pro-choice position, which replaces the egalitarian recognition of the mystery of all human life with judgments concerning the quality of life, reflects the tendency of the extreme division of labor, as Marx said, to reduce the mass of people to nothing.[80]

Lasch accepts the position of contemporary American Catholic Thomists such as Percy that the unrealistic denial of human mystery and human goodness leads to tyranny and murder. The rule of law and limited democracy depend on respect for the personal mysteries of sex, love, and death, and for the ordinary person's capacity to live well with them. So they also depend on the primacy of a kind of democratic moral responsibility over the willfulness of experts.[81]

With its acknowledgment of limits of choice, the working class is modest in its expectations for life. Its members accept the barrier the body poses to projects for nature's conquest and personal re-creation. They are more easygoing about exercise and diet, or more accepting of the inevitability of the body's decay. From the knowledge class's perspective, they are slackers when it comes to the body, but too tough when it comes to the soul or virtue. But for Lasch, because they accept the body, they are more free to cultivate the soul.[82]

The individual, ordinarily, is saved from the "crippling emotional conflict" that comes from self-obsession by love and work, meaning love of other, particular human beings and work that is challenging, somewhat spontaneous, and concrete or not purely mental or endlessly creative. But even love and work disappoint if we expect too much from them or give too little of ourselves to them. Both connect us with others and the world. Love is of particular men and women, not of humanity in general. So it, even more than work, is the foundation of our personal responsibility and moral realism.[83] Abstract, Rortyan talk about solidarity and even the universal doctrine of rights is unrealistic, if taken to be a replacement for love as a foundation for responsibility.[84]

Bourgeois virtue or self-restraint on behalf of worthwhile work and one's familial and civic duties is indispensable for all lives worth living. Without the concrete, particular experiences associated with love and work, without especially the joys and longings connected with the many forms of eros,[85] the human experience of reality really is unstable and uncertain. So only someone well rooted in "particularism" can experience the "true cosmopolitanism" that is realism.[86] For hypermen, hyperreality or escapist self-denial seems better than what we really know about ourselves and the world.[87]

Lasch contrasts the ordinary or common world formed by love and work, which includes the political world, with Rorty's postmodern combination of private fantasies or narcissism and a limited, calculated public concern with protecting the space that makes equal-opportunity fantasizing possible.[88] Rorty, Lasch admits, is distressingly close to describing America's elite-dominated civic life as it actually exists today. What Lasch finds missing is "almost everything . . . that makes life worth living." The therapeutic erosion of the social joys of love and work may mean that we are losing the capacity not only to govern but even to amuse ourselves.[89] The knowledge class is so obsessed with control, or finally mere survival, and consumed with self-pity about the futility of its efforts, that it has no appreciation for the experiences that make merely human life good. Rorty's suggestion that the common human good become endless conversation divorced from real content is pitiful to anyone who has anything—love, work, politics, nature, morality, death, or God—real to talk about.

The working class views the dominant knowledge class as whiny, self-indulgent, and needlessly unhappy. The elite's moral permissiveness or tolerance is really personal weakness, a lack of courage in one's convictions even within one's own family. Its members are "endlessly demanding of life," expecting more than anyone has a right to expect. And they expect so much without demanding much of themselves in return. They do not restrain their pursuit of happiness or self-fulfillment on behalf of, or in acknowledgment of, their dependence on others.[90]

From the working class's perspective, the knowledge class is unadmirable and unhappy because it believes it has a right to be happy. The working man can distinguish between a real man, a person of character, and a hyperman. He knows how thoughtful and courageous, how heroic, any human being must be who lives well. Lasch sided with the working man, finally, because he too was a real man. He worked, loved, and died well. In his life and in his writing, Lasch "made what was extraordinary seem ordinary."[91]

RELIGION

The real but incompletely satisfying human joys of love and work both point in the direction of God. All of Lasch's thought points to the question of religion's truth, or the compatibility of truthful self-examination with revealed or biblical religion. Lasch holds that the tradition of introspection is in substantial agreement with Augustinian psychology. He agrees with the Christians that dialogic self-examination may not be enough to live well in light of the truth, which is not to say that religion is untrue. He rejected radically Freud's view that religion is merely a "hoax" to be perpetuated for the benefit of culture. For Lasch, "an honest atheist is always to be preferred to a culture Christian."[92]

Religion can function as a refuge, as a source of illusory security. But "the most radical form of religious faith," which is Christian, can also be "a challenge to self-pity and despair." Its affirmation of moral realism and responsibility opposes itself to victimization and resentment. Its understanding of human freedom as a limited, mixed, but genuine good opposes itself to the modern, atheistic extremes of the fantasy of self-sufficiency through control and apathetic passivity. By protecting the good that is human individuality, "Submission to God makes people less submissive in everyday life."[93]

The "deepest variety" of religion always "arises out of the background of despair." The "prelude to conversion" often is "[b]lack despair" or "melancholy." Faith is finally in "the goodness of being in the face of suffering and evil." It is not a negation of suffering and evil. Lasch's final word in his last book is that the future of the modern project is much more problematic than religion's future. The latter reflects the perennial human truth that "life and its negation" are "inextricably bound together." The acceptance of that truth and the practice of the "true virtue" it engenders is what separates a real man from a hyperman.[94]

The last section of that final book Lasch called "the dark night of the soul." It is composed of three chapters articulating in different ways the limits of secular views of the human soul. The phrase "the dark night of the soul" Lasch takes from the American Catholic Thomistic writer Flannery O'Connor, who used it to show that even saints sometimes experience "the truth as revealed by faith" as "hideous." Lasch adds "the whole world now seems to be going through a dark night of the soul."[95] It is reasonable to hope that the despairing awareness of the futility of that rebellion may be a prelude to faith based on a courageous and joyful affirmation of the goodness of being, including the alienated being who is mysteriously equipped to perceive that goodness.

It is only reaching a bit to say that Lasch's concluding use of O'Connor's authority points to Thomism as the authentic postmodernism, or genuinely thoughtful, truthful reflection on the failure of the modern project. Lasch did write that a genuinely postmodern thinker would have to be "philosophically a realist." In light of the failure of modern and all human rebellion against nature, he "respects not only the 'intransigence' but the 'eloquence' of things."[96] And he sees the compatibility of philosophical and religious insight, and so he is open to the truth of revelation.

NOTES

1. This chapter is based on Lasch's last five books, which contain his fully developed views as a social critic: *The Culture of Narcissism: American Life in the Age of Diminishing Expectations* (New York: Norton, 1991, revised edition [original edition, 1979]), hereafter referred to as CN; *The Minimal Self: Psychic Survival in Troubled Times* (New York: Norton, 1984), hereafter MS; *The True and Only Heaven: Progress and Its Critics* (New York: Norton, 1991), hereafter TOH; *The Revolt of the Elites and the Betrayal of Democracy* (New York: Norton, 1995), hereafter RE; *Women and the Common Life: Love, Marriage, and Feminism* (New York: Norton, 1997), hereafter WCL. The last book is an edited collection of Lasch's essays by his daughter, Elizabeth Lasch-Quinn, after his death. RE was finished while Lasch was very near death.

2. "History as Social Criticism: Conversations with Christopher Lasch," *The Journal of American History* (March 1994), 1313.

3. Alexis de Tocqueville, *Democracy in America,* volume 2, part 1, chapter 1.

4. See Lewis A. Lawson and Victor Kramer, eds., *More Conversations with Walker Percy* (Jackson: University Press of Mississippi, 1995), 232–233. This view of Percy is, of course, defended in the previous two chapters.

5. See my *The Restless Mind: Alexis de Tocqueville on the Origin and Perpetuation of Human Liberty* (Lanham, Md.: Rowman & Littlefield, 1993).

6. Lasch, RE, 114.

7. Ibid., 90–91.

8. Lasch, TOH, 530.

9. Lasch, RE, 69.

10. Ibid., 58.

11. Ibid., 89.

12. Ibid., 88.

13. Ibid., 105–107.
14. Ibid., 105.
15. Ibid., 210.
16. Ibid., 85.
17. Lasch, WCL, 126–136.
18. Lasch, RE, 107.
19. Ibid., 82.
20. Ibid., 161–162.
21. Ibid., 180.
22. Lasch, WCL, 168.
23. Lasch, RE, 95–98; CN, 232–234; TOH, 518–519.
24. Lasch, WCL, 182–183.
25. Lasch, TOH, 532; CN, 238.
26. Lasch, TOH, 532.
27. Lasch, CN, 235.
28. Lasch, MS, 58.
29. Lasch, RE, 216.
30. Lasch, MS, 209.
31. Lasch, CN, 209.
32. Lasch, RE, 201.
33. Ibid., 212.
34. Ibid.
35. Ibid., 201.
36. Lasch, CN, 240.
37. Lasch, RE, 207.
38. Ibid., 234.
39. Ibid., 202.
40. Lasch, MS, 58.
41. Ibid.
42. Ibid., 215, 217.
43. Lasch, CN, 248.
44. Lasch, MS, 209.
45. Lasch, CN, 230.
46. Lasch, RE, 20.
47. Ibid.
48. Lasch "After the Foundations Have Crumbed," *Commonweal* 119 (20 November 1992), 22–23.
49. Lasch, RE, 20.
50. Lasch, CN, 249.
51. Lasch, RE, 106–108.
52. Lasch, CN, 239.
53. Ibid., 244.
54. Lasch, RE, 243; TOH, 529.
55. Lasch, RE, 244.

56. Lasch, CN, 242–246.
57. Lasch, RE, 246.
58. Lasch, CN, 245.
59. Ibid.
60. Lasch, MS, 236.
61. Tocqueville, *Democracy,* volume 2, part 1, chapter 6. I take the term *pantheism* from Tocqueville, not Lasch. But Lasch is clearly describing what Tocqueville calls pantheism.
62. See the remarks about Buddhism in Walker Percy, *Lost in the Cosmos: The Last Self-Help Book* (New York: Farrar, Straus, and Giroux, 1983), and throughout Percy's work.
63. Lasch, CN, 240.
64. Ibid.
65. Ibid., 70.
66. Ibid., 48.
67. Lasch, MS, 257–259.
68. Tocqueville, *Democracy,* volume 2, part 2, chapter 16.
69. Lasch, RE, 244, 246.
70. Lasch, RE, 223.
71. Lasch, TOH, 530–532.
72. Lasch, RE, 82.
73. Ibid., 83, 233–234.
74. Ibid., 70, 95–98.
75. Lasch, TOH, 450–452.
76. Lasch, RE, 237.
77. Ibid., 242.
78. Ibid., 246.
79. Lasch, TOH, 489–491.
80. Ibid., 490–491.
81. For this argument, see chapter 4.
82. Lasch, RE, 28.
83. Lasch, CN, 248–249.
84. See Jean Bethke Elshtain's nice summary of Lasch on love in "The Life and Work of Christopher Lasch: An American Story," *Salmagundi* (Spring 1995), 154.
85. For an excellent account of Lasch on the therapeutic "domestication of eros," see Diana J. Schaub, "Girls Just Wanna Have Fun," *Public Interest* (Fall 1997), 116–124.
86. Lasch, MS, 264.
87. Lasch, CN, 244, 249.
88. For a defense of the view of Rorty found here and there in this chapter, see chapter 2.
89. Lasch, RE, 128.
90. Lasch, TOH, 493.
91. Lasch's daughter, Elisabeth Lasch-Quinn, quoted by Jean Bethke Elshtain, 157.

Elshtain was a good friend of Lasch, and her article contains many moving observations concerning his remarkable life and good death. See also the remarks by Lasch-Quinn in her introduction to WCL, xxv–xxvi.

92. Lasch, RE, 228.
93. Ibid., 245; WCL, 159–160.
94. Ibid., 243–246.
95. Ibid., 246.
96. Lasch, "After the Foundations," 23.

6

THE RETURN TO REALISM

R ealism, Christopher Lasch and Walker Percy agree, is postmodernism rightly understood. It is the view of both human nature and morality that returns with reflection upon the failure of the modern project to extinguish the mystery of being and human being and bring history to an end. Death has not been put to death. It cannot be talked to death, as Richard Rorty hopes. It even resists scientific efforts to suppress the self or soul with chemicals. Human beings, when they tell the truth to themselves about themselves, remain aware of their ineradicable limits as thoughtful beings with bodies.

The failure of pragmatism is also the failure of existentialism. Alexandre Kojève is right to say that the existentialist cannot explain why he knows anything about himself and the world. But we can no longer say, with the Hegelian, that the human being might come to know the truth about himself as a result of his struggle to make himself free. Human beings, in fact, cannot free themselves from their natural limitations.

Nor can we say that human nature is an oxymoron. There is a natural foundation for what distinguishes the languaged being, for the self or soul. There really is a connection between mind and body, and that connection is language. Human beings can know something about themselves and the world, because they are equipped by nature to do so. So human distinctiveness is not simply accidental or absurd, and the truth discovered by the languaged being leads not only to miserable anxiety but joyful discovery. Because we can really know something about ourselves and each other, we are not necessarily miserably isolated. Love is not an illusion.

Walker Percy and Christopher Lasch explain, each in his own way, that the modern world is a world split apart. Percy calls that split Cartesianism. The Cartesian only recognizes or is satisfied with the existence of rational systems, and so he both denies and aims to eradicate all that is unsystematic. The Cartesian defines the human being as two systems, mind and body, both impersonally

179

rational but with no connection to each other. The Cartesian modern philosopher incoherently both denies the reality of and aims to eradicate the disorder of the being with language. He tends not to come to terms with, much less attempt to account for, the reality of human alienation. He will not acknowledge that man is a stranger in the cosmos.

Lasch explains the split with class analysis. He analyzes the extreme division of labor between mental and physical laborers that John Locke and Karl Marx knew to be characteristic of a free, modern society. One result is the elitist hyperman who denies both his own human limits and responsibilities and the humanity of most other human beings. The intention of the intellectual elite that Lasch describes is the same as that described by Percy—to deprive others of their freedom and dignity, to reduce them from citizens to animals to be predictably controlled.

Both Lasch and Percy see that B. F. Skinner's expert-directed, joyless, virtueless behaviorist utopia expresses with embarrassing candor and consistency the deepest, elitist aspirations of modern thought. As Kojève makes clear, the goals of behaviorism, Marxism, and therapeutic liberalism are the same— to deprive human beings of their specifically human discontent and so their specifically human content. They aim to make the human being completely at home in the world, no longer a stranger or alien. The goal, Percy and Rorty say, is to deprive them of language.

Lasch and Percy trace the degradation of modern thought through the history of psychoanalysis. It begins as the last part of the Socratic tradition of the introspective and dialogic search for the truth about oneself. Psychoanalysis so understood is, as Percy says, psyche-iatry, or the healing of the soul through the exploration of the significance of the experiences of self-conscious mortals. The intention is not to do away with these experiences but to understand them, not to purge human existence of its distinctive misery but to ameliorate it through understanding. Psychoanalysis at its best leads to the discovery of the connection between morality and the reality of the existential constraints that always characterize human nature. For Lasch, the key psychoanalytic discovery is the connection between shame and curiosity: Both science and morality depend on the mysterious human experience of natural limitation.

The scientific, or Cartesian, objections to psychoanalysis, Lasch and Percy agree, are powerful. The method is uncertain, time consuming, and at best only partially successful. It is inappropriate for large numbers of people, making it hardly an adequate replacement for religion. A more scientific remedy apparently is needed for the anxious disorder or alienation in our seemingly post-Christian or postreligious time.

So psychoanalysis is displaced by psychotherapy. Psychotherapy better than psychoanalysis achieves the latter's intention of replacing religion. The uncertain and limited success of psychoanalysis, contrary to its intention, makes human beings more aware than ever of their need for God. Psychotherapy, one form of which is linguistic therapy and another chemotherapy, aims to eradicate the longings that brought religion into existence.

The therapists or mental laborers become pop Cartesian experts. They insist that the self or soul is an illusion. Experiences of anxiety and alienation can be explained and cured by the proper sort of therapy. Experiences of self or soul are symptoms to be treated through linguistic manipulation, environmental alteration, and finally chemical suppression. The truth is, as Rorty says, human beings are clever animals and nothing more.

Psychoanalysis is oriented toward individuals, psychotherapy to whole societies. The latter aims to cure social disorder, to produce a classless society of nice, gentle, agreeable, cosmopolitan beings. It compassionately aims to free human beings from their human misery. They are better off not as active citizens but as clever animals subject to expert control.

Both Lasch and Percy see the danger to democracy and the rule of law from the therapeutic rule of experts. The experts deny the truth and goodness of traditional accounts of human choice and moral responsibility. The experts are, officially, pro-choice in the sense that they dismiss all accounts of moral limits as reactionary prejudice. They add that, given that there are no limits to choice, we should choose against death and human misery. We should choose against the illusion of personal responsibility or sovereignty. We should trust the experts, not ourselves, for the content and meaning of our experiences. The pro-choice position is anti-life in the sense that it tends to choose against human life as it actually exists. The choice is for a world without choice or virtue.

Our genuine choice, as Lasch presents it, is between therapeutic elitism and moral populism. The moral populist tends to be pro-life, to affirm the mysterious goodness of all human life. The populist does rank human lives according to personal accomplishment and practice of virtue. But the fundamental distinction still remains between self-conscious and unconscious life, and the purpose of democracy and the rule of law is to protect all citizens in the exercise of their freedom from expert tyranny of one sort or another.

The expert both makes judgments concerning the quality of life and denies that anything about human existence is beyond human comprehension and control. So only two types of lives are worth living. The knowledge of the wise expert places him above the troubles and limitations ordinarily associated with self-conscious mortality. Ordinary people would have lives of quality only if freed by the expert from their troubled disorder and human misery. The goal of the experts, as Percy says, is euthanasia, the good death human beings cannot experience without their help.

This pursuit of euthanasia leads both to efforts to suppress self-consciousness and to the killing of human beings judged not worthy to live. As Lasch says, pro-life moral populists understand that the pro-choice, quality-of-life argument leads to the elimination of whole classes of human beings. The extreme division between mental and physical labor, as Marx contended, tends to reduce the great mass of people to nothing. That certainly was the intention and for a while the result of the chemotherapeutic experiment of *The Thanatos Syndrome,* and clearly Rorty's cosmopolitan, classless society will be so agreeable because it is so empty.

Compassion, Percy and Lasch agree, is what the intellectual and scientific elite claims to feel for the condition of ordinary people. Lasch explains that compassion is paternalistic. It is not what one feels for free, equal, competent, and dignified citizens. Those who deserve compassion cannot be expected to earn respect. They are exempted from the requirements common to all citizens. They are excused from the practice of virtue and allowed to become dependent on the government. They are allowed to do and so to be nothing much.

Percy's emphasis is on the connection between compassion or sentimentality and cruelty. Seemingly cruel means are perfectly appropriate for the eradication of the cruelty that is human liberty. For those who can see nothing good in being merely human, compassion becomes a perverse imitation of Christ. We are saved from our misery not by God but by political projects for human transformation originating in modern science.

Nothing is more obtuse, from Percy's perspective, than Rorty's view that the antidote to cruelty is sentimentality. We, in fact, live in the most sentimental and most murderous of centuries. The deepest cause of the cruelty of our century is the suppressed anger or fury of the theorist at what he believes he really knows about his own existence. He is unable to live well with the realities of his contingency and mortality.

The view that human distinctiveness is some sort of cruel, miserable accident, and that human beings might work to eradicate that fundamental cruelty, both Percy and Lasch trace to Rousseauean romanticism. The natural human longing for regression, they explain, is what inspired this misanthropic theory. Percy thinks that Rousseau misunderstands this longing and its natural foundation. Human beings do long to be freed from their alienation, and they cannot help but experience the pain of loss that comes with the acquisition of language and so self-consciousness. But they most deeply really do not want to be freed from the experiences connected with the twinship of love and death.

The joys of love and knowing and communicating the truth are more than ample compensation for the anxious misery of death. But love of another human self is always elusive and imperfect. It can reduce but not eradicate alienation. Human longing points to the unalienated unity of man transparent before God, the Person who can know and love us as we truly are.

Whether or not there is a personal God, human beings cannot really satisfy their longing for unity through their own effort. Kojève is wrong to say that historical work and struggle can really produce in this world what the imaginary Christian God promises in the next. Even regression to a subhuman, sublinguistic, or submoral existence is not within the power of human effort. The antidote to cruelty is tough-minded acceptance of human nature as it actually is, an inseparable mixture of joy and misery, the good and the perverse or grotesque, and love of and alienation from others. So part of the antidote is realistic theory. Human existence is much better than either the pragmatist or existentistist believe it to be.

Percy says that the fundamental human choice, in one way, is between the empirical conclusions of psyche-iatry and those of expert psychotherapy. The psyche-iatrist notices how troubled, strange, and courageous seemingly ordinary lives are. Contrary to the expert, he knows that most people are mysteriously given the capability to live well enough in light of death. So he knows that linguistic therapy or chemotherapy actually diminishes the quality of their lives by depriving them of love, curiosity, anger, and all the other qualities that constitute human liberty.

Lasch observes that ordinary working people are more death-accepting so more truthful and admirable than the elitist knowledge class. They are better able to practice virtue, accept responsibility, and to experience the joyful compensations for human alienation in love and work. They better come to terms with what they know about the limitations of beings with bodies, and so they are less concerned with their bodies and more with their souls. They are less concerned with happiness or materialistic self-fulfillment and more with duty or responsibility. By not demanding the right to be happy, they are actually more happy. Their practice of virtue is what protects them from elite manipulation. Despite the best efforts of therapists, ordinary people, to a remarkable extent, retain their personal sovereignty.

Allan Bloom and Richard Rorty, despite their great differences, both seem to affirm the therapeutic view. They agree that most human beings would be better off if they did not know they were going to die. Bloom here exempts not a scientific elite but the rare philosopher, who can accept all that is implied in the truth about death and enjoy the compensatory pleasure of "insight." Rorty may do the same for the liberal ironist, such as himself. And both Bloom's Socratic ironist and Rorty's liberal ironist practice linguistic therapy to protect ordinary people from the truth about death. Rorty contributes to and Bloom opposes, on the philosopher's behalf, the modern project to put death to death. But Bloom's opposition concedes too much to Rorty's pragmatism, and so is too questionable and too elitist to be effective. Perhaps more precisely, Bloom and Rorty share an incorrect description of ordinary Americans that might be explained as the product of Lasch's knowledge class. They both, from the perspective of that class, exaggerate, with considerable self-deception, the success of pragmatic therapy.

Lasch and Percy both note that members of the knowledge class exempt themselves from the therapeutic treatment they impose on others. So they refuse to recognize or respect the human liberty or dignity of those they treat. By reducing them to nothing more than readily controllable bodies, they seem to elevate themselves to gods. But they remain merely human, with the imperfectly suppressed awareness of one's natural limitations that characterizes human existence as such. Their doctrine that all human reality is a social construction is contradicted by their futile obsession with youth and bodily health. Their mental construction of a hyper- or abstract world in a gated community is a pathetic attempt to escape from the realities of a common human nature and morality. They try to make Cartesianism true, to divide human reality into bodies and minds, to free themselves from being affected in any way from the limitations of, which is why they have trouble experiencing the human joys connected with, embodiment. The compassion they claim to have for others, they really have for themselves. They are miserable in spite of their wealth, health, freedom, and great intelligence. Their pretense of divinization masks a childish inability to come to terms with their desire for regression.

For Percy, the members of the scientific elite impose therapy on others in the hope of alleviating their own anxiety. They incoherently aim to create an untroubled but still human world. Their treatment's success, Percy shows, would leave them more anxious than ever. They would be dissatisfied with the exploitation of subhuman beings. They still really would not know how to live. They would be, like Kojève, Rorty, and Captain Marcus, ironically or inexplicably superfluous, aliens in the world they can otherwise perfectly understand. Their need for genuine or Socratic introspection and dialogue remains, even intensifies. The scientific therapist's inability to cure himself is a certain limit to his pragmatic project. Another is his inability to explain how science could perpetuate itself without the anxiety and curiosity of the scientist.

Elite self-deception produces a naive belief in progress, which both Percy and Lasch never tire of mocking. This belief also comes from Rousseau. Man is naturally good, but he accidentally made himself perverse and miserable. Progress is evidence that he is returning to natural goodness as he overcomes perversity and prejudice through scientific enlightenment. He is moving toward a world of peaceful, affectionate promiscuity and easygoing wisdom where virtue and morality will simply be obsolete. As Rorty observes with approval and Bloom with dread, people are becoming nicer because they are becoming less morally serious. Maybe they are regressing to a prehistorical existence, becoming clever animals and nothing more.

The future "heaven" hoped for by progressive utopians, for Bloom, Lasch, and Percy, would actually be hell. There would be no place for moral, death- and God-haunted, and curious human beings like themselves. There is nothing to admire, no one to love, and no work to be done in a world without virtue, Kojève's end of history. There would be, as Percy shows, no joy in New Ionia. But Percy and Lasch do not really believe that Rorty's hopes and Bloom's fears are warranted. There really is very little evidence that history has or is about to come to an end.

Self-deception is what keeps the therapeutic elite from accepting the distinctive experiences of the human self or soul as authentic and ineradicable. Pop Cartesian therapy, Percy and Lasch agree, is actually failing. For Percy, the experts' failure either to explain or to eradicate the experiences of self have made contemporary Americans more dislocated than ever. The attempt to put death to death has produced people who are more anxious, angry, and death-haunted than ever. Contemporary looniness or pervasive mental disorder is actually a sign of hope. There are natural limits to human manipulation, and experts cannot free even a seemingly postreligious people from their experiences of deprivation and alienation. For Lasch, hope is found in the extraordinary persistence of moral realism among ordinary working people. Both Lasch and Percy locate the future of personal sovereignty, the foundation of democracy and the rule of law, in the realism of one's own judgment concerning the significance of one's own personal experiences.

Finally, Percy and Lasch show that reason or realism points in the direction of the possible truth of religion, meaning biblical religion. Modern science, in fact, has not banished superstition from the world. It has become compatible with the therapeutic intention of modern science. Elite superstition is a form of New Age or Buddhist pantheism. All is divine, and so our experiences of alienation or individuality are an illusion. Pantheism, a theological attempt to satisfy the longing for regression, is particularly seductive but still degrading and incredible for beings who cannot help but experience themselves as individuals. It is a denial of the greatness and misery of being human articulated so well by the best Christian thinkers. Percy and Lasch, together, point to Augustine, Thomas Aquinas, Blaise Pascal, Jonathan Edwards, Søren Kierkegaard, Reinhold Niebuhr, and Flannery O'Connor. The last author, arguably the best contemporary American Thomistic artist, seems to have impressed Percy more than any other. And her name, cited as an authority about the God- and reality-denying character of our age, concludes Lasch's last and best book.

Lasch and Percy show the compatibility of the results of Socratic introspection and what is taught about human psychology by the great Christian thinkers. Human beings are necessarily alienated. They cannot be "saved" from the misery of their mortality or the limitations of their nature through their own effort. *The* fundamental human experience, O'Connor says, is of human limitation. Acceptance of this truth and the personal responsibility or virtue it makes possible and necessary is one consequence of faith. Their denial is typically one cause or consequence of the absence of faith.

For Percy, human beings are by nature "lost in the cosmos." The soul or self cannot really be integrated into nonhuman nature, but there is plenty of evidence for the natural foundation of human distinctiveness. The human being is the languaged and so social and self-conscious being by nature. The longings of alienated lovers point in the direction of each other and finally toward the personal Creator. The postmodern Percy says that the failure of pragmatism or pop Cartesianism is evidence man is incurably God-directed. Revelation perhaps provides the most plausible explanation for the mystery of the elusiveness of one's own soul. Reason or science cannot demonstrate the existence of the Creator, but the denial of that possibility is scientism or dogmatic atheism.

Postmodernism, from one perspective, comes into being with the awareness of the inability of modern scientists to eradicate the mystery of their own being. From another, it is the abolition of the untrue Rousseauean distinction between nature and history, and so the view that human liberty is miserable and accidental. For the Socratic realist, there is authentic joy in discovering what is real because language has a natural, or not merely a historical, foundation. Living in the truth imposes responsibilities on social beings who die. The moral realism that is the product of the Socratic search is authentic and humanly worthy whether or not the Creator actually exists. So is the love for one troubled alienated being for another.

Aleksandr Solzhenitsyn's famous postmodern remark that if human beings were born only to be happy, they would not be born to die, is realistic. They were born to be happy, but human happiness comes as a result of truthfully accepting the responsibility one has been given. A life of simple happiness or contentment alone, Rousseau was perhaps right to say, is for unconscious beings without language. But that option will never be open for us, and we have reason to be grateful for all that has been given to us. We are invigorated by being required to live a morally demanding life. We can, on occasion, glimpse, Percy says, the goodness and gratuitousness of created Being. Human happiness in this way depends upon human alienation, and no human good is or can be unmixed with the fact of one's own death.

INDEX

AA (Alcoholics Anonymous), 102
abortion, 107–108, 132, 141–142, 145,
170–171, 183
Adorno, Theodor, 55
alienation, 12, 36, 88–89, 97, 108, 138,
180–181, 185–186; and being,
82–83; from the cosmos, 80, 110;
and goodness, 174; and happiness,
187; as normal condition, 162, 169;
from original unity, 137–139, 162;
pantheism vs., 168; Pascal on, 4;
Sagan's, 86
America, 5, 10, 12–13, 16, 41, 48, 50,
52–53, 55–56, 59, 63, 66, 70, 72, 78,
84, 91, 96, 105, 108, 115, 142,
158–159
American Founders, 6–8, 159
American Psychological Association,
141
Americans, 1, 3–4, 6, 11, 17, 36, 71,
92–94, 97–99, 157, 184–185
Anthony, Saint, 106
Arcilla, René, 44, 46
Arendt, Hannah, 95
Aristotle, 5, 20, 31, 33, 79–80, 91
Aron, Raymond, 46, 49
Athens, 133
Augustine, Saint, 5, 173, 186
Australia, 81
authenticity, 81–82, 88, 95–96, 106, 187
autonomy, 95–98

Bacon, Francis, 19, 47
Beethoven, 89
Benedictines, 101
Bible, 47, 90, 99, 101

Blackmum, Harry, 142
Bloom, Allan, 9–10, 13, 41–43, 54,
64–72, 105, 108–109, 115, 128,
184–185
Bloom, Harold, 44
Boétie, Etienne de La, 70
Bruell, Christopher, 121
Budd, Billy, 89
Buddhism, 8, 90, 106, 186

Calvinism, 107
Carnap, Rudolf, 44
Chartres, 97, 105
chemotherapy, 116–117, 119, 122,
125–126, 128–129, 133, 143, 146,
181–182
Christianity, 186; Kojève on, 32–34,
183; Lasch on, 12, 158, 169,
172–173; More on, 146; O'Connor
on, 148; Percy on, 11–12, 78, 85,
90–91, 94, 98–100, 103–109, 121,
147, 151; Rorty on, 52, 56, 62; Van
Dorn on, 134
citizenship, 27–28, 30, 33, 50, 63, 109,
159–161, 170, 181–182
Comeaux, Bob, 130–134, 136, 138–139,
143–145
communism, 1, 18, 31, 36–37, 49, 51,
55
contentment, 2, 6, 23–24, 29, 35–37,
42, 55, 58, 72, 118, 123, 128, 131,
187
Cooper, Barry, 32
cosmos, 10–11, 28, 57, 72, 77–78, 80,
85–87, 90–92, 96, 100, 110, 118–119,
121, 128, 180

ABOUT THE AUTHOR

Peter Augustine Lawler is a professor of government at Berry College in Mount Berry, Georgia. He is the author of two books, editor of six more, and has written well over one hundred scholarly articles and chapters on a wide variety of topics. He was chair of the politics and literature section of the American Political Science Association and is associate editor of *Perspectives on Political Science*.